WORKING DOGS

True Stories of Dogs and Their Handlers

BY KRISTIN MEHUS-ROE

PHOTOGRAPHS BY KEITH MAY

BOWTIE™
PRESS

A DIVISION OF BOWTIE INC.

Irvine, California

Nick Clemente, Special Consultant
Karla Austin, Project Manager
Ruth Strother, Editor-at-Large
Michelle Martinez, Assistant Editor
Book design and layout by Keith May

The following photographs in this book are courtesy of Karen Keb Acevedo, p. 6; U.S. Army Quartermaster Museum, pp. 18, 164, 168, 171, 172, 177, and 178; © Corel, pp. 114, 116, 119, and 120; Ernie Ayala, p. 178.

Library of Congress Cataloging-in-Publication Data

Mehus-Roe, Kristin.
  Working dogs : true stories of dogs and their handlers / by Kristin
Mehus-Roe ; photographs by Keith May.
     p. cm.
Includes bibliographical references (p.   ).
  ISBN 1-931993-04-1 (pbk. : alk. paper)
  1. Working dogs--United States--Anecdotes. 2. Dog specialists--United
States--Anecdotes. I. Title.

SF428.2.M44 2003
636.73'0973--dc21
                          2003006968

BowTie Press
A DIVISION OF BOWTIE INC.
3 Burroughs
Irvine, California 92618

Printed and Bound in Singapore
10 9 8 7 6 5 4 3 2 1

To the dogs in my life, Desi, Tramp, Muddy, Patsy, and Sunshine, who have given me far more than I gave them. Through Desi, especially, I've learned to respect what dogs are above what I want them to be. I'm grateful to my family for indulging my love of dogs and listening to me ramble on about this project and others.

To the staff at BowTie Press, especially Nick Clemente, thank you for allowing me to write this book. Without the help of photographer Keith May this book would not be what it is; his work inspired me. Most of all, thanks to my best friend and husband, Andrew.

CONTENTS

Desi.

LOOKING FOR WORK

I never really thought much about working dogs until I adopted Desi. I found her in a humane society in Tacoma, Washington. She looked sort of like a German shepherd dog–Doberman pinscher–rottweiler mix, but when I brought her to my vet he said right away, "Nope, she's some kind of heeler mix."

I'd never even heard of a heeler but after some research found out it was an Australian cattle dog. She did look like one, but she looked even more like the cattle dog's close cousin, the Australian kelpie. In dog lore, the cattle dog is a descendant of the kelpie and both are purported descendants of the dingo. No one really seems to know the exact lineage of the breeds but both have been and continue to be used as herding dogs on ranches across Australia and now in North America and Europe.

When Desi was eight or nine months old, we met a woman who insisted that Desi was a kelpie. "Where did you get that dog?" she demanded. "That's a kelpie—how much will you take for her?" I demurred and the woman gave me a stern talking-to, lecturing that a kelpie is a working dog and that living as a pet would break her spirit. Of course, I didn't hand Desi over to this stranger; however, this incident did give me pause.

Had I done the right thing for Desi? Well, yes and no. Desi is 11 now and she's had a fine life with a lot of walks and playtime, two annoying little "sister" dogs, and a lot of people who love her. She's even had stints as a therapy dog and agility dog. Still, Desi has never been particularly happy. She's loyal to me and enjoys playing and cuddling, but honestly, she's really only content when we're out doing something. Over the years I've learned a lesson I wish I'd taken to heart that day: Some dogs are made to work. That's not to say I would have given Desi up to the nearest rancher, but had I taken her working dog spirit more seriously, I certainly would have made a deeper effort to involve her in canine activities.

Not all dogs are working dogs. There are many dogs bred to be companions and there are older dogs who no longer have the same passion burning in their souls as a one-year-old. Many are best made for cuddling and fetching balls. But for the dogs who are born to perform, work is their most cherished activity. A real working dog never needs to be forced to work; he lives to work.

Thousands, even millions, of dogs are relinquished to animal shelters each year simply because their families don't understand their need to work. After years of working as an editor and writer for pet magazines, I've heard hundreds of stories about high-energy Border collies or Jack Russell terriers being abandoned or euthanized because they'd become destructive after being left in a backyard all day. Few people do sufficient research when choosing a dog breed, and many end up with animals that they don't know how to care for properly. It is tragic when a dog is abandoned simply for doing the job we bred it to do. This happens every day in the case of herding dogs who herd or nip, pit bull–types who fight, and sled dogs who run.

> **For the dogs who are born to perform, work is their most cherished activity. A real working dog never needs to be forced to work; he lives to work.**

Irresponsible breeders are unlikely to dissuade an inappropriate purchaser. So what if an urban family with three kids buys a high-energy Australian shepherd pup? It's not the breeder's problem anymore. Of course, when the harried family finally, tearfully brings the Australian shepherd to the shelter, this dog becomes a problem for all of us: taxpayers who support animal shelters and the shelter workers who face the stress of euthanizing a perfectly healthy dog.

Ironically, at the same time that we as a society continue to give up on dogs we don't understand, many of us are skeptical of using dogs for work. Working dogs just don't fit into our concept of a dog's life. We're caught in a crux between the

The author with her always active companion, Desi.

dogs who get nothing and the dogs who spend their days in doggy spas. We cater and coddle our pets, question the idea of making dogs work as ranch dogs, but still euthanize more than four million dogs each year. This dichotomy interested me: I instinctively cringed away from the idea of using a dog as a beast of burden, but is that really what it is? I started to question my knee-jerk reaction to working dogs and began to wonder, if some dogs are unsatisfied with the lives we give them, would a working life be better? It would certainly be better than abandonment or a life relegated to the backyard.

Desi wasn't the only dog I'd had in my life who lacked for a job. Tramp, my German shepherd–Lab–pit bull mix, spent her first four years of life bouncing off the walls. My family's Irish setter, Sunshine, was legendary for her jailbreaks and food theft. I started to rethink the use of dogs in work; might a dog be happier

Desi, like many dogs, is hard-wired to work and is happiest when performing a task.

spending the day working closely with his person while using both his mind and body to complete a task?

Working isn't right for all dogs, but it is for some. While we continue to breed dogs in the image of what we want, we're shocked by their desire to do the work they were bred for. To happily coexist with our dogs, we need to learn what our dogs need to do, and make better decisions about the right dogs for our homes. If you are not willing to provide a dog with work, including canine activities such as flyball or agility, you should not bring home a Border collie.

In the process of writing this book, I met dozens of working dog handlers and interviewed more than 80 of them. Some handlers I related to more than others; some jobs sounded like a dog's dream come true while others placed dogs in constant danger and relegated them to a life in a kennel. I learned that working dogs'

Looking for Work

lives aren't necessarily all good, but neither are they all bad. My hope is that you will come away from this book with a sense of dogs' capabilities as well as a better barometer to judge the work they do.

On another note, dogs do work all over the world, but I've limited my coverage to the U.S. Although I provide a general sense of the work dogs do for us in this country, space and time restrictions have kept me from addressing every job a dog does. There are some truly innovative jobs for dogs that I haven't covered, especially in the area of detection work, simply because these jobs aren't widespread or well researched. I've limited coverage to those jobs that dogs have a measured period of success doing. I've also excluded some work because of ethical reasons.

> *My hope is that you will come away from this book with a sense of dogs' capabilities as well as a better barometer to judge the work they do.*

The addition of multi-mix "Tramp," provided Desi a constant companion (and occasional nemesis).

INTRODUCTION

A HISTORY OF WORKING DOGS

Dogs have worked for humans since the beginning of recorded time. Although there is disagreement over how dogs came to share their lives with us, it's clear that we have been close companions for the last ten to twenty thousand years. Recent studies conducted by the National Museum of History and the University of California in Los Angeles (UCLA) indicate that dogs walked across the Bering land bridge with the first human settlers to the American continent approximately twelve thousand years ago. These studies place dogs' domestication in East Asia about fifteen thousand years ago.

According to most theories, dogs were the first domesticated animals, and they remain the only animal to so completely share the lives of humans. Cats may live in our homes, but they are largely independent of our needs or preferences, and we've never been able to manipulate their genes to serve our needs. Dogs, on the other hand, truly live with us. Anyone who has had a dog knows how closely our canine counterparts bond with us and how they look toward humans for sustenance, shelter, entertainment, and safety.

What happened to make dogs so intrinsically linked to our lives? Many believe dogs first came into our lives when they scavenged from ancient tribal villages. They were attracted to the villages by refuse piles and scrap food and would slink at the outskirts of an encampment at night, gnawing on the bones of that evening's dinner. If another animal approached their scavenging ground, they would bark or growl at it to protect their food source. Over time, the villagers probably came to depend on these vocalizations to warn them of approaching animals or people. Although the dogs weren't strictly protecting the humans, their food protection behavior served the same purpose.

As the dogs continued to coexist with the villagers, predatory and scavenging animals, including vermin, may have become less of a problem. As villagers appreciated this, perhaps they invited the accidental guards to come closer; the dogs may have even been fed extra scraps from time to time. Perhaps the step toward true guarding came by chance, when a dog warned of an invading enemy, allowing the village to protect itself. At the same time, familiarity probably led to some of the bolder dogs approaching village children to cadge a snack. Over time, this interaction led to petting and playing. Children may have begun to recognize particularly affectionate dogs and given them names or tried to tempt puppies with bits of meat to come closer. Ultimately, a particularly cute puppy was adopted as a playmate. Living within the village circle, this dog would have naturally bred with other dogs living around the village, resulting in equally agreeable animals.

However it happened, dogs began to infiltrate the lives of villagers, and it wasn't long before humans learned that dogs could perform more tasks than guarding. Once dogs were established as part of the village pack and regularly used as guards against other humans and animals, the next task was probably hunting, followed by herding or flock protection activities. Humans gradually learned that the dogs' dependency on them could be manipulated into training.

A dog may have first accompanied a lone human on the hunt—surprising her master by trailing the scent of prey and leading him to it. The human would have rewarded this find with a chunk of the meat: the first positive reward-based training. Or a shepherd lonely for company may have brought a dog with him to tend his flock (what came first, domesticated cloven-hoofed livestock or domesticated dogs, no one seems to know). The dog may have inadvertently protected the livestock from predators by barking at roaming animals in the night. The shepherd would have come to depend on his dog, perhaps even leaving the dog with flocks grazing for long periods of time in remote areas while he worked closer to home. In another part of the world, an enterprising or bored shepherd must have found that by using his dog's prey drive he could train the dog to chase his flock from

A History of Working Dogs

point A to point B. Over time, this initial training became an integral part of the canine-human relationship and paved the way for the future role of working dogs.

As dogs learned new ways to serve humans, humans learned methods to genetically manipulate dogs. People, accidentally or intentionally, realized that breeding one great herding dog to another great herding dog would lead to puppies who grew up to be tremendous herding dogs. And as humans are prone to doing, they took this idea and ran with it.

Amazingly, even with the tremendous range of behaviors and physical characteristics among dog breeds, they're all basically the same animal. If you put 20 dogs of varying breeds on a desert island and left them there for several generations, the offspring would look quite similar to the native dogs found across the world: the dingoes of Australia and the pariah dogs of Asia, eastern Europe, and the Middle East.

Doggy genetics tend toward overriding characteristics: medium-sized; neutral colored; prick or tulip ears; slightly curled tail; and small, catlike paws. As a friend told me excitedly after a recent trip to Costa Rica, referring to my multimixed dog, "I saw Tramps all over the place!"

At some point in our relationship with dogs, people discovered that they could breed to their needs and rapidly began creating an extraordinary number of breeds—all for different purposes. In different parts of the world, humans bred their dogs for work suited to the region. Spain produced a number of flock protecting and herding dogs; Asia bred tiny companion animals for royalty and stout, fierce dogs for guarding; and Rome bred huge mastiffs as war dogs.

Based on archeological findings, guarding, hunting, and companion dogs appear to have been used throughout the world. Dogs, apparently family pets, were even found tethered in Pompeii. In *A Celebration of Dogs*, the author Roger Caras comments that the inscription Beware of Dog found etched in the stone above thresholds of ill-fated Pompeian homes was probably not a warning of guard dogs, but rather a caution not to step on the family pet.

During the last millennium, our domestication of the dog reached a new height.

By the 1700s, hundreds of breeds of dogs with hundreds of different jobs had been developed. There were dogs bred for hunting birds, bears, lions, and vermin; there were dogs bred to herd and protect livestock; there were dogs bred to kill, guard, and scout. Not all dog jobs were noble; some dogs were bred to fight one another or to fight bears or bulls for humans' entertainment and other dogs were bred for food.

In the latter half of the nineteenth century, as the modern world edged toward industrialization and urbanization, working dogs fell out of favor in many countries, including the U.S. In New York City, there was no place for a herding or hunting dog to do her work and the use of urban dogs to pull carts and do other drafting work was largely outlawed. Although we continued to breed for looks and temperament, we forgot what each breed was originally intended to do.

For a hundred years we've cherished our companion dogs but struggled with what sometimes seems to be boundless energy and fruitless yearning. We feed them, love them, and play with them; what more could they want? Unfortunately, many of the breeds we are most taken with are those that were never bred to be companion animals. The dalmatian, for example, was bred to run alongside horse-drawn coaches. At the end of the day, when the passengers rested in a roadside inn, the dalmatian guarded the horses, carriage, and its contents. Dalmatians also accompanied the early horse-drawn fire engines and watched over the horses and equipment at night. No wonder these dogs never seem content now that we expect them to sit by the fire looking cute all day.

A History of Working Dogs

The working background of dogs is inextricably linked to the unfulfilled lives of many so-called companion dogs. We breed dogs for specific tasks yet do not provide them with a life wherein they can do those tasks. Although some dogs were bred to be companions, most were not. Considering this history, it's no surprise we find ourselves struggling with the role of dogs in our lives.

Ironically, although we live our lives strongly intertwined with dogs—they live in our homes, even sleep in our beds—we are often surprised to learn that they ever had jobs. Most Americans look at guide dogs and are amazed at the work they do, not realizing that this is not a new talent, just a role rediscovered.

We can thank guide dogs, however, for redefining the use of dogs in the twentieth century. It was probably this job, more than any other, that put working dogs back on the American map. The mind-boggling discovery that a dog—that lazy animal who sleeps on our couch—can provide such a complicated and useful task has reawakened the public's eyes to the fact that dogs are much more than just our friends.

Guide dogs first came to the U.S. in an article published in the *Saturday Evening Post* in 1927. They were further popularized after World War II, when returning soldiers blinded through injuries sustained in battle refused to accept a lifetime of infirmity, instead using guide dogs to help rebuild functional lives. These specially trained dogs allowed blind people a level of independence difficult to attain otherwise, and they allowed the public to see a dog at work in their everyday lives.

When guide dog teams first ventured out, they were greeted with surprise and, often, resistance. Many in the general public couldn't fathom that dogs could serve such a vital role, and restaurant and hotel managers were unsure whether to allow the dogs into their establishments. As time passed, however, and guide dogs proved to be a permanent and essential part of society, the public became better educated and more accepting. The passage of the Americans with Disabilities Act (ADA) in 1990 further increased the acceptance of guide dogs and other assistance dogs in public, giving handlers a legal foothold.

Since guide dogs came into use, dogs have been incorporated as tools for people with many different kinds of disabilities. There are service dogs who assist the mobility impaired, hearing dogs who alert deaf handlers to doorbells and fire alarms, even medical response dogs who can be trained to stay by the side of an epileptic, seek help, or call 911.

Working Dogs

The ADA has legitimized the use of assistance dogs in a legal sense and has given those with assistance dogs access that they were not able to count on before. Although there are times that assistance dog handlers still have to contend with an ignorant or hostile public, the tide has changed and through the efforts of individual and organized advocates, the use of assistance dogs is slowly becoming customary.

In the past 50 years, our relationship to dogs has changed markedly. Ironically, as we have gained a deeper appreciation of the ethical treatment of dogs and animals in general, we have lost the respect for our dogs as working partners. Sometimes it's hard to say whether the influx of doggy spas and doggy aromatherapy helps or hinders our canine companions. In one sense it leads to a great appreciation of dogs as sentient beings. On the other hand, it reinforces the idea of dogs as come-to-life stuffed toys. An apartment-bound pooch would probably prefer a day of exercise than a reflexology massage. Feeling like we've done the best we can for our dogs because we've spent the most money or given them something we would want pays scant attention to their needs as dogs. That's not to say that every modern dog amenity is bad. Doggy daycare provides a safe outlet for a high-energy dog who would otherwise be relegated to a crate, and the increase in dog sports has certainly served both dogs and their human companions well. In many ways, these types of activities serve to replicate the more natural life of dogs, but it's crucial we balance their needs with what we want to provide them.

My late father-in-law used to joke that dogs were the ultimate example of socialism: they are dependent on humans for everything. What we often lose sight of is that dogs provide a great deal in exchange for food and shelter. They give us companionship, security, and affection. They lower our blood pressure, keep us

A History of Working Dogs

active, and protect us from predators—now, largely other humans. Under the right circumstances, our canine companions can also serve us in many additional ways, fulfilling roles that are constantly expanded and strengthened.

In the past 20 years, our knowledge and appreciation of dogs' abilities have expanded dramatically. For example, the research by advocacy groups such as the Delta Society, an organization that conducts research on the human-animal bond in addition to serving as an accrediting body for therapy dogs, has given us quantifiable results to back up our gut feelings about the human-dog bond. Because of the Delta Society's work, therapy dogs are now a common sight in hospitals and nursing homes, and are being regulated to protect their safety and the safety of patients, while expanding their ability to serve in an increasing variety of ways. And as small farmers try to preserve a way of life, dogs are returning to use as herders and flock protectors. That a good herding dog can do the work of several ranchers is not lost on those who are struggling to keep their farms and ranches viable. As we continue to learn about the potential of working dogs, their roles only broaden. The possibilities seem infinite as education and research expand.

Media have played a major role in the legitimization of working dogs, from the disaster search and rescue (SAR) dogs in Oklahoma City in 1995, and at the World Trade Center and Pentagon attacks on September 11, 2001, to the much-discussed Vietnam War dogs documentary, *War Dogs: The Untold Story of Dogs in Combat.* As the events of 1995 and 2001 unfolded, TV viewers were amazed to learn that disaster SAR dogs can find bodies hidden even when the most technologically advanced equipment can't. In the aftermath of September 11, the public was further enlightened to the important role of explosive-detection dogs in airports. It's become clear that dogs protect us both inside and outside our homes.

War Dogs not only illuminated the fact that there would likely have been ten thousand additional names on the Vietnam War Memorial Wall but also exposed another shameful legacy of the Vietnam War; the dogs were largely euthanized or abandoned after their jobs were over; a practice that was not only sanctioned but required by the military until 2000. Although the treatment of war dogs and disaster dogs is far different from one another, the use of dogs in Vietnam and at the bombing sites had an interesting psychological effect on thousands, even millions, of Americans. After September 11, SAR groups were amazed to discover not only a new respect for SAR dogs but financial support of them as well. Thousands of American citizens donated dog booties to protect the disaster dogs and many projected the emotion of the tragedy onto the dogs. The exploration of the treatment of dogs in Vietnam has had a cathartic affect on Vietnam dog handlers in much the same way that the release of the movie *Platoon* had on many Vietnam vets. Since *War Dogs* was released, handlers have rallied for acknowledgment of their dogs and managed to fund several Vietnam dog memorials.

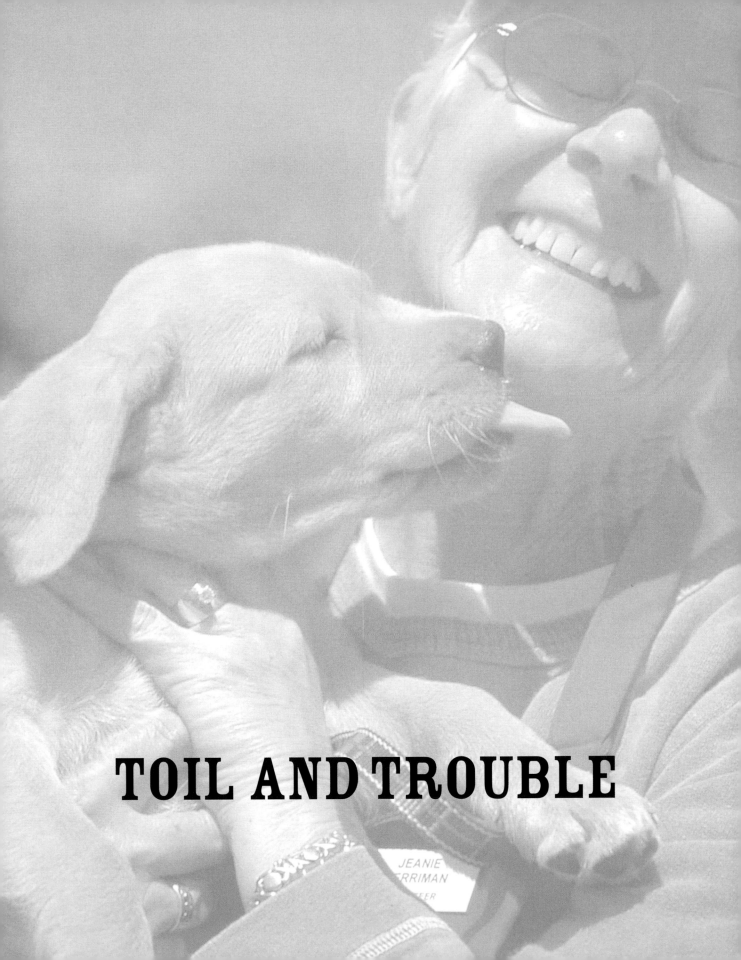

TOIL AND TROUBLE

CHAPTER 1

THE HUMAN-DOG BOND

Anyone who's ever had a dog knows that there is bond between dogs and people. Some outsiders, though, are surprised to learn how much that bond means in a human–working dog partnership. Most working dog handlers say that the bond they have with their dogs means everything to their work. Whether it is being able to read what a dog is telling them or that the dog is able to pick up their signals, the connection is imperative.

Sometimes, the bond is the work in itself. Therapy dogs, for example, take the human-dog bond to a new level, bringing normalcy, acceptance, and affection to a variety of clients, including hospital patients, nursing home residents, and at-risk or otherwise challenged children. There is something about what an animal, particularly a dog, does for our self-confidence and happiness that cannot be undervalued. At the same time, therapy dogs seem to find fulfillment from the work. Handlers say that when the therapy vest comes out, the dogs are giddy with anticipation—much like a pet dog when his owner pulls out the leash.

Although assistance dogs do a great deal toward helping disabled people live more fulfilled and independent lives; many recipients assert that the most important service their dogs provide is to create a social bridge between themselves and others as well as provide them with companionship and affection. Many disabled people, especially those with disfigurements and those who have experienced a traumatic spinal cord injury, become socially isolated and depressed. As much

Working Dogs

as a dog helps them with basic functions, having an assistance dog also helps them to reconnect with the world and provides a nonjudgmental companion. An assistance dog gives some a reason to get up in the morning and motivates them to come out of a shell that is far too easy to live within. The assistance dog, in turn, receives his

attention and affection from the handler, with the added bonus of being able to spend twenty-four hours a day, seven days a week with his favorite person.

Search and rescue and detection dog handlers live by one motto, Trust your dog. If you don't trust your dog, you can't do the work. If you don't have a close bond with your dog, you can't trust him.

Even flock protector dogs must form a bond; for them, however, it is with their livestock rather than with a human. As pack animals, dogs live to serve their pack. If they don't feel that connection, they will not do good work.

With some dogs such as SAR, police, and military dogs, the human-dog bond becomes even closer due to the stress and danger inherent in their tasks. Police dog handlers think of their dogs as their partners and say that their canine partners would give up their lives to protect them. This allows them to trust their dogs with their lives. At the same time, they know that they are equally responsible for their dogs' lives. Military dog handlers, especially those who have served in a war, consider their dogs their battle buddies—fellow soldiers who get them through the tough times and help celebrate the good. As Vietnam War handlers remember the heroic moments, they also remember the mundane: reading letters from home to their dogs, sleeping with their heads next to their dogs', and feeding their dogs treats from care packages.

We cannot forget the most common jobs dogs have, being our companions and protectors; dogs serve us in informal ways every day. Some people can point to con-

The Human-Dog Bond

crete examples of a dog's devotion such as a dog who alerted his owner to an impending heart attack or a dog who rescued his owner from a burning fire. But most of what dogs do is less dramatic. They stay by our sides day in and day out, comforting us when we're down, motivating us to get out and walk, lowering our blood pressure by their presence. They keep us healthy physically and mentally; they bark at intruders; they keep us safe on nighttime walks. In turn, we reward them with

affection and treats, security and comfort.

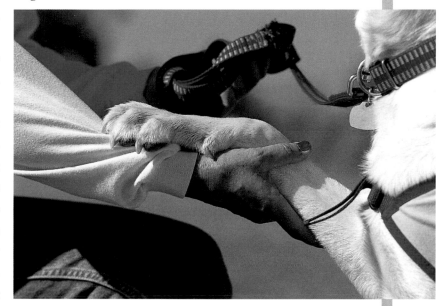

You cannot underestimate the strength of the bond between a working dog and his human. Often, the two are together twenty-four hours a day, seven days a week. They go to work together, usually come home together, and often sleep in the same room at night—some in the same bed. Most handlers say they spend more time with their dogs than with their families. When it comes time for a dog to retire, due to age or illness, the decision can be agonizing. Handlers invest huge amounts of time and often money into the training and development of a dog, but they also invest huge amounts of themselves. According to avalanche dog handler Patti Burnett, the two worst days of working dog handlers' lives is when their dogs retire and when their dogs die.

In "The Truth About Dogs," an article published in *The Atlantic Monthly*, the author purports to give the true story of dogs, arguing that dogs take far more from us than we take from them and that any purpose they do serve is merely a byproduct of their parasitic relationship with us. Although there's no question that dogs were drawn to us for what we could provide them, they stay with us because of what they provide us. Rather than parasitic, the relationship is symbiotic. After reading this book, I think you'll agree.

CHAPTER 2

THE ETHICS OF WORKING DOGS

In nineteenth century United States and Britain, dogs performed the meanest of labors: pulling carts laden with milk, cargo, or passengers, and pacing endlessly on dog wheels used to power cooking spits, water pumps, and even grain mills. The value of their labor far outweighed their value as companions and dogs. As it was for all animals, dogs had yet to be perceived as sentient beings in the industrial west. Some scientists even argued that dogs were merely animated mechanisms with no real sense of pain or deprivation (Coren, 2002). In fact, the dire conditions of working dogs were largely the incentive for the formation of the Royal Society for the Prevention of Cruelty to Animals (RSPCA) and the American Society for the Prevention of Cruelty to Animals (ASPCA).

The world of working dogs has changed drastically since then, but does that mean that it is ethical for dogs to work for humans? Aren't dogs supposed to be digging holes and chasing sticks? Do modern dogs enjoy the work they do and do their handlers truly have their best interests in mind?

Stories are told about such horrors as sled dog mushers culling dogs from litters by euthanizing them, humanely or inhumanely, and disreputable greyhound tracks where dogs are beaten and malnourished and then killed when they can no longer run. Some working dogs do suffer cruelty. Fortunately, these incidents are the minority in the world of working dogs. Although there are sled dog mushers who kill underperforming dogs, provide inadequate veterinary care, and use cruel training practices, there are also sled dog mushers who provide their dogs with plenty of social interaction, promote positive training techniques, and keep their dogs no matter what.

Many working dog advocates dismiss accounts of cruelty by arguing that abused working dogs won't perform well so working dogs aren't abused. Despite

this, abuse does happen. Good trainers and handlers, however, work hard to educate others to appropriate training and humane treatment of all dogs, including working dogs. Ideally, ethical handlers take it upon themselves to report or educate others who do not treat their animals well.

And just as there are good and bad working dog handlers, there are good and bad forms of work for dogs. There are some forms of work that promote animal cruelty by their very nature, and there are jobs that provide dogs with the physical and mental stimulation they relish. Whatever you feel about dogs doing work, you can't paint the picture with one brush.

Individual handlers, welfare organizations, and the general public each have varying levels of tolerance and support when it comes to working dogs. While some organizations don't approve of dogs working in any situation, others, such as the Humane Society of the United States (HSUS), support the use of working dogs where appropriate and humane. The American Humane Association (AHA) even has a division that focuses exclusively on the welfare of animals used in film and TV.

"At AHA, we often celebrate working dog–human partnerships because it is one aspect of the relationship that humans and dogs have," says Jodie Buckman, of the AHA. "But there has to be a constant awareness of the balance between work and the best interest of the dogs. Are the dogs handled well, are they trained well, are all

The Ethics of Working Dogs

their needs met, is there appropriate equipment available for the animals' protection? When a person works with a dog, it brings [their relationship] to a whole other level."

Some organizations have official statements on the welfare of working dogs. The People for the Ethical Treatment of Animals' (PETA) statement indicates the organization is neither vehemently opposed nor in support of working dogs:

> *Relationships of mutual respect and benefit are truly wonderful. However, working dogs are often used as a substitute for innovative programs that intelligently address human needs. . . . Optimally, human services for the disabled should be improved rather than relying on the breeding and exploitation of animals.*

The PETA statement also mentions concerns about dogs being used to do work that is too dangerous for humans and that working dogs are not always cared for humanely before, during, or after their careers.

The HSUS has an official policy supporting the use of assistance dogs with some strict tenets: assistance dog organizations must accept full responsibility for ensuring that the dog's "medical, physical, behavioral, and psychological needs are met." Dogs must be willing and able to do a job without physical manipulation such as teeth pulling or debarking; programs must provide adequate housing and care for animals; training must be based on positive reinforcement; and "humane disposition must be assured for animals who fail to qualify for the program or become unable to perform required tasks." Career-change dogs and retired dogs must be adopted by a well-screened home or, if there is no other option (due to illness or severe temperament problems), be humanely euthanized.

Many animal welfare organizations support work for some dogs because they know that many

> **Just as there are good and bad working dog handlers, there are good and bad forms of work for dogs.**

high-drive dogs end up in shelters and are ultimately euthanized. For dogs who are unhappy or destructive living as companions, work can be a legitimate alternative. And for the many dogs who end up in shelters, living as a working dog is a lot better than being euthanized. The San Francisco Society for the Prevention of Cruelty to Animals (SF/SPCA), for example, began a hearing dog program in the 1970s as a way to place more dogs. Many other assistance dog programs regularly turn to local

shelters for potential dogs, even training shelter employees in the characteristics to look for when a promising dog comes their way. U.S. Customs and the U.S. Department of Agriculture (USDA) also use rescued shelter dogs in their dog programs with the support of most shelters.

The HSUS even has a program in association with the Marshall Legacy Institute, the K9 Demining Corps. Although dogs who detect mines are put in danger through their work, they also serve to educate other cultures as to the value of dogs. Randall Lockwood, Ph.D., who is the HSUS liaison to the K9 Demining Corps, explains, "Part of our interest in helping countries establish local canine demining projects is that we feel it does improve the overall perception and treatment of dogs in countries where they have not traditionally been valued as partners and companions, e.g. in parts of Asia and the Middle East."

The Ethics of Working Dogs

The demining dogs work closely with their handlers—they are never put in situations more dangerous than those their human partners face. According to the Marshall Legacy Institute, mines kill tens of thousands of humans and hundreds of thousands of animals each year. The dogs' ability to detect mines has proven to be far safer than alternative demining methods and saves both the lives of humans and animals.

The HSUS and AHA also support other types of dog work, including recreational sledding, SAR, and detection work, as long as the dogs are cared for humanely, not just fed and sheltered, and enjoy the work. In general, they'd rather see a Siberian husky tearing up a trail than a house.

Animal welfare groups caution, however, that not all working dog programs or handlers are as good as others. Nancy Peterson of the HSUS advises anyone who is considering fostering an assistance dog puppy, donating, volunteering, or applying for an assistance dog of their own to research the organization carefully.

Some working dog advocates argue that if a dog is born to a job, then the dog should do that job. That argument clearly doesn't hold up in the case of fighting dogs such as pit bull-types who are bred to fight one another to their deaths. It also doesn't hold up in regard to greyhound racing, a gambling industry in which money far outweighs the health or happiness of the dogs. Greyhounds may be born to run, but greyhound racing has few safeguards and little interest in the well-being of the animals who participate in the sport. "Competition is where we see the most problems," says Buckman. "The welfare of the dog should come first rather than winning."

Being bred to a job doesn't mean a dog should do it; it only means the dog has the potential and the drive to do it. Whether the dog should work or not all depends on the appropriateness of the particular job, the handler's skill, and the dog's willingness. If all the elements line up: a good handler, a good job, and a happy and willing dog, a job can be the best thing to ever happen to a dog. If not, it can be the worst.

Animal welfare laws have made a big difference in working dogs' lives, as they have in every aspect of animal welfare. That doesn't mean they serve to protect every dog in every job, however. As many advocates point out, dog work is newly rediscovered in the U.S., and as Peterson says, "it's been a big learning curve." Some dog work, such as illegal dog fighting rings, flies beneath the radar, and other organizations just don't do a good enough job protecting the animals.

> **Being bred to a job doesn't mean a dog should do it; it only means the dog has the potential and the drive to do it.**

Unfortunately, U.S. military dogs do not have the quality of life most of us would like to see. They live in kennels and until 2000, military dogs were routinely euthanized when they could no longer work. A bill passed unanimously in congress prodded the air force to begin an adoption program, but the number of dogs euthanized still far outnumbers the dogs adopted by private homes. The United States Department of Agriculture (USDA) and U.S. Customs also require their dogs to live in kennels, although the dogs are adopted by private citizens when they retire, usually to their handlers, who often make a strong emotional connection with their dogs. These are all areas where advocates hope to see improvements.

There's no doubt that many dogs love to work and aspire to the activity bred into them. Hunters want to hunt, fighters want to fight, and runners want to run. It is our job to guide their instincts in a way that keeps them occupied and others safe. The challenge is, then, to find ways to decide whether a dog's work is safe and humane. If it is not, the handler must introduce the dog to another more suitable job or activity that can channel some of her energy and drive.

The thing is, of course, that the appropriateness of a particular job can change based on the human mores of the time. We don't let our mastiffs go into battle with spikes on their collars, but despite its illegality, there are still plenty of people who find it reasonable to send dogs into fights. Hunting with dogs is also legal, although there are some restrictions on the type of hunting that can be done with dogs. Many states have laws against treeing (chasing animals into trees so the hunter can easily shoot them) animals with hounds. Fox hunts with huge teams of foxhounds or beagles have largely gone the way of the big game hunts.

The Ethics of Working Dogs

During war, dogs have been used both to save lives and to take lives. As much as we celebrate the devil dogs of World War II, we abhor the Nazis' use of dogs in concentration camps, the use of dogs by East Germany at the Berlin Wall and by southern police against Civil Rights marchers. Dogs don't choose sides and they don't have a moral barometer. They work for those who feed and train them.

So, when is it okay for a dog to pursue her instincts? Who decides and what is the decision based on? Are there times when it is appropriate to manipulate an animal for our own benefit? Is the HSUS right in saying that working dogs help gain a public acknowledgement of the dog's value and lead to better treatment and stronger laws for animal welfare? What about breeding dogs for their respective jobs—is it appropriate for us to genetically manipulate our canine companions to do the work we want them to do, especially given the number of dogs euthanized each year? Is it inherently wrong to breed dogs for our purposes when so many are dying due to our

lack of responsibility as a society every day? There are good arguments against any work, according to some. Hunting is an archaic blood sport, SAR can be dangerous, herding can traumatize the livestock, and guiding is a humorless poor excuse for what should be a carefree dog's life.

Ultimately, the answers to our ethical questions are largely subjective and ruled by our own moral barometers. We can protect dogs from obvious mistreatment through legislation and laws, but when it comes to the ethical complexities of dogs—and all animals—in our society, we each set our own standards.

Aside from the obvious—jobs in which dogs are mistreated or jobs that cause grievous suffering to humans or other animals—the types of work for dogs that we do or do not support are determined individually. If we care, we look at each situation and judge both our own and society's values while determining whether the dog is safe and healthy, and, as importantly, whether the dog seems to enjoy what she's doing. While dog racing, for example, may bring pleasure to the dog during the actual run, it is a profit-motivated gambling activity that encourages the culling of dogs and inexpensive care to increase profitability. Any job where someone profits directly from the dogs, rather than from the assistance a dog provides (for example, a herding dog can help a ranch be profitable without the rancher receiving a direct payment for the dog's work), cannot ensure a humane and healthy existence for participants.

Further complicating the question of working dogs are individual ideals. For example, many people do not believe in hunting for sport. But many dogs continue to be used for hunting and most of the work we do with dogs stems from their hunting roots and the predatory instincts that drive them to hunt. People who hunt with their dogs say their animals are most happy when flushing a bird in a field or streaking through the woods after a deer. I've seen my own dogs chasing seagulls with the fiercest abandon and joy. At the same time, I'd never hunt with them because of my own personal feelings about sport hunting. That said, hunting is important in the evolution of working dogs and hunting dogs capture what it is that working dogs do: sniff, chase, and follow a human's commands to a tee.

The best argument for working dogs is that some dogs are born to be companions and some aren't. Working dogs who aren't given a job, be it a "real" job or a play job such as agility can have a range of reactions, from depression to anxiety to destructiveness. This isn't exclusive of purebreds; random-bred dogs, or mixed breeds, can be as much in need of a job as a working line Australian shepherd. What's more cruel, leaving an energetic, intelligent dog locked in a crate all day because she can't be trusted in the house, or giving that same energetic, intelligent dog a job that lets her burn up energy, utilize her intelligence, and be with her person day in and day out, twenty-four hours a day?

Ironically, it is the dogs who make the best working dogs that pet owners have the most difficult time with. Intelligent and energetic dogs who are left alone all day often develop behavioral problems. Siberian huskies are notorious for being far-roaming escape artists. When not given ample exercise, their crafty minds will figure out some way, any way, out of their confines. Huskies have been known to break through metal fences, chew through 2-inch-thick wooden doors, and destroy homes in the quest for freedom. When expected to be companions without any form of energy release, they can become anxious and stressed, which leads to destructive, skittish behavior. Idle Border collies often turn to herding neighborhood children and animals—sometimes roughly. Another breed with high energy and high intelligence, the Border collie's boredom can easily become destructive.

There are hundreds of other breeds just like these, whose innate characteristics necessitate they receive intellectual and physical stimulus beyond their role as a family pet. Their unreleased potential can lead to despondency or even aggression. A dog allowed to fulfill her potential is enriched and far happier than a dog dumped in a shelter because she's "unmanageable" or left to entertain herself in the backyard. "The more I know about dogs and the lifestyle that we've inflicted upon them I realize that they weren't made to just sit around all day and do nothing," says Peterson. "What would we do all day? We have computers, we can read, we have televisions, we have things to entertain us. Dogs have very fertile minds; if they

> **For dogs who are unhappy or destructive living as companions, work can be a legitimate alternative.**

don't have something to entertain themselves, they're going to create something."

Ultimately, the jobs working dogs do reflect our own values at any given time. As we continue to develop our appreciation and respect for the dogs in our modern society, our treatment of working dogs will reflect that. There's no doubt dogs love to work. It's our job to ensure that their well-being, and the well-being of other animals and humans, is never compromised in the process.

CHAPTER 3

WORKING BREEDS

Every breed of dog has a purpose. After humans originally domesticated the dog thousands of years ago, our ancestors eventually realized that breeding for specific qualities could create dogs to do specific work. Deliberate breeding followed, producing dogs developed specifically for guarding, herding, and companionship. Four hundred breeds of dogs exist today, and there are hundreds of additional breeds of dogs that no longer exist.

Now, the breeds are largely divided by the work they were bred for. The American Kennel Club (AKC) divides them as: miscellaneous, hound, terrier, working, herding, sporting, non-sporting, and toy. Other registering bodies divide the breeds by more specific working designations, such as gun dogs, herding, guards, and companions. Regardless of how they're divided, the dogs within each group were born and bred for specific purposes, and it behooves pet owners to know which dog does what. Too few people research the breeds before choosing a dog and many end up with an animal they don't understand or can't control.

Owners who find out what their breed of dog is "supposed" to do before bringing one home are much better equipped to deal with any and all of its distinguishing traits, both good and bad. Knowing your dog's background, whether he's a mix or a purebred, can also help you integrate your dog into your life. If you understand why your dog exhibits a particular behavior, you can address it or channel it into work or worklike activities that will give him a more fulfilled life.

Working Dogs

For this book's purposes, I'm using the United Kennel Club's (UKC) breed divisions, which include companion dogs, guardian dogs, herding dogs, gun dogs, northern breeds, terriers, sighthounds/pariah dogs, and scenthounds. Although the UKC's divisions sometimes don't make any more sense than the other registries', I

find that it is a bit more logical and inclusive in terms of work than the AKC or the Kennel Club, in Britain. The groups are mostly based on traditional work; the work of modern working dogs often spans the groups. For example, most SAR dogs are from the gun dog or herding groups.

Many of the companion dogs were originally bred for work but now function solely as companions. Most are small and have minimal exercise requirements, although they still have many of the same needs and desires of other, larger dogs. Among the companion dogs are the toy and miniature poodles, Yorkshire terrier, pug, English bulldog, and even the large dalmatian. Without proper training and socialization, a companion dog can become a tyrant.

The role of most companion dogs is just as their name implies—household pet. Companion dogs may also serve as informal watchdogs—many have a highly developed sense of hearing and will bark madly at any invasion of their territory. Companion dogs may work as actors and hearing dogs as well. Their small size and great hearing ability is especially welcome for older people with hearing difficulties. Some companion dogs participate in dog sports.

The guardian dog group is an apt name for these dogs, who were bred to protect people and other animals from intruders, as well as to find and recover lost or injured people. They are, sort of, canine guardian angels.

Among the guardian dogs are the livestock guardians such as the Maremma sheepdog, the akbash dog, and the Great Pyrenees, as well as those dogs bred to protect humans such as the rottweiler, the Doberman pinscher, and the mastiff. In addition, the UKC's guardian group includes the traditional lifesaving dogs: the snow-loving Saint Bernard and the water-loving Newfoundland. (Known traditionally as the lifesaver dogs, ironically neither of these two breeds is commonly used in SAR today. Their large size and poor longevity negates their use in most modern SAR mediums.) Today, guardian dogs do other jobs besides guarding humans and livestock. These breeds are also found doing patrol, detection, and therapy work. There are even a few service dogs among their rank.

All of the guardian dogs are large, sometimes fierce animals who will lay down their lives to protect what they feel is theirs. As the livestock protectors go against bears and mountain lions to save their sheep or goats, so will the rottweiler and Doberman pinscher go against an intruder threatening to bring harm to the home or family. In work settings, the livestock guardian dogs are often discouraged from bonding to people in order to establish their relationship with the animals they guard. Despite the ferocious reputation of the guardian dogs, however, many make excellent pets and will bond tightly with their people as long as they are raised

> **Many of the companion dogs were originally bred for work but now function solely as companions.**

with them. Rottweilers, Doberman pinschers, Newfoundlands, and Great Pyrenees are common and well-loved pets. All guardian dogs must be well trained and socialized so that their brawn can be controlled, and, although they really don't require a huge amount of exercise past the age of two or three, participation in agility, obedience, or other canine activity will keep their keen minds busy.

The herding dogs are energetic, smart, and instinctual dogs who were bred to herd livestock through eye contact or by nipping at the heels of the animals being herded. Among the herding dogs are the Australian cattle dog, Shetland sheepdog (sheltie), Border collie, and German shepherd.

Herding dogs do best as pets when they have some sort of job to do; they excel in herding trials, agility, and obedience. They can become bored and destructive if their busy minds and bodies aren't occupied. Happiest when they are in the mix, these dogs will often herd whatever they can find; that might mean your kids, your cat, or you. If you expect to have small animals in your home, it's important that you socialize your herding dog early, before the prey instinct is fully developed. The urge to herd can lead to biting, so a no nipping rule is imperative.

Aside from their physical and mental energy needs, herding dogs are amazing companions. A herding dog generally picks one person in the family as his own and is devoted to that person for life. Allegiances aren't switched easily. Herding dogs are still used on ranches, but may also serve as SAR, therapy, and detection dogs.

Gun dogs include super-friendly family dogs such as the golden and Labrador (Lab) retrievers, the high-energy Irish setter, and the harder, or more work-oriented, German shorthaired pointer. All of the gun dogs are aligned by one thing: their love of hunting birds. The gun dogs are divided among the pointers, the flushing dogs, the setters, the retrievers, and the water dogs. If there is one dog among the UKC's gun dog group that doesn't quite seem to fit, it is the web-footed Portuguese water dog, which was and is used to retrieve nets and lines on boats rather than hunt birds. The Portuguese water dog, however, is said to be the forebear of several gun dogs, which is probably the reasoning behind its inclusion in the gun dog category.

> *Regardless of the breed, all working dogs possess certain characteristics: intelligence, boldness, and the drive to play the game.*

All of the gun dogs are high-energy animals with considerable exercise needs. An unexercised gun dog is an unhappy, out-of-control dog. Because of their amenable nature, love of play, and keen sense of smell, golden retrievers and Labs are probably the most common working dogs in the U.S. today. These two breeds make up many of the SAR, detection, and assistance dogs in service right now.

The northern breeds have been bred for a variety of work, including sledding, draft work, herding, hunting, and guarding. Among the northern breeds are the spitz dogs, those animals with prick ears, wedge-shaped heads, and heavy coats that are ubiquitous to northern climates. They are said to be among the closest of domestic dogs to their early dog ancestry, and many modern breeds are purported to include occasional additions of wolf interbreeding.

All of the northern breeds are high-energy dogs who have a tendency toward being independent. Incessant roamers, Siberian huskies, for example, need jobs in order to expend their boundless energy. Without something to keep them busy, they often turn to finding their own work.

Working Breeds

Northern breeds may be used for sledding, skijoring, herding, or flock guarding. These dogs absolutely love the snow, so they are really best suited to a northern climate. If you don't have snow in your region, consider getting your northern breed involved in a weight-pulling or drafting activity. You can get involved in competitions or keep it casual by merely hooking up a harness to your bicycle or to yourself while in-line skating and giving your pup the okay to pull. No dog should ever be expected to pull exorbitant weight, however, and proper safety equipment is essential. Know your dog's limits and use common sense: ensure your dog is healthy by giving him a thorough veterinary exam, always keep your northern breed on a leash in unfenced areas, and only do weight-pulling activities in areas where your dog cannot dash into traffic.

Terriers were bred to hunt and kill vermin, and many of their modern-day tendencies bear this out. Because they are often small in stature, many people are confused about terriers' activity needs. They are not merely companion dogs; rather, they are tenacious, intelligent, and high-energy animals. Because of the work they were bred for, they also have a tendency to dig, bark, and chase—even kill—small animals.

Among the popular terriers are Jack Russell terriers, rat terriers, American pit bull terriers (APBT), and Staffordshire bull terriers (Staffies). These breeds may sound different from one another, but in fact they are quite similar, apart from size and muscle mass. All the terriers are bred to quickly dispatch the animals they are hunting or fighting; this is where the signature terrier shake comes in. Without significant socialization, there are few terriers of any breed who are completely reliable around other animals.

Fearless animals, terriers need a lot of exercise and a lot of training. Traditional trainers often find themselves at a loss when it comes to terriers; these aren't eager-

to-please Labs. Still, terriers can make great pets; surprisingly, the best companion terriers are often the larger Staffies and APBTs, who some find to be more interested in their human companions than are the smaller terriers.

Pariah dogs and sighthounds are grouped together because they encompass the ancient dog breeds. They are often depicted in early art. The pharaoh hound, for example, is significantly similar to the drawings found in Egypt dating from 4000 B.C. Pariah dogs are the ultimate ancient dogs from which all other dogs seem to be descended. Allowed to breed indiscriminately, all breeds eventually lead back to the look of pariah dogs, with their prick ears, medium size, and indiscriminate coloring. Among the pariah dogs are the New Guinea singing dog, Canaan dog, dingo, and basenji. Some of the pariah dogs have become increasingly popular companion animals, although many pariah dogs continue to exist on the periphery of civilization.

Working Breeds

Among the sighthounds are the greyhound, saluki, and Afghan hound, all dogs bred for thousands of years to run fast and long. As the name *sighthound* indicates, these dogs track prey through sight. They have been used for racing for over a millennium and continue to be used for racing on both professional and hobby levels.

Because of their predilection to chase, many sighthounds are not trustworthy around small animals, including small dogs and cats. Sighthound fanciers with small animals in the home must be sure to socialize their dogs to live among them. Unfortunately for cat-owning greyhound lovers, most of the greyhounds kept as pets are retired racing greyhounds. Most don't adjust well to cat households, although there are exceptions. A good greyhound rescue program can help a cat-loving greyhound adopter find the right dog.

Sighthounds have high exercise needs, although greyhounds, the most famous of the sighthound runners, tend to have moderate exercise needs. Many call greyhounds the consummate couch potato. Some people opt to get involved in lure coursing but this doesn't seem to be necessary for the happiness of most sighthounds. That said, they are true runners, so it's important they be kept on leash when on walks or at the park. Once a sighthound catches sight of an in-motion rabbit, all bets are off. For the health of neighborhood pets, wildlife, and the dog, leashes for a sighthound are a must.

Scenthounds are the hounds of our imagination: big, slobbery, nose-to-the-ground dogs, whose olfactory senses are legendary. Among the scenthounds are the ubiquitous bloodhound, basset hound, and beagle. Included in the group is the dachshund, which is really better suited to the companion group.

> **Scenthounds are the hounds of our imagination: big, slobbery, nose-to-the-ground dogs, whose olfactory senses are legendary.**

The drawbacks to scenthounds are that they are slobbery, independent, one-minded, often stubborn, and prone to howling. Bred for tenacity and stamina, scenthounds also need a good amount of exercise. Many people, however, are addicted to the peculiar nature of scenthounds and their love of play and sense of humor.

Scenthounds do well in a variety of activities, especially in tracking and scent discrimination. Bloodhounds are commonly used by law enforcement and are famous for their ability to track a cold trail through all types of distractions.

Working Dogs

People are sometimes surprised by the amount of exercise these dogs need, deceived by the myth of the lazy southern hound, hanging out on the porch all day long. In fact, these dogs are true hunters and are built for veracity. Once they pick up a scent, they're off and running, so a leash is imperative. In addition, a hound on scent is unlikely to look up to see where roads start and stop, so an unleashed scent-hound often leads to a short-lived dog.

When considering breeds and working dogs, it's important to realize that few dogs actually do the work they were originally bred to do. Search and rescue dogs are often from the gun or herding groups. Hearing dogs are often terriers, and prototypical guide dogs are German shepherd dogs or Labs. Labs and golden retrievers are considered to be ideal working dogs mostly because the breeds combine a love of play, a superior sense of smell, and amenability.

Mixed breeds also do a great deal of work from detection to herding to SAR. Some assistance dog programs even breed Lab–golden retriever crosses. A dog's breed in no way limits his ability to do a job, although certain breeds do excel in one type of work over another.

Regardless of the breed, all working dogs possess certain characteristics: intelligence, boldness, and the drive to play the game. They work for the love of it; and as a result they save and enrich innumerable lives. Although the dogs in the following chapters don't tell the whole story of working dogs, they represent just what makes these animals so invaluable to us as workers and as pets.

WORKING LIKE A DOG

CHAPTER 4

HUNTING DOGS

If there is one job a dog does that is the root of all other jobs, it is hunting. Despite the ethical questions that some people pose regarding killing wild animals, there's no doubt that hunting fulfills most dogs' destinies. Without the predator-prey hunting instinct, dogs would not herd or rescue or sniff out contraband, and they probably would never have been domesticated by humans in the first place. Dogs have been trained to hunt almost every animal on earth, big and small. The hunting breeds range from the Rhodesian Ridgeback used to hunt big game, including lions, to the diminutive Yorkshire terrier bred to find and kill vermin.

Aside from their natural guarding tendencies, dogs' first explicit partnership with humans was to hunt. Some scholars speculate that humans first followed dogs as they stalked prey, taking advantage of their superior olfactory and tracking skills to find game. Then humans began to manipulate the dogs' skills, training them to serve as hunting companions. Over thousands of years, humans eventually manipulated these skills into other jobs: herding, flock guarding, SAR, even truffle hunting. All of these jobs use the basic hunting skills of dogs: a predatory instinct coupled with amazing olfactory and aural senses.

The hunting breeds, because of their instincts and senses, are used extensively in almost every avenue of work, not just to hunt. In herding, the predatory instinct is redirected to gather animals rather than to kill them. SAR dogs are trained with traditional hunting techniques, and many SAR handlers argue that hunting dogs are the quintessential search dogs. A. J. Frank, who has handled two disaster SAR dogs, says that his first dog, Ohlin, now retired, was originally bought as a hunting dog, "Only now he hunts humans." Bloodhounds are used by the police to search out missing children as well as fleeing suspects, and another little hound, the beagle, uses its considerable hunting skills to find contraband fruits, meats, and vegetables for the USDA.

Hunting dogs are also being used in the most surprising of ways, for example to chase birds off airport tarmacs and scare wandering bears from populated areas. Dogs once bred to kill wildlife are now working to save wild animals or serve as an alternative to euthanasia as humans continue their encroachment into the territories where wild animals make their homes. As always, dogs have adapted to meet the evolving needs of humans.

There is something stirring about watching a dog's innate hunting drive, even if we don't use that drive for hunting.

Although dogs are still used to hunt big game, their use has declined dramatically as diminishing wildlife populations and increasingly restrictive laws have limited this type of hunting. The use of traditional treeing hounds such as coonhounds, for example, is illegal in many states.

Hunting, in general, has been largely relegated to privately stocked hunting preserves that are mostly limited to birds and to field trials. As wildlife populations have declined to the point that there are few animals to take, hunters are becoming quasi-environmentalists, working through conservation to preserve the legacy of hunting.

Hunters who use dogs say that they wouldn't hunt without their dogs. As hunter and bird-dog breeder Dan Larose points out, few hunters hunt for subsistence and even during hunting season bag limits are small, usually two a day. The real point is being outdoors and working with your dogs. "My real joy isn't going out and killing these things," he says. "It's going out and working with my dogs and doing this as a team. The enjoyment I get out of it is when the dog does it all right, when all this time and training come to fruition and the two of us are working together as a well-meshed team; we communicate without hardly talking."

Larose describes bird hunting as though he were a sportscaster giving a play-by-play commentary, with a rat-a-tat delivery, uncontained excitement, and true love of

Hunting Dogs

the sport. "I carry a whistle in my teeth and I can give him a tweet-tweet and a finger point and he's to that side and he's running to this side and, boom, I can see the excitement in his tail and all of a sudden his pace slows right down. I know he's in a stalk, he's got scent in his face, I can read bird all over his body. I step out to one side and watch him work and, boom, he locks up and says it's right there."

Garrett Lockee, 80 years old, has been hunting with dogs since he was a little boy, "We've had bird dogs in my family since I was born," he says. A principle founder of The Bird Dog Foundation, Inc., in Grand Junction, Tennessee, Lockee is busy with volunteering and family but still has time for a month and a half of hunting each winter. He and his wife, Sally, whom Lockee characterizes as a "fairly decent quail shot," take their 12 hunting dogs to south Texas for much of December and January of each year to hunt to their heart's content. "We feed 12 dogs for one month of satisfaction," remarks Lockee. Like Larose, Lockee is in it for the dogs. "If I didn't go with the dogs, I wouldn't go," he says. "The older you get, the more you appreciate your dogs. I would never take a gun out or anything if I didn't have the dogs. We have probably found as many as 10 or 18 coveys of quail in a day and probably won't kill but 1 or 2 birds. We hardly even shoot except as a super reward for a super job for a dog. We let the dogs point and if everything is completely perfect, their work is perfect and we feel like it's time to reward them by shooting a bird, we do."

Lockee adds that his joy in working with the dogs comes from his ability to communicate and work smoothly with them, "You feel good that your dogs are responsive enough through the training you've given them to go to the areas you'd like them to go. It's sort of an ego thing, like a child that does well in school is a pride to the parent; the dogs do the same thing for guys like me. You enjoy the response you get out of the dogs whether you caused the response or they respond naturally."

There is something stirring about watching a dog's innate hunting drive, even if we don't use that drive for hunting. I remember as a girl how I would watch our Irish setter, Sunshine, suddenly stop and stand on our beach for long moments, her head and chest thrust forward, back legs braced, and one front leg bent and pointed toward seagulls searching the tidelands for clams. Then, just as suddenly, she would leap, streaking toward them, scattering them into the sky.

It's not surprising that for centuries authors and painters have tried to convey the spirit of hunting dogs; it is a wonder to behold. A hunting dog and its handler manifest the central relationship between dog and human, the evolution of our relationship and the core of its expanse. As Lockee points out, a good handler is always looking to see if the dog is acting on instinct or on skill, "Is it really hunting or is it really running?" he laughs. "I had a dog who I could never understand why it didn't find many birds in areas where other dogs were finding birds plentiful. The dog was not hunting, it was just running. If it stumbled onto a covey of birds, it would point."

Handlers revel in being able to form basic instincts into skills used by a well-trained hunting dog. "Hunting dogs are capable of a lot more than people realize," says Lockee. "The dogs will do a lot of things for you if you give them the opportunity." Lockee, for one, doesn't believe in pushing a dog. "We have two dogs who we've hunted almost two years but they're not solid broke yet," says Lockee. "Each time we take them out we notice they're learning and developing. Just like a kid in school, you don't expect it to read in kindergarten.

"I don't do any rush techniques, trying to overburden the dog; I have one out for thirty minutes and put him on two or three covey finds and do the same thing the next day," says Lockee. "By slowly doing that day in and day out, in a couple years you've got a fairly decent dog."

In general, hunting dog trainers don't train with treats or toys; rather verbal praise and the hunt itself is the reward. Finding a bird is the culmination of the hunt, and the ultimate reward is to allow the dog to retrieve the bird after it's been shot—in fact, dead or injured prey is what most dog toys simulate. Larose raises pigeons that he uses in training, but many hunters rely on the use of dead birds, or, more commonly, rubber retriever bumpers.

Like most handlers of working dogs, these trainers tend to believe in a mixture of positive reward and correction-based training. Larose explains that when his dogs do well, he pets them and praises them in a high tone of voice. When they don't follow a command, he reissues the command with a firmer tone of voice. Larose also judges which training method is appropriate for each dog. Depending on how amenable the dog is, he says, it may require a soft, cajoling voice, a stern voice, or a physical correction.

As much a believer in corrective training as Larose is, it's clear that he relishes the reward. "Positive reinforcement is a much higher tone of voice and a lot of praise and scratching them up on the back of the butt where they can't reach. When I'm happy, I'll get down on my knees and hug 'em and they love it; they're licking my ears and my face and just love that attention, love that you're down on their level. I play with them on the ground like a dog and that's what makes that trust relationship; they trust me and when I tell 'em good dog they know I mean it."

Lockee also adheres to a reward and correction training regimen, "I think when a dog is a good dog you have to have a simple way of rewarding him that registers with the dog. When the dog does something wrong, you can detect it

> **Aside from their natural guarding tendencies, dogs' first explicit partnership with humans was to hunt.**

in the dog, *Hey, boss, I think I did something wrong and I don't want you to punish me, but if you do I expected it.*" That said, Lockee quickly cautions, "I don't think you have to punish dogs the way the old timers did to get them trained."

Handlers' philosophies run the gamut from dogs who are kept in large kennels and socialized little to hunting dogs who live in the house and, aside from the time in the field, are pets in every way. Hunter Bruce Hummel's vizsla, for example, sleeps on the bed and accompanies Hummel's wife, who is a grade school teacher, to the classroom as a special reward for well-behaved students.

Larose believes that a strong human-dog relationship makes for a good hunting dog. "I think to make a good hunting dog you really do have to have a relationship with him; I think that relates to any dog doing any purpose. It's a trust relationship between the handler and the dog." He explains that this is important day-to-day and in the field, "A good dog is always checking to know where you are; otherwise he's a self-hunter, he's out there to hunt that predator/prey situation totally on his own. In a good relationship, he's doing it with you, for you. That's why he's always checking to make sure you're there." Although Larose has nine dogs, seven Braque do Bourbonnais and two English springer spaniels, he makes it a point to have a relationship with each dog. He points out, though, that having a pack of dogs makes them less dependent on him for their social interaction. All live in kennels during the day and in the basement at night, where they have individual crates, but he's attentive to providing one-on-one interaction with each dog every day.

A hunting dog and its handler manifest the central relationship between dog and human.

Lockee takes a firmer view: his dogs, he asserts, are "hunting dogs" and live in a kennel full time. "They're fairly obedient but these are hunting dogs and we treat them as hunting dogs. We give them the best food that's made and we have a very good rapport with our dogs and I think we take very good care of them. I've already given them a biscuit this morning," he tells me when we speak early one afternoon. "Still, it's not the type of things you do with pet dogs in the house."

Despite the size of most hunting dog packs and varying philosophies about their upbringing, it's a rare hunter who has not had a special attachment to at least one of his or her dogs. For Lockee it was an English pointer who he didn't even want. He'd loaned a dog for stud and the breeder insisted he take one of the pups. "I took her everywhere with me and every time we went hunting she would find something. She was one of those dogs who you could take up into big grouse woods where you can hardly see the dog so you have to run with bells. She would run half a mile, then come right back looking for me, and then when she'd find me she'd go off again. When the bells stopped I knew she was on point and I'd go kill her bird. She was just something you had to fall in love with."

Hunting Dogs

Not all hunting dogs actually hunt, many are only used in field trials or hunting tests. Some hunters, as is the case with both Larose and Lockee, participate in trials and tests as well as hunt. Lockee, who is active in field trials, has devoted much of his life to honoring and commemorating the dogs in this competitive sport. The Bird Dog Foundation, Inc., he tells me, includes the Field Trial Hall of Fame and the National Bird Dog Museum. He was inspired to start the organization after finding out that the only museum commemorating the great bird dogs was a couple of walls in the back of a grocery store.

Field trialing is a popular sport that many who would have been involved in hunting a few years ago now participate in. It gives dogs a chance to indulge in their innate love of the hunt, while allowing handlers to compare their dogs' prowess against others. For many hunting dog handlers, bringing home a ribbon means more than bringing home a bird. Field trials occasionally use live tethered birds but usually use dead, or "cold," game or rubber retriever bumpers. American Kennel Club field trials do not allow the use of live game.

The fact is dogs love to hunt. Almost everything they do for us is based on this love. It's hard to say that the hunting life is the best for a dog, given the somewhat isolating conditions in which they live. It's an old-fashioned job, and training and living conditions reflect that; they tend to be archaic in comparison to those that many modern working dogs experience. Still, I'm not sure that the life Lockee's and Larose's dogs live isn't the ultimate dog's life. Dogs who get to live together in a pack and get to run and kill are probably doing what they like best, and there proba-bly isn't a happier dog on earth than the bird dog racing through the brush after her prey.

After almost 80 years of hunting, Lockee has learned the signs of a dog who will make an excellent hunter. One setter who his wife raised "died to find birds," he says. "Every minute on the ground she was looking for birds; she'd put a spasm on," he laughs. For a true bird dog, that drive is everything. "There's an incentive, a motivation, a burning desire to say, *Let me out of here,* and then when you let them out, man, they are streaking across the country looking for something."

CHAPTER 5

RANCH DOGS

Ranch dogs are the cowboys of the dog world. They're a quintessential part of the western landscape. According to their enthusiasts, it was the herding dogs' tenacity and intelligence that paved the road for settlers moving west. As in Australia, where they say the country was built on the back of kelpies, herding dogs allowed American farmers and ranchers to do work no one person could do on his own.

There are two roles that ranch dogs fulfill: herding and guarding. One bonds so tightly with his human that he takes direction from the blink of an eye; the other bonds so tightly with the livestock on the farm that he will protect his charges with his life.

On a misty Sunday morning in northwest Washington, Jan Wesen is bringing her sheep into the paddock. She directs one of her nine dogs, a red and tan kelpie named Slip, to bring the sheep around and in through the narrow opening in the fence. With nary a stray sheep and practiced aplomb, Slip crouches in prototypical herding dog stance and eyes the sheep. With quick directions Wesen tells Slip "come by," sending the dog clockwise around the stock. Occasionally, Wesen gives a command and Slip bursts into a quick run toward the sheep, causing them to push forward, then just as quickly Wesen says, "stand," and Slip is crouched and still again.

Watching Slip, it's hard to tell whether he wants to herd the sheep or eat them; his statue-stillness and obsessive stare is disquieting. But that's the thing about herding dogs; for millennia, savvy

ranchers have taken the natural prey drive in their dogs and molded it, through breeding and training, to develop a dog who herds rather than kills.

Wesen is a dairy farmer as well as a herding instructor, trial competitor, and kelpie and Australian shepherd breeder. She bought her first kelpie, Bear, to help work the cows on the farm, especially when moving them inside the barn for milking, feeding, and veterinary care. Much of Bear's work was done inside the barn, says Wesen, laughing that when she and Bear first started competing, their tendency to work close in wasn't considered impressive. Competitive herding dogs are prized for the ability to work far away from their handlers, who give fluid, barely detectable commands. She points out, however, that Bear did the work that needed to be done. He wasn't a show dog or a hobby dog; he was a true worker. Tasks that at one time seemed unmanageable became routine with Bear's help. When she bought Bear in

Ranch Dogs

1985, admits Wesen, she was green and he had to rely mostly on his instincts, "He figured it out, quite honestly."

Although Bear wasn't from the best lines or a recipient of Wesen's now-immense knowledge of herding, he taught her the value of a working dog: a lesson that has substantially changed her life.

A little before 9:00 A.M. Wesen's students begin to trickle onto the muddy grounds of the dairy farm. Herding dogs of all shapes and sizes leap out of trucks and four-wheel drives. Here, about an hour north of Seattle in the agricultural Skagit Valley, many of the dogs are both competitors and day-to-day working dogs, although Wesen professes to a fair share of one-timers: Seattleites who make the trek to test their herding dogs' prowess with livestock. She always cautions them before introducing their dogs to sheep, "If you're not going to do this you need to understand that introducing the dog to sheep will awaken its chase drive, which may be misdirected toward cars or cats." Most of Wesen's students, however, are experienced herders. Some take classes from her regularly while others show up now and again to work on problems that crop up in competition or on the farm.

Using garden rakes rather than the traditional crook—these are real working dogs, after all—Wesen's students shepherd their dogs through their paces as Wesen watches and guides. She corrects and encourages occasionally, nodding when a move is particularly fluid. In a small paddock, a corgi and his handler herd for the first time under Wesen's close supervision. The session was short and the sheep were particularly gentle, but when it's over, the little white-and-tan dog is shivering with excitement and adrenalin. This is a moment that handlers cherish: the amazement of seeing their dogs herd for the first time and seeing that their dogs have a burning desire to do this work.

Linda Jaquish, who has four cattle dogs, remembers the first time she took her female, Sadie, to a farm, "I had a herding instinct test done on her," remembers Jaquish. "Basically, they just threw her out there on some sheep and observed certain things they think are important: whether they gather the stock, what they do. She absolutely did unbelievable. It was as if she knew what to do. She wasn't frantic, she gathered all the sheep, she never bit—it was like watching poetry in motion, I just stood there in awe and watched her." Jaquish knew at that moment that Sadie was born to herd.

Working Dogs

When Jaquish started herding with Sadie, it was only because the dog had taken an uncanny interest in the cattle kept in a pasture behind their house. A friend had warned Jaquish that unless she absolutely didn't want Sadie to herd, she shouldn't squelch the interest, "It gave me the opportunity to perfect a really sound recall," laughs Jaquish.

Once Jaquish saw Sadie in action, however, she knew it was a done deal. In the five years since, this cattle dog has not only become an experienced trial dog but a working dog as well: to keep up with her love of herding, Jaquish bought Sadie her own sheep. "For years I went to Jan's and worked her sheep," explains Jaquish. "When you first work a dog it's important you have docile sheep, but then you go to your first trial and you have sheep from hell. When Sadie got to a certain level Jan suggested I get some sheep that hadn't been worked so she could get used to it."

Now, 12 sheep later, Sadie utilizes her competitive skills at home, helping to move the sheep when needed and generally keeping them in line. Jaquish laughs that when she and her husband first got the sheep they tried to get them into a stall to trim their hooves, "We could not get them into the stall. Finally in desperation we got Sadie. She walked in there, looked at the sheep and they ran into the stall. Once in the stall, Sadie kept the sheep to one corner so we could pull them out one at a time. We thought, *Boy, we're never doing this without her again!*"

Other herding dog handlers get their dogs with the intention of working them. Carol Hummel, who owns a cattle ranch in southern Oregon, knew a herding dog would be a tremendous boon. Although she'd never had a working dog before, when she bought Border collie Callie she did her research, investing in a puppy from a proven working line and beginning classes with the dog by about eight months of age.

Now Callie is part of the working life of the farm; when the cattle move, so does she. Callie and the cattle are a tandem team working together to make the farm a success. When we spoke, Hummel was planning a cattle drive from their ranch to a neighbor's, about nine miles away. "We're 'preg checking' the cows," she says, "Keeping the pregnant ones and selling the others, then moving them back. We work off of horseback when we move them like that. There will be four of us on horses and three dogs. We just kind of go to different places to gather them up, then as a group move across country. The dogs keep the animals moving. If there's a straggler, they'll bring it back.

Ranch Dogs

"They just keep the momentum going," says Hummel. "Part of it is that the cattle learn to respect the dogs. They know that with the black-and-white dog behind they need to keep moving. The older cows have learned that this little dog is going to make them move. She's just this tiny little thing and she'll go out in a bullpen with 15 bulls in it and round them up and move them where she wants."

Hummel adds that of the three dogs they'll be using, one is Callie's littermate and the other is an older herding breed mix. "When we're moving, the dogs just sort it out—one will take the middle and the other two take each side, and they'll stay within their boundaries." She adds that she and Callie may also divert from the group and go and collect 10 head on their own and then bring them into the group.

> **Competitive herding dogs are prized for the ability to work far away from their handlers, who give fluid, barely detectable commands.**

Hummel is quick to add that due to her inexperience with working dogs, it's often Callie teaching her. "I think she really knows more than I do; her instinct is so strong." That said, both dog and handler are continually learning. When I first met Hummel at Wesen's clinic, she was returning for a little help on problems she'd encountered on the ranch. Callie is only three years old, and she and Hummel are still a couple years away from being a well-oiled machine, something that experienced handlers say doesn't happen until about the fifth year of working together.

Jaquish also hastens to assure me that Sadie is the one doing all the work, "She really does know more than I do. She sees the reaction of the stock and senses it long before I do." Although Jaquish doesn't call Sadie disobedient, the cattle dog will do what she knows is right, even if Jaquish doesn't.

"Often I'll be out there and I'll give the wrong command, getting mixed up, and my herding instructor will say, 'You know, you were giving her the wrong command: bless her heart she didn't listen,'" Jaquish tells me, laughing. On one occasion, shortly before we spoke, Jaquish was in Canada for a herding trial. They were coming to the end of the course when Jaquish gave Sadie a command to bring the sheep off the fence, although Sadie was already moving in the opposite direction to control the sheep. Sometimes the instinct of the working dog is more in tune than that of the herder. "She gave me one look over her shoulder, not in a sassy way but to tell me it's not going to work. She went around, took the command, and brought them off the fence right to me." As soon as Jaquish left the field, a more experienced trial handler confided, "Your dog really saved your butt."

Jaquish doesn't mind this give and take with Sadie, although it's taken her time to get to this point. "I used to demand that she do it my way and things would go awry. Finally somebody told me that I had to stop doing that to my dog; she's an independent thinker and you have to trust her when she's right. She's not trying to beat me at the game; she's just reading things better than I am. I've learned to let her do that—that's been my greatest learning experience with her."

Hummel agrees, "I have to trust Callie for her to trust me." She adds that on a working ranch, trust between the dog and handler is imperative, "They have to believe you're a partnership. Trust is especially important when you're working with bulls: those are big animals and you need to believe that she's going to do her job and she needs to believe that you're going to do yours."

"I'm utilizing their instincts to their full advantage; the teamwork is what makes that work," says Wesen of her dogs.

Herding dog handlers caution that these dogs are independent-minded, sensitive animals who do not respond well to punishment, harsh words, or abandonment in the barn. Herders pick their people, usually just one person in the family, and they want to be with them whenever they can. Negative reinforcement such as shock collars doesn't work on the herding breeds, says Wesen, "They'll just say, *I'm not going to play.*" Instead, Wesen works to find the key that will unlock each dog's potential. She's skeptical of the emphasis so many American trainers put on negative training methods, pointing out that Australian handlers are light spoken with their dogs. "All this nonsense that Americans are doing just doesn't have to be there," she says.

Ranch Dogs

"I'd like to say I'm 100 percent no-correction, but I do still have to protect the livestock," adds Wesen, "I try to keep it gentle." She points out that herding dogs are moving large powerful animals but are undaunted, even when kicked or rolled during their work.

In general, most herding dogs are pets as well as workers, and handlers doubt that it could be any other way. Even Wesen brings her nine dogs in the house at night. "I do all the stuff as a pet owner," says Wesen. "Part of a good working relationship is that they are a companion and a friend. You can't get as much out of a dog without that bond."

I'm captivated by my trip to Wesen's farm, and on my return home I can't help wondering how my own cattle dog mix, Desi, would fare with livestock. No matter that she's 10 years old and has never been closer to a sheep than through the car window; I'm not worried about bringing out her prey drive, that's there in force. She's been known to herd a cat or two, and I take her somewhat obsessive/compulsive staring as fair warning that she's about to take off after something.

So I contact a local Southern California herding instructor and competitor, Jerry Stewart, and find myself in a paddock on another spring day—although this time it is hot and dusty. Wilting in the heat, Desi and I take refuge in the shade and listen as Stewart explains the mechanics of herding: the "come to mes" and the "go bys" and the various and sundry other abstruse herding terms. While we chat, his "dog broke" sheep huddle in a corner, sending wary glances Desi's way, and his current dog, a Border collie named Choice, lounges under a shady tree.

> **Herding dog handlers caution that these dogs are independent-minded, sensitive animals who do not respond well to punishment, harsh words, or abandonment in the barn.**

Stewart explains that he entered the world of herding through a sheltie named Easy. A well-mannered gentleman, Easy would turn into another dog whenever Stewart and he passed cattle or sheep, scratching at the windows of the car and generally making a racket. Stewart thought this drive could be channeled into herding, and he was right. Easy eventually went on to become a herding champion. WTC Stewart's Easy Storm, UD, HX, HTD-III, PC earned all of his championships by the time he was four years old, and then he became Stewart's work partner, helping to train several generations of dogs until he died in

1999. Most working dog handlers say that their best dog was their first, and Stewart is no exception. He attributes everything he's done in herding to Easy and the relationship they shared.

After chatting for almost an hour, Stewart peers down at Desi, who is now done exploring and sacked out like Choice. "Okay, let's give her a turn," he says. As soon as Stewart rises, Desi's up and walking a little cautiously toward the sheep. Her ears are cocked forward and I wouldn't have been able to break her concentration if I had tried. Guiding her with his crook, Stewart directs Desi toward the sheep, and she looks focused and confident as she trots from the side to the back of the flock, stopping when they stop and maintaining some distance from them. All bets are off, however, when an errant sheep takes off across the pen. In a cloud of dust Desi follows it at a dead run, in sheer prey mode now. Stewart calls her off and I leash her. Her hind legs are quivering with exhaustion and adrenalin, although she's really only been herding for a few minutes.

> **I'm captivated by my trip to Wesen's farm, and on my return home I can't help wondering how my own cattle dog mix, Desi, would fare with livestock.**

Stewart explains that the wayward sheep brought out Desi's prey drive, "That's when accidents happen," he says gruffly. He attributes her shakiness to a combination of adrenalin and exhaustion. The dogs work hard, he says, both mentally and physically. After seeing the toll a couple minutes of sheep minding takes on Desi, I have a better sense of herding dogs' stamina and endurance. She's an older girl, it's true, but she's also in good shape with regular agility training and long daily walks.

Seeing the innate skill of a herding dog, even a mixed-breed one who spent her first 10 years of life largely ignorant of the concept of livestock, is astonishing. The experience of 10 years wasn't able to condition out of her what hundreds of years of breeding put in. And that's the beauty of herding dogs, their handlers will tell you. Herding isn't about training; it's about watching the dog and learning how to help him do his job. As Jan Wesen tells me, "If the dog can control the stock, I can control the dog."

Herding dogs aren't the only canine workers returning to ranches and farms across the U.S. Although livestock guardians have been used extensively in Europe and Asia for thousands of years, the tradition didn't arrive on this continent until the 1970s when the USDA initiated a predator study. Before that, farmers protected

Ranch Dogs

their livestock with any technology available, struggling to stave off wolves, cougars, coyotes, and bears with shotguns, electric wire, motion detectors, and anything else that might work. Sometimes, however, new doesn't always mean better and what's worked for two thousand years may have lasted for a reason.

Predators are a major part of life for ranchers and farmers, especially now as civilization encroaches on the traditional hunting grounds of wildlife. When a sub-division erases acres of wild land, the resident animals need to find a new source of food: often that means a farmer's livestock.

Although the concept of livestock guardian dogs stems from the practice of leaving animals to graze in areas away from the farm, many modern-day ranchers and farmers use them even in small fenced-in pastures. Although flock protectors tend to look like large lovable teddy bears, they are fierce warriors when it comes to defending their flocks. And the flocks are just that: theirs. True livestock guardians are born and raised with their flocks and kept at a distance from humans and other dogs. Right from the start, they are encouraged to see the flock as part of their pack, so they are willing to protect them to the death. While most livestock protectors will allow human contact only from their handlers, and that may be grudgingly, they coddle their livestock with affection and often become so attached to the babies that they try to steal them from their mothers.

Ironically, there is probably no bigger difference among all working dogs than between herders and guardians; these dogs truly operate on opposite ends of the spectrum. Herding dogs thrive on the bond they share with their handlers; without that bond they will not work. Guardians, on the other hand, are good workers because they do not share a strong bond with humans. Their bond is with the livestock.

Working Dogs

On Doug Maier's goat farm, about 60 miles north of Jan Wesen's dairy farm, live five large, furry white dogs. The Maremma sheepdog is an ancient Italian breed, bred for two thousand years to protect livestock, mainly sheep and goats. Although these dogs look like cuddly and lovable pet dogs, on approach they quickly make it clear that they are not.

Maier bought his first dog shortly after starting his farm. In the wooded area where he lives, he knew that it would not be long before predators began visiting. It's hard to imagine anything trying to get past these dogs, as all five bark out warnings to us as we approach the goat pens. The large male, Maximillian, is interested in our presence, posturing and shifting his position constantly to keep between the goats and us.

Maier explains that he raises his dogs with little human contact except from him and his wife because he doesn't want strangers approaching the goats. "You raise the dogs to your situation," he says. "We don't want them friendly to people because we don't want people to go in there when we're not around." That said, when Maier goes in with the dogs to move them, they immediately soften, nuzzling him and trying to maneuver a butt scratch or two while he's there. "With humans they know they're real subordinate, they're big babies, they'll roll on their backs and want their tummies rubbed," says Maier. "Anything strange, though, they're real suspicious. If someone went in there alone they'd be taking their chances."

When new puppies are born, the first thing they see is their goats, so the process of bonding to their livestock starts from the very beginning. They quickly view the animals as part of their pack and become protective over them. "You have to walk a fine line," says Maier. "You want to be alpha but you want them to bond with the animals, to have a desire to be with the animals. They're so cute but you can't give them too much attention and affection. You don't treat them as a pet dog but you don't totally ignore them." Maier generally limits his interaction with the puppies to feeding time, when he checks them over, plays with them, and gets in a few cuddles. This way, the dogs will allow him to touch them when they're adults but they won't rely on him for their social interaction. He points out, however, that dogs in pastures or on large ranges of land often don't see people for a month at a time. They can become so human-shy that even their owners are unable to get near them.

Farmers who want their dogs to be friendly to people raise them with more human social interaction but still keep the emphasis on the dog's relationship with the livestock, "You have to treat them like a livestock dog who is there to protect the animals," says Maier.

Maier is convinced that he would not be in business today if it were not for the dogs. "We've never lost a goat to a predator but if we didn't have

> **Right from the start, they are encouraged to see the flock as part of their pack, so they are willing to protect them to the death.**

the dogs, our goats would have gotten ate up a long time ago," he says. Often, he and his wife wake up to barking in the night. "The dogs have different barks, they have a woof-woof warning bark, but when there is something there they have a real fast bark. We've been in the house and heard them do that and growl. We come out and shine our spotlights and see these beady little eyes looking at us from the woods back there."

Working Dogs

To point out just how valuable these dogs are to his operation, Maier tells me about a neighbor down the road who had a resident cougar who was killing her sheep and alpacas. She stopped to ask Maier about buying a dog but was apparently unconvinced because she never returned, "She's out of business, but the cougar's still there," says Maier. "Now he's eating the neighbor's Black Angus cattle."

Although Maier had no intention of becoming a dog breeder, he had so many inquiries that he now breeds two litters a year, one from each female. All of his dogs are placed as working dogs, and he's had a waiting list since the first litter. He's sold dogs to people with everything from alpacas and llamas to cattle. "They'll protect whatever they're raised with."

> **Had I, or anyone, made a threatening gesture toward Bridgett's goats, her response would have been swift.**

Predators range from cougars and coyotes to bears. "The dogs will go up against anything. Whether they'll win or not, that's something else. With most predators, unless they're really serious, that's enough deterrent to make them want to go away." Maier explains that with a guardian dog the first line of defense is intimidation: the size and barking are usually enough, but there are always the exceptions. There was one dog who he almost didn't sell because it was born without a tail. Convinced by a rancher who was having severe predation problems, Maier finally sold the dog with the caveat that he be neutered. "The dog's now 150 pounds and went up against a black bear and won," he laughs.

A livestock guardian's life can be a tough one. Whereas Maier's Maremmas are in a fenced area with few large predators in the area, other flock guardians are exposed to cougars and bears on a regular basis. Predator stress can lead to a shortened life span for guardian dogs, either as a result of physical and mental stress or as a direct result from an attack by a large predator.

A livestock guardian's instincts to protect come from his love of the livestock. Guardians sometimes become so attached to the livestock that female dogs will even allow the babies to nurse from them. "When kids are born, the dogs' protectiveness goes up a couple of notches," says Maier. "Sometimes they get into fights over who's going to sleep in front of the pen with the kids." The dogs will even fight the mother goats over the kids, "Sometimes the dogs will get overprotective, and they'll get in there when the mom's kidding [giving birth] and interfere."

Ranch Dogs

Maier explains that when the does are kidding he keeps a baby monitor in his bedroom. One night he heard a kid screaming bloody murder and went out to the barn to investigate. There, he found a little black kid alone in the middle of the barn. "When we went to bed we didn't have any black kids so right away I knew what happened. Max had stolen this newborn kid. I went around to see whose kid this was, and one of my older does had blood on her so I could see she and Max had gotten into a fight over it." Once Maier started checking over the doe, he discovered that she had a second kid that was breech. If Max hadn't stolen the first kid, both the doe and the breech kid would have died. "He kind of redeemed himself," says Maier, adding, "Now when we have a goat kidding, he has to be with the bucks."

As Maier gives me the tour of his farm, he points out the dogs and describes each personality. Max is the alpha male and Sophia the alpha female. Leonardo's

neutered because he has an overbite, but that hasn't affected his instinct for the goats. "He likes his goats. When the goats lay down at night he has to go right in the middle of them and lay down." Bianca's a gentle touch with her charges, while Bridgett is the friendliest of the lot. Maier wants to prove his point and takes me into the paddock Bridgett is watching over. She postures a bit and gives some warning barks, but eventually comes over to give me a thorough sniffing. She seems serene enough, and as we visit I'm fairly comfortable that she's not going to attack me if I turn my back.

The white dog with her meek charges, however, is deceptively serene. Had I, or anyone, made a threatening gesture toward Bridgett's goats, her response would have been swift. As far removed as she is from her Italian forebears, Bridgett and the rest of Maier's Maremmas are the same animals—in appearance and devotion.

CHAPTER 6

ASSISTANCE DOGS

Many terms are used to describe the dogs who serve people with physical disabilities, be they are related to sight, hearing, or mobility. Those who serve the blind or sight impaired are called guide dogs, those who serve the deaf or hard of hearing are called hearing dogs, and those who assist with mobility as well as medical response are called service dogs. *Assistance dogs* is an umbrella term that can be used for all dogs doing this type of work.

Other types of assistance dogs include those who serve to alert their handlers to oncoming medical crises such as seizures or high blood pressure. At this point, however, there is no established way to train dogs for this purpose, so I have not designated these jobs separately nor have I discussed those dogs characterized as support dogs who are trained to serve people with emotional or mental illness. The Delta Society is currently developing a program to provide guidelines to train support dogs.

Assistance dogs in general have many similarities, including their training, function, and population served. Assistance dog teams (a human handler and a dog) also face many of the same challenges, especially in relation to access. The Americans with Disabilities Act (ADA), which was passed in 1990, provides disabled Americans "reasonable access" to all public places, including hotels, restaurants, retail stores, airplanes, and public buildings. That means that an assistance dog by herself doesn't have access but the person using the dog has access with the dog, as people do when using a wheelchair or walker. The ADA does not require that an assistance dog wear a vest or collar identifying her as a certified assistance dog or carry papers verifying her use as an assistance dog, although most assistance dog handlers choose to use these identifying items.

Guide dogs were the first of the assistance dogs to gain recognition in the U.S. and inspired other types of dog assistance work. Most assistance programs follow

the essential protocol first established by the guide dog programs, meaning the dogs are trained by professional or volunteer trainers and then are placed with the recipients. Since the first American guide dog organization was established in the 1920s, the use of assistance dogs has expanded greatly. Service and hearing dogs first came into use during the mid-1970s, then hit their stride in the 1990s, with larger established organizations.

Assistance dogs are either bred by the organization, found through animal shelters or rescue groups, or donated by breeders. Organizations that specially breed assistance dogs—such as the service and hearing dog training organization, Canine Companions for Independence (CCI), and all guide dog organizations—work hard to breed only healthy dogs with a good working attitude. Many organizations employ geneticists to determine the most successful breedings.

The number of dogs entering a program who actually become assistance dogs is about the same for all the organizations: 25 to 40 percent. These numbers, however, can be misleading. For example, CCI has about a 35 percent placement rate for all puppies; however, not every dog becomes a service dog, some become hearing dogs, and others become facility dogs. Facility dogs are owned by institutions or volunteers who have a commitment to various institutions and either work to educate community members about service dogs or do animal-assisted therapy (AAT). Dogs for the Deaf, Inc., on the other hand, has a placement rate of 25 percent, but not all of its dogs are certified for public use, some are only certified for use inside the home.

To make matters more complicated, many assistance dog organizations now work together to place career-change dogs in working situations. For example, Guide Dogs for the Blind may place a career-change dog with the SF/SPCA hearing dog program. So, while Guide Dogs for the Blind's guide dog placement rate is 25 to 35 percent, its general assistance dog placement rate is higher.

Assistance dog organizations shy away from labeling one dog better than another, but guide dog programs probably have the most rigid standards for placement, followed by service dogs then hearing dogs. The nature of the guide and service dogs' work requires that standards such as size, strength, health, soundness, temperament, intelligence, and amenability are met.

Guide dogs and service dogs need to be fairly large, sturdy animals because of the physical work that they do. In general, the programs that breed their own dogs use golden retrievers, Labs, and German shepherds for guide dogs; and golden retrievers and Labs for service work. For example, CCI opts to use golden retrievers and Labs not only because of their size and strength but also because of their affable nature, retrieving instinct, and the public's comfort with these breeds.

Hearing dogs can be of any breed because the nature of their work is much less physical. According to Ralph Dennard of the SF/SPCA, dogs as small as five pounds have been placed in homes; and Dogs for the Deaf, Inc., has a number of Yorkies on its roster.

> **The number of dogs entering a program who actually become assistance dogs is about the same for all the organizations: 25 to 40 percent.**

Dogs who do not make it through the programs fail for a number of reasons, including temperament, drive, and interest in work. Some dogs are deemed best suited as companions, while other dogs have such a high work drive that they are more appropriate working in SAR or police work. Other dogs may not be comfortable enough to work in crowds or under stressful conditions. Some dogs are cut from a program because they cannot adapt to kennel life during training.

Working Dogs

Dogs who do not make it through a program become career-change dogs and are either put up for adoption or placed with another organization. For example, sometimes a career-change service dog can make an excellent hearing dog. Since dogs in these programs are well trained and generally well socialized, there is usually a waiting list for adoptions. All reputable assistance dog organizations place career-change dogs in well-screened homes.

> **Dogs who do not make it through a program become career-change dogs and are either put up for adoption or placed with another organization.**

Dogs who are bred by an organization stay in their whelping home for about eight weeks. They then come to the kennels for about a week of general health care, shots, and tests. They're then placed in their puppy raiser home, where they will live for about a year. Both breeder, or whelping, homes and puppy raiser homes are provided by volunteers. Despite the heartbreak of having to give up a dog who has lived in their homes for an entire year, many puppy raiser families become addicted and return over and over again for puppies. They explain their commitment, saying that to cope with giving up a dog you love, you need to be able to focus on the person who will receive her rather than your attachment to the dog. Puppy raisers are always given first option to adopt a career-change dog.

The puppy raisers return the dogs at about 15 months of age. The dogs then live in the kennels for another 3 to 12 months while they undergo intense training. Their final formal training comes when a new class for assistance dog recipients begins, which lasts from one to four weeks. Depending on the organization, its size, and facilities, the recipients may stay in dorms on campus, in area hotels, or the trainer and dog may go to the recipient for training. Some programs serve only a regional area while others are nationwide.

Programs that use shelter or rescue dogs place young dogs or puppies with puppy raisers until they are old enough to begin their formal training, but generally they look for dogs who are at least a year old so they can begin the training process right away. Fortunately, or unfortunately, many of the dogs in rescues or shelters are this age, because many families find they are unable to cope with a dog when she enters her adolescent stage, sort of a mixture of human terrible twos and rebellious adolescence.

Assistance Dogs

In assistance programs that utilize rescue dogs, the same general concept follows: service dogs are larger, sturdier dogs who can retrieve, provide balance support, and even pull a wheelchair. Lab and golden retriever mixes tend to be an organization's first choice, but due to the types of dogs available in shelters, this isn't always possible, so they can be of almost any mix—it's the individual dog who must be judged. Most programs have a trainer who works with local shelter volunteers or staff to watch out for eligible dogs. When a shelter receives a dog who is healthy, friendly, and high energy, the trainer, or another representative, visits the shelter and tests the dog for temperament, play drive, and amenability.

Hearing dogs are almost always rescues; the nature of their work does not require a breeding program for several reasons: most of the work hearing dogs do is in the home; they do not do any physical work, so mild hip dysplasia does not mean automatic rejection; and their work is appropriate for almost any high-energy, reactive dog. The preferred dogs tend to be smaller, so terriers and terrier mixes are the most common. That said, CCI does place hearing dogs from their breeding program. These are dogs who are deemed better suited to hearing work than service work.

Training techniques vary for assistance dogs but generally are based on a mixture of reward-based and corrective training. Most programs give food rewards coupled with verbal and physical praise. Corrections are generally verbal or involve the use of mild leash and collar corrections. Half-check collars, a modified quick-release choke chain, are becoming increasingly popular because of their humane nature. The Prison Pet Partnership Program, at the Washington State Correctional Center for Women, for example, uses these collars to train their dogs.

Whether looking for an assistance dog or looking to volunteer or donate money, do your research into the organization; not all are equally effective or humane. Stick with organizations that are members of a larger body, either Assistance Dogs International, Inc., or the U.S. Council of Dog Guide Schools. Organizations associated with either of these two bodies function under some basic expectations of training hours and skills, as well as ethical treatment for both canine and human partners.

Guide dogs are used both by people who were born blind and those who lost their sight later in life. It's rare, however, for a guide dog to be placed with a child under 18 years old. Handlers must be proficient at using a cane before being placed with a dog and must be able to train and care for the dog once she's placed. Although popular perception is that guide dogs lead their handlers; in fact, the relationship is truly symbiotic.

After Arial Gilbert lost her sight 14 years ago, she spent six months in her room. Blinded by eye drops that had been tampered with, she went from a fully sighted person to a blind person in a matter of minutes. A nurse and an athlete, she couldn't do her job or participate in the activities she loved. She felt like her life was over. Overwhelmed by her circumstances, she retreated, but not for long. "After I lost my sight, life came to a screeching halt," says Gilbert. Eventually, however, "I started thinking about what I needed to have a normal life." She realized that she faced a long and boring life if she didn't do something, and there was one thing that she thought would help her: a guide dog. "Once I got started thinking about guide dogs I had a mission," says Gilbert. Since then, Gilbert has had four guide dogs and is the volunteer coordinator for Guide Dogs for the Blind, where she oversees over three hundred volunteers. She's married and is an avid athlete: a rower and hiker.

Once she'd decided that a guide dog was what she needed, Gilbert contacted Guide Dogs for the Blind but was told that first she needed to learn to live as a blind person, using a cane, reading braille, and otherwise learning to navigate a new world. After six months at the Orientation Center for the Blind, in Albany, California, she almost immediately began a month's training at Guide Dogs for the Blind, where she was matched with Webster, a Lab.

"When I took my first walk with Webster, that was a revelation. He gave me the confidence to do what I needed to do," says Gilbert. Although it takes six months to a year before a guide dog team is fluid, "like dance partners," says Gilbert, they are street and traffic safe when they leave the school after one month. The final test includes a portion where the dog and handler cross a street and a Guide Dogs for the Blind vehicle comes screeching around the corner. The dog must back the handler out of its path. For many guide dog handlers, this is when everything comes together and they truly learn to trust their animal. "It's a very transitional moment," says Gilbert.

Unfortunately, Webster was diagnosed with a debilitating health problem and Gilbert's next two guide dogs also had health problems requiring their early retirement. "That's the heartbreak of working with a dog," says Gilbert.

Almost seven years ago, however, Gilbert went back to the school and made a request; she wanted a German shepherd dog, "That was the dream of my life," she says. She was placed with German shepherd Deanne and the two have been together since, working as a team in the true sense of the word. They even carried the torch in the 2001 Winter Olympics.

Gilbert and Deanne work together. Gilbert tells Deanne what to do while Deanne interprets visual cues for Gilbert. "Guide work is team work," explains Gilbert. Handlers use the *find* command often. For example, when entering an office build-

> **Crossing streets is one of the most important things Deanne does, but contrary to popular belief, it's not the dog telling the person when to go.**

ing a handler may tell the dog to find the elevator. When leaving, she'll tell the dog to find the outside door. Although Gilbert needs to know where she's going to tell Deanne how to guide her, Deanne looks out for the many obstacles such as changes in elevation, holes in the ground, and overhanging obstacles that sighted people rarely even think about. When Deanne stops at an obstacle, it's up to Gilbert to feel and decide how to proceed around it; if Gilbert does not find the obstacle and tries to continue, Deanne will not move. "It's intelligent disobedience," says Gilbert.

Crossing streets is one of the most important things Deanne does, but contrary to popular belief, it's not the dog telling the person when to go. "I have to listen to traffic and then tell her to go, but she'll back me out of the way if a car is coming," explains Gilbert, adding, "She's backed me out of the way of oncoming cars; it's those times that you realize, boy, oh boy."

As teams progress, their work together becomes stronger and more nuanced, "A lot of the guide work is very fluid," says Gilbert. Handlers also add to their dog's repertoire over time; Deanne, for example, knows how to find the nearest chair for Gilbert and also where to find a cash machine. At home, Gilbert has trained Deanne to find the cordless phone when it's not on its base.

It's almost impossible to overstate what these dogs do for their handlers. In addition to the day-to-day activities of life, guide dogs also allow their handlers to pursue activities that they would not otherwise be able to do. Before Gilbert lost her eyesight, she was a passionate athlete. When she lost her sight, going for the long solitary hikes she loved was out of the question. With Deanne, however, she has that part of her life back. "With a cane you just don't go for fun walks," she says. "Now, we go for two- or three-hour hikes, just the two of us. It's the most beautiful freeing thing."

> **Trying to make eye contact with a guide dog, tempting her with food, or making sounds to get her attention are all dangerous distractions.**

Gilbert also returned to rowing, and although Deanne can't help her there, the guide dog has become something of a boathouse mascot. She's even been on the escort boat during long races, and other rowers tell Gilbert that Deanne never takes her eyes off of her.

Not all guide dog recipients take to the idea so immediately. Kenneth Altenberg, who also works for Guide Dogs for the Blind, has had his guide dog, Honcho, for five years. When he first lost his sight to diabetes-related retinopathy, he wasn't interested in using a guide dog. "I needed to do some adjusting," he says. He attended a school to learn braille and became comfortable using a cane. Although he could no longer work in his field of automotive engineering, he was beginning to adjust to his new life.

One day, however, he met up with a blind friend with whom he often took short trips. That day, his friend quickly left Altenberg in the dust. Something had changed: he had a guide dog. Always competitive, Altenberg saw the advantage his friend had with a dog and quickly set out to get his own.

Since getting Honcho, Altenberg has experienced his world opening back up for him. He works full-time for Guide Dogs for the Blind and is married. He's also able to travel and walk in a way that was impossible with a cane. "With a dog you're walking at a normal pace," says Altenberg. "It's very natural, and that's an uplifting feeling. Having a dog feels like a relief; mentally, it's a big lift off of you." Altenberg says Honcho is like a conscience with feet and fur.

Assistance Dogs

Altenberg explains that his moment of truth came before the simulated one that Guide Dogs for the Blind had in mind, "During the class we were crossing the street and had to avoid a car. That was when I knew it was going to work." Since then, says Altenberg, he and Lab Honcho's relationship has only grown stronger. Now, Altenberg feels that he can rely on the dog in almost any situation. "I have no problem getting to the airport and on a plane," says Altenberg. "I wouldn't do that with a cane but with Honcho there I'm confident enough." He adds that the biggest thing Honcho does for him is provide safety: navigating uneven sidewalks and crossing streets, as well as finding doors, elevators, and escalators. "On any day some or all of these can be used," says Altenberg. "We've been together for six years. He knows me, and I know him. The nice thing about becoming a seasoned team is that everything's just automatic."

As with all teams, the effectiveness is in the match: while Deanne and Gilbert are athletic and fast moving, Altenberg and Honcho are a slower, more thoughtful team. When Altenberg takes a seat on a bench, Honcho lies beside him, seemingly slipping into a quick snooze. But when Altenberg rises, Honcho quickly joins him. "Some dogs take breaks, and some stay on all of the time," explains Altenberg.

Altenberg points out that guide work is hard on a dog, "It's very draining, and he's mentally and physically tired at the end of the day." When Altenberg and Honcho return home, it's Honcho's off time, and he knows the difference. "At home he's a pet. There's a big distinction between work and play. When the harness goes on, it's a different attitude," says Altenberg.

When at work, guide dogs must stay focused. Altenberg explains that petting or otherwise distracting a working dog is taboo for a reason. "Petting the dog breaks their focus and it can take fifteen to twenty minutes to regain their concentration." When a team is trying to cross a street, a break in concentration can be fatal.

At the same time, public interaction is good for both the public and guide dog teams. Guide dogs are natural public relations representatives. Meeting and interacting with a guide dog team helps to educate people about guide dog use and its value. In addition, part of what a guide dog does for a blind person is to serve as a social bridge. For many, it is easier to interact with a blind person when a dog is there. "Honcho serves as a bridge, an icebreaker," says Altenberg. "He also makes people more aware when you need help, which is a definite plus."

Working Dogs

It's a fine balance that both guide dog handlers and the public often struggle with. Even when a dog doesn't look like she's working, she often is, "When we're in a restaurant, Honcho is working; not going after food is working," says Altenberg. "When someone asks to pet him at a restaurant, I tell them if they're still around when we leave they can pet him outside."

Because it's impossible for an outsider to know when a dog is or isn't at work, it's essential that people ask before petting a guide dog and refrain from distracting her in any way. Trying to make eye contact with a guide dog, tempting her with food, or making sounds to get her attention are all dangerous distractions. Most guide dog handlers are happy to talk about their dogs, as long as they are not working or busy. But if you politely approach a guide dog team and ask if you can pet the dog and the handler declines, don't take it personally. Not all handlers are comfortable allowing strangers to pet their dogs, or they may be doing work that you can't see.

After several years of working together, guide dog teams become tightly bonded so the death or retirement of a dog is devastating. Guide dog handlers experience both the pain of losing a pet and the sudden loss of independence from losing their partner. Although most handlers wish to keep their dogs after their retirement, it often isn't possible. Guide dogs are no longer exempt under the ADA after they've retired and are not allowed to live in no-pets apartments. Some retired dogs do poorly living in a home with a new guide dog, and some handlers simply aren't equipped to care for two dogs. When the retired dog is given up, guide dog programs are committed to finding good homes for them; if the dog doesn't go back to the puppy raiser, or a close relative or friend, there is a waiting list of potential adopters. In fact, many guide dog programs have a five-year-long adoption waiting list.

None of that, however, makes it any easier for a guide dog handler who is losing his or her best friend, "The relationship becomes deeper as time goes on," says Gilbert of Deanne. "It's sort of like a cross between a spouse and a child; I'm with her 24-7 and we trust our lives to each other."

Hearing dog handlers also become highly dependent on the help their dog provides them. Although the work hearing dogs do isn't as obvious as the guide dogs', it's no less significant or life-changing for their handlers.

Imagine what it feels like to be deaf or hard of hearing. Outside, you do not hear the sounds of passing airplanes, honking cars, or car alarms. Inside, the TV is mute, the teapot whistle is silent, and you do not hear the telephone or the doorbell ring. Now imagine that the cable man is coming "sometime between 8:00 A.M. and 5:00 P.M.." This is irritating to most of us who must take a vacation day from work to wait at home. We make the most of it, perhaps getting some work done, cleaning the house, or reveling in a day of bad soap operas and TV talk shows. Now imagine you are deaf. You can't watch TV, clean house, or catch up on work because you might miss the cable man. You can't even read because you need to look out for him constantly. What about the bathroom; what if he comes while you're gone? The cable man shows up at around 3:00 P.M. and you've spent your entire day staring out the front window for him. This is the scenario

> **Although the work hearing dogs do isn't as obvious as the guide dogs', it's no less significant or life-changing for their handlers.**

that hearing dog handlers and organizations want hearing people to imagine, so they'll understand the power of a hearing dog.

Robin Dikson, head of Dogs for the Deaf, Inc., a hearing dog organization in Southern Oregon, gives an example, "One of our recipients was in college before she had a dog, and she had arranged for a ride home for Thanksgiving vacation. They were coming to get her early in the morning and she didn't want to miss the knock at the door, so she decided she'd sit up on the edge of the bed all night waiting. Sometime during the night she fell asleep and missed the knock on the door and ended up spending her Thanksgiving alone in the dorm. That's the real world for somebody who's deaf."

A hearing dog can mean even more in the case of fire or other dangers. "We have a young adult man who lives with his elderly mother; he's deaf, she is not," says Dikson. "He wrote and told us that one day he wasn't feeling great and he was going to sleep in. His mom was going to a church activity, so she had a friend over for breakfast and they were heading on their way to church. She got done with breakfast, put everything away, put the little burner cover on the stove, and off they went. Pretty soon the dog comes and starts hitting him and trying to get him up, 'No, no I don't want to get up.' He just thought the dog wanted to go potty or play, but the dog would not give up; she just kept on and kept on. Finally he got up and the smoke alarm was going off—his mom had forgotten to shut the burner off and the burner cover was on fire. He said, 'I'd have burned up in the house.' "

Working Dogs

Most of a hearing dog's job is less dramatic but no less important. Hearing dogs are taught to give an alert in response to specific sounds, usually within the home but occasionally at work and in public. Every hearing dog, whether she's trained at Dogs for the Deaf, Inc., the SF/SPCA's hearing dog program, or CCI, learns to

respond to a few basic sounds: an alarm clock, a door bell and door knock, a timer buzzing, and the phone ringing. Other dogs are customized for additional sounds, including a baby crying or a particular phone or alarm tone. Some dogs even teach themselves things; for example, many recipients find that their dogs begin alerting their handlers to off-balance dryers or other buzzing noises.

"Before I got Billy, my wife had to jump up and down to get my attention," says Ronald Goosman, who has had a hearing dog for five years. "If I was alone and expecting a phone call, I had to sit and have my hand on the phone or I would miss the call. Billy makes me feel more independent and at ease because I know he will help me when needed."

In general, the alert is the same no matter where the dog is trained: the dog runs to the source of the sound and then to the handler, then back and forth until the handler responds. For a smoke alarm, the dog may do a one-directional alert, running only to the handler, or she may run to the handler and then to the vicinity of the smoke alarm and back. Alerts usually consist of a poke with the nose or a paw, although some small dogs are actually taught to jump up on the handler. Jill Exposito's CCI dog, Uriah, has two alerts: one to use in the house and one outside. In the house, Uriah runs to Exposito and when she says, "Where?" he runs to one of the many small area rugs throughout the house: there is a rug for the oven timer, for the telephone, and for the smoke alarm. Because CCI dogs are large, they are taught to alert with a nose nudge at the knee level. In public, Uriah does a passive response to name calls, sitting at Exposito's feet to alert her when someone is calling her name.

Not all hearing dogs are used in public. Dogs for the Deaf, Inc., for example, graduates two types of dogs: home dogs and public dogs. The idea is that many hard-of-hearing or deaf recipients want to use their dogs only in the home, so it is unnecessary for those dogs to have public access. Dikson explains that many dogs were being washed from the program for public access reasons, such as dog aggression or discomfort in crowded public settings. Now the organization talks to recipients about their needs and when it is clear a dog will not be used outside of the home, they place an in-home hearing dog with that person. The in-home hearing dogs are not allowed to wear the Dogs for the Deaf vest when in public.

Many retired people or at-home parents are only interested in a hearing dog at home, as bringing the dog outside can be more troublesome than helpful. A mom with two toddler-aged children isn't likely to bring her hearing dog to the grocery store. On the other hand, hearing dog handlers who are employed full-time may have use for their dogs at work, where the dogs can alert to the phone or the handler's name

> **While service and guide dogs must be of a certain size and physically sound to do their work, hearing dogs do not need the physical stamina of the other assistance dogs.**

being called. Active hearing dog handlers often want their dogs with them in public to help keep them alert to dangers and to ease social interactions. Exposito relies on Uriah to alert her when a friend calls her name.

"Even though dogs aren't trained specifically for honking horns or sirens, the dogs' natural reaction helps," says Dikson. "We tell people, 'When you're out in public, watch the dog, pay attention to what the dog is doing. If the dog all of a sudden looks, if the dog stops, if the dog jumps, you better look and see what is going on around you because there is something happening.'" One recipient, for example, was walking through a grocery store when her hearing dog suddenly stopped. She looked up and saw that a shelf had collapsed in her path.

Exposito has had Uriah for two years, "I have no doubt in my mind if I was out in public and something was happening, even if it wasn't a specific thing he was trained to, he would let me know and he would take care of me. This dog is more than just a helpmate, he's my life mate."

Working Dogs

Knowing the dogs are there, not only to alert the handlers to trained sounds but also to give them a gauge of what is happening around them, provides recipients with an enormous sense of confidence. "I am more independent because I don't have to depend on my husband or my kids yelling at me to get the door or get the phone. They love it too. I just have to wait for my wonderful Uriah to come and give me a nice little nudge around my knee and he lets me know what is happening," says Exposito. "I have tons more confidence. My self-esteem is higher. I feel better about myself because of the independence he's given me. I really feel safer. My husband just loves it—he sees how much happier I am having him with me. My mom calls him my sidekick."

While service and guide dogs must be of a certain size and physically sound to do their work, hearing dogs do not need the physical stamina of the other assistance dogs. Hearing dog programs use shelter dogs of any size, shape, and breed, although CCI uses golden retrievers, Labs, and Lab–golden retriever mixes. The important thing is that the dog be reactive to sounds and interested in working. Hearing dogs can be five pounds on up, although it's rare for a dog bigger than a golden retriever to be trained for hearing work, only because there are fewer recipients interested in or able to care for a larger dog.

Knowing that they don't constantly have to be on alert gives hearing dog recipients the chance to completely relax—something that most of us take for granted. "They can go out in public, they can do things, they can be in their own home, and they're secure knowing that if something goes on around them, the dog will let them know about it," says Dikson. "The other thing we hear constantly is that the dogs let them relax. You and I and other hearing people, we can kick back and relax and we know our ears will let us know if something happens. We can go to sleep, we can read a book, we don't have to worry about it, but deaf people are constantly on the alert."

Hearing dog handlers often have an unintentional benefit from their hearing dogs. In public, people notice the dog and make a better effort to be understood. "With Billy by me it alerts hearing people that I'm hearing impaired and they speak more loudly and direct their speech more directly to me," says Goosman, who is about 95 percent deaf.

Carl and Eleanor Cates, who received their hearing dog, Sierra, from Dogs for the Deaf, Inc., value the information she provides others, "When the public sees the dog with us, they volunteer any information they think we need to know, like missing the intercom system at the airport," they say. The Cates add that Sierra also seems to open social channels for them, "The presence of the dog indicates to the public that we are not too shy, inviting them to open communications with us."

As with all assistance dogs, bridging the social gap seems to be a major role in the work hearing dogs do; especially, hearing dog professionals say, with children. Although the parent must be the primary caretaker, Dogs for the Deaf, Inc., will place dogs with children as young as 10. "Dogs with kids help with socialization, they help make the children more socially acceptable," Dikson explains. "They also work smoke alarms and the name call: those are the two things that seem to affect deaf children most. When they go to bed at night, they get very afraid and nervous, *If mom and dad can't get to me and something happens I'm going to be cooked meat.*"

Although many hearing dog handlers indicate that the dog helps open up social interaction, some express concern that the presence of the dog deters people from approaching them. Exposito, for example, has one lament when it comes to Uriah, "I think people see that it says Hearing Dog on his vest and think, *well, she's deaf, she won't be able to hear me.* So they don't talk to me." Other times, she laughs, "People approach me and want to know if I'm training him to be a guide dog."

Access issues are often more difficult for the deaf than the blind because many people assume that only guide dog teams have access. In restaurants and hotels, hearing dog teams are sometimes denied service by employees who don't understand that ADA laws cover all assistance dog handlers. Fortunately, this is the exception to the rule.

Many recipients become dependent on their dogs, and losing their dogs is devastating, emotionally and practically. "The worst thing is when we get the call that a dog has died suddenly in an accident or sudden illness," says Dikson. "What we hear on the other end of the phone is, 'I'm deaf again; I'm deaf again.' They've been deaf all along, but they've had sound awareness and now that sound awareness is suddenly gone. You lose your best friend and your hearing all over again. It's a double whammy."

Losing a hearing dog to illness or retirement is an individual thing for handlers. The transition can be difficult, and tough decisions must be made when a dog retires. Many programs are wary of recipients having more than one dog in the home. "If the old dog can't handle it or the person can't handle two dogs, then we tell them you have an option: you can keep your old dog until it dies and then we'll get you a new dog, or you find a home for your old dog with a friend or a relative," says Dikson. While some recipients are philosophical about giving up a hearing dog, others can't even fathom the idea.

"I have to be honest with you," says Exposito of her dog Uriah, "I hope I die before he does. I know that's an awful thing to say, but that is how close our bond is and I don't think I could cope if anything happened to him."

Service dogs are multitaskers; they're type A personalities with a dose of good nature to balance them out. They pull, they push, they fetch, they balance, and they provide a fair measure of affection and support.

A service dog may help a mobility impaired person gain his or her balance, pull a wheelchair, turn on lights, open doors, or retrieve dropped items. She may also help with daily chores such as doing the laundry (opening the dryer door and pulling dry clothes into a basket) and fetching things from the cupboard. A service dog can also be used for medical response: trained to call 911 or attract attention if her handler falls, loses consciousness, or experiences another traumatic event.

Assistance Dogs

Some dogs even serve as medical alert dogs. Although there is no way to train for this, some service dogs are able to alert their handlers to an impending crisis such as an epileptic seizure, insulin coma, or blood pressure drop. Purely by coincidence, some service dog recipients have found themselves doubly blessed with one of these highly attuned dogs.

As with hearing and guide dog recipients, service dog recipients receive a great deal from their dogs: the dogs not only help them with mobility but they also serve as loyal companions who help their handlers deal with loneliness and serve as a social bridge. Unfortunately, many mobility challenged people find that other people have difficulty speaking to them or approaching them, but the dogs fill in that gap. "In fact," laughs service dog recipient Nancy Sawhney, "sometimes it's a problem." People are so interested in her dog, Union, that they interrupt her work. Sawhney has a neuromuscular disorder that affects her ability to walk. She alternates between using a wheelchair and a walker. Union helps her to open doors, picks up dropped items, and turns on lights. When Sawhney doesn't want to interact with the public she avoids meeting eyes, and if that doesn't work she lets people know she's busy but that she'll talk to them next time. She's also adamant about people asking

> *While guide dog handlers are generally understood by the public, service dog handlers often have to explain themselves and argue for access rights.*

before petting Union. "This is a working dog," she emphasizes. In fact, when I meet Sawhney at a CCI event, she quickly chastises me for putting out a hand for Union to sniff. "I have no shame!" she boasts to a friend, "I'll even tell journalists to ask first." As mildly embarrassing as it may be to have this outspoken woman correct your etiquette, Sawhney's made it something of a life's mission to let the public know what does and does not go with service dogs.

Unfortunately, she's had to make it a mission. While guide dog handlers are generally understood by the public, service dog handlers often have to explain themselves and argue for access rights, although under the ADA they are as protected as guide dog teams. As service dog recipient and retired lawyer Carl Zerbe points out, public knowledge is generally five or six years behind the law. He's had to use his mediation skills plenty of times since receiving service dog Truman from CCI. "I can talk people into allowing him, explaining why and handing them materials on

ADA. They get used to it, and I help people get used to it. Once they understand the dog, they get on the bandwagon."

Service dog handlers often point to national chain motels as being the worst flouters of ADA, mostly because clerks are not educated by their employers about the law. In a case of true serendipity, however, Sawhney was playing with Union at a park when she happened to meet the executive vice-president of the California Hotel & Lodging Association, Jim Abrams. He offhandedly asked if she ever had any problems with access, and, well, as she says, she had a few stories to tell.

Since then, Jim Abrams has initiated two educational videos addressing access issues for all assistance dog handlers. One is directed toward the hospitality industry and the other is directed toward law enforcement. As Sawhney relates, knowing that you are on the right side of the law doesn't always work for assistance dog handlers, even with police officers. "I've had police officers who said, 'No, this dog can't come in unless you're blind.' It just so happened that it was my 50th birthday that day; I tell you, I don't cry easily but I started crying and I guess the tears sort of did it to them and they said, 'Well, just this one time.' I was very careful to get their information and then when we got home we wrote a letter to the sheriff's department in San Luis Obispo [where the incident occurred]." As a result, the head of the sheriff's department initiated an in-service, conducting a workshop in collaboration with CCI.

> **Service dogs are multitaskers; they are type A personalities with a dose of good nature to balance them out.**

There've been other incidents in which the responses Sawhney's been met with have been so begrudging even once it had been made clear that the law was on her side, she opted not to stay at a hotel or eat at a restaurant, "I tell them, 'I want to leave you this material but I'm not going to stay here because I don't like to spend my money where I'm not wanted.'" She also confides she's afraid they'll spit in her soup.

Service dogs come to their handlers through a number of routes, from large organizations with breeding programs to prison-based training programs that may place only a couple dozen dogs each year. In general, service dogs are trained to respond to about 40 commands before they are matched with their handlers. "Half are functional and the other half are operational," explains CCI's Pete Rapalus. The dogs know all the essential obedience commands such as *come*, *stay*, and *heel*. They also learn skills specific to service dog work, such as turning on lights and opening doors.

Assistance Dogs

In the team training when a recipient is matched with his or her dog, the recipients are not only trained to take advantage of what their dogs have learned but they also learn to train the dogs themselves. "We customize the commands for each client," explains Rapalus. "That's why it's important we don't just hand dogs out; it wouldn't do them any good. When you're disabled, the last thing you want is another burden."

In team training, recipients usually come to the training facility, although some very small organizations send the trainer and dog to the client's home for training. While CCI has large campuses with dorms, smaller organizations house recipients in local hotels during training.

Service dog recipients can have a range of disabilities. While Nick Danger is a quadriplegic as a result of a spinal cord injury, Carl Zerbe has post-polio syndrome and is partially ambulatory as is Nancy Sawhney. Because of their range of mobility, their needs from each dog differ. For Zerbe, Truman primarily "retrieves things that I've dropped and opens and closes doors." Truman is a sometimes independent dog who needs a handler strong enough to have some physical control over him, so they are a good match. Danger, on the other hand, cannot control Rica physically, so he needed a dog who was turnkey. "The biggest thing she does for me is pick up things I drop, which is like every minute," explains Danger. "My hands work a tiny bit, just enough to grab something and drop it, and I can't bend over and grab." Rica also opens and closes doors for Danger and turns on and off lights, but Danger adds, "Really the biggest thing she does is the emotional lift she gives me. Having her here is so comforting; she's opened up doors, both literally and figuratively."

The relationship a service dog team shares is intrinsic to the work they do together. "Rica will do anything for me if I can communicate it," says Danger. "She's so intuitive;

she often knows what I need before I say it. She's on alert, watching for me to give the command."

"The functional stuff is great," Danger adds. "She's really helped me out of a jam by picking things up; it's sitting right there but I can't get it and she always finds a way to get it for me. But even that doesn't compare to just her presence."

Zerbe points out that although technology can do many of the things service dogs do, including remote-controlled lights and doors and electric wheelchairs, it can never replace the friendship.

> **Those who expect to give up their dogs in retirement, do it under duress and after some agonizing thought.**

As Danger reminds me, being disabled can be a lonely experience. It is socially isolating because people are less likely to approach a disabled person, but there is also a measure of self-enforced isolation that the dog helps eliminate. "A lot of people that have been traumatically injured find it comforting to sink into a dark room and not be part of life anymore," explains Rapalus. "The dog changes that."

"Union is my motivator," adds Sawhney. "She motivates me to get beyond the front door. Just because you're disabled doesn't mean you can't be lazy too. It's easier to be lazy and passive and sedentary when you're disabled because everything takes more effort. These dogs make things so much more enjoyable."

Through a program called Skilled Companions, CCI and other service dog groups place dogs with children. These dogs have an adult caretaker but work for a child. Much of the work the dogs do for children ultimately comes down to the social aspects. Danger describes a severely deformed child who was in his team training class. His mother confided to Danger that in public people stared and whispered or were afraid to approach him. Once the child had the dog, however, all that changed. "It's like night and day," says Danger. "Now, people come up to him because they focus on the dog and forget what he looks like."

Danger and Rica are active, despite his injury. Danger is a sports announcer for college and minor league baseball, and Rica accompanies him. "She's a pretty gutsy dog," he says. "When I do baseball we are right behind the backstop, sometimes there's a foul tip that comes back and nails the backstop—wham—and she'll have her head right next to it. She'll sort of wake up and look and I'll look at her and she'll have that *Oh, Daddy!* look and she'll come up on my lap for a minute and then she'll go back down. She's very calm."

Assistance Dogs

Danger explains that whenever he's out doing volunteer work, going to concerts, eating a meal, he and Rica are representing CCI. "Rica just lays there and puts the moves on people," he laughs. "They really gain an appreciation for the program."

As with all working dogs, there comes a day when the service dog can no longer do her work, no matter how much she wants to. That day is heartbreaking on many levels. For many reasons service dogs often aren't kept by their handlers once they retire: Many people with severe disabilities just aren't capable of caring for two dogs, or the dogs themselves may have difficulty adjusting to retirement in the home where they've worked all those years. Says Rapalus, "CCI dogs only rarely stay with the recipient. Most are adopted by the same people that apply for puppies."

Rapalus is pragmatic about the transition, "It's emotional and upsetting, but it's not the end of the world; it's something you get used to. If your wheelchair breaks, you get a new one." This is the philosophy that worries some animal welfare advocates who are concerned that viewing an assistance dog like another piece of equipment can lead to inhumane treatment of the dogs. However few recipients or advocates, including Rapalus, are really that blasé. Despite the bluntness of his sentiments, Rapalus accedes that losing a dog can be traumatic for recipients. "The disadvantage of using dogs in this capacity is that they do die. If you get used to the services that that dog provides and it dies, it's going to be a major disruption in life, beyond the emotional."

Service dog handlers themselves are unlikely to characterize their service dogs as equipment. Those who expect to give up their dogs in retirement, do it under duress and after some agonizing thought. Retirement is an inevitability all service dog handlers must prepare for. "Union is nine years old and I'm well aware that at some point we'll have to retire her and that's going to be a tearjerker," says Sawhney. "Knowing this dog the way we know her, we'd love to keep her as a pet, but she won't understand she got the gold watch. I need to think about what's best for Union."

Others, such as Nick Danger, sweep the possibility of retirement or death from their minds. He chastises me that I've gotten ahead of myself, then adds, "She'll be with me forever; we'll never be apart." Since Danger's accident in 1995, he has felt a void that wasn't filled until Rica came into his life. "Every night I prayed for God to bring me a cool, beautiful woman that I could share these feelings with, and in his infinite wisdom, he gave me Rica."

CHAPTER 7

THE PRISON PET PARTNERSHIP

The Washington State Correctional Center for Women looks something like a prison and something like a well-fortified high school. What it doesn't look like is a place where abandoned dogs are turned into highly trained service dogs for the disabled. Yet inside the fences and barbed wire and low-slung buildings is a big room decorated with pictures of puppies. Here, prisoners perform miracles for the disabled, the dogs, and themselves. This is the center of a program that has been replicated around the country: the Prison Pet Partnership Program.

In 1981, a nun by the name of Sister Pauline Quinn set out to save women who, like herself, had encountered many trials in their lives. In the process, she hoped to save a few dogs too. She had an idea: why not use inmates to train rescued shelter dogs to help the disabled. She knew the power a trained service dog could have on both the trainer and the recipient. A dog had saved her life, teaching her to trust and giving her confidence and a sense of strength she'd never known before. She approached Dr. Leo Bustad, then head of the Delta Society. Bustad had already had success starting innovative dog-human programs, and he was immediately interested. With his help, Sister Pauline approached the Washington State Department of Corrections, and, extraordinarily, they were given a chance to implement the program at the Washington State Correctional Center for Women.

Working Dogs

The pilot program at the Correctional Center was so successful that it has expanded dramatically since then. Several years after its inception, it became a non-profit organization with a contract with the Washington State Department of Corrections for vocational education. The Prison Pet Partnership Program now incorporates the training of service dogs with a well-respected grooming and dog boarding vocational program. Eligible inmates not only train dogs for the disabled but also

groom and kennel community dogs. The money from these services helps to keep the program in operation, and the women learn skills that can be taken with them upon their release, as well as earn a small stipend: $1.46 an hour for grooming and kennel work and an additional $75.00 a month for service dog training as of 2003.

After establishing the program, Sister Pauline moved on and replicated it in men's and women's prisons across the country. Some are large self-sustaining programs such as Washington's Prison Pet Partnership Program; others are smaller programs that place service dogs with the help of another larger umbrella group such as the National Education for Assistance Dog Services, Inc. (NEADS).

The dogs in the Prison Pet Partnership Program are all rescued from area shelters. The head trainer, Susie McGhee, looks for dogs with high drive and high energy, as well as a willingness to fetch a ball and an amenable, easygoing disposition. The dogs should be about one to two years old; not a problem, McGhee points out, as many dogs are turned into shelters during the sometimes difficult teenage years. Shelter volunteers often contact the program to let them know when they have an appropriate dog, but the final decision is made only after McGhee has seen the dog for herself and has considered all the criteria. She explains that the screening process is rigorous because once a dog is placed in the program, they take complete responsibility for him, whether he makes it as a service dog or not. "Once we bring a dog into the program...we're not going to give him up," says McGhee. In fact, of the approximately 25 dogs the program adopts each year, usually only four are placed as service dogs. The others become what they call paroled pets and are adopted by good homes.

Some high-drive and ball-crazy dogs are referred to the McNeil Island Prison, in Washington, where they are trained as drug detection dogs. About six or seven of the Prison Pet Partnership Program's career-change dogs end up at McNeil Island each year.

Once McGhee chooses a dog for the program, the dog goes to the prison and is kept in quarantine for two weeks. A dog can be at the prison anywhere from six to 12 months, shorter if paroled. Some dogs are paroled just weeks into the training if they exhibit cat or dog aggression and are found homes almost immediately. Others are paroled after spending several months in the program and then aren't found homes for several additional months. The training time itself depends largely on how easily a dog is able to adjust to prison life, how much pretraining must happen, and how easily the dog grasps the service dog training.

Each dog is matched with an inmate who will be his trainer and companion during his stay at the prison. The dog trains with this inmate each day in the dog training center, and then returns with her to her unit at night, sleeping in her cell. The inmate is not only responsible for the dog's training but his exercise, affection, feeding, grooming, and any additional care.

Once several dogs are trained and ready for placement, McGhee assembles a team training class, generally four recipients and four dogs. The recipients are carefully screened for their physical need, ability to care for a dog, and support system.

> *Each dog is matched with an inmate who will be his trainer and companion during his stay at the prison.*

All of the dogs are trained as service dogs, so most recipients are in wheelchairs. The recipients stay in an area hotel for a week while they work at the prison daily. McGhee admits that it can be intimidating for the recipients when they first arrive at the prison, but they quickly become comfortable. The dog's trainer works closely with the dog and the recipient throughout the week's team training. The experience is beneficial for all parties involved.

Working Dogs

The Prison Pet Partnership Program is a win-win-win solution, according to advocates. Dogs are rescued from animal shelters, often days or hours from euthanasia; prisoners are taught patience, selflessness, and a valuable vocational skill; and disabled people are paired with dogs who will help them in almost every aspect of their lives.

Beth Rivard, director of the Prison Pet Partnership Program, explains that they do such a good job of training the women here that almost everyone is assured of a job when they are released. Groomers and kennels often contact the program in search of prospective employees. Rivard adds with a laugh, the only time the grooming isn't perfect is when there's a sudden lockdown and the staff has to finish up the dogs. "We try to tidy them up and don't charge the owners," she says sheepishly.

When a woman is getting close to her release date, the program helps her to get a job in the community. A program staff member even goes to job interviews with her. For those who choose to work as groomers, the program provides them with $800 worth of grooming equipment with which to start their new careers.

Training time is clearly what the women and the dogs look forward to. Even the women who are not currently training a dog take part during training time, keeping up their skills or preparing for a future dog. When the dogs are brought in from the kennel or released from their crates, they dance happily, while the prisoners cajole them in joking, sing-song voices, "C'mon girl, c'mon!" The program clearly relies on positive reward-based training, working to redirect distracted dogs rather than punishing them.

> **Although they certainly gain from the program, ultimately they're doing it for someone else.**

As anyone who's ever trained a dog knows, dog training is a repetitive task that can be frustrating. Repeating a command over and over until a dog finally gets it, only for him to forget the command ten minutes later, can lead anyone to pulling her hair out. It is just this kind of activity that tries the prisoners' patience and might have caused them to react in anger in their lives before incarceration. The prison has a zero tolerance rule. No hitting, no yelling, no violent behavior of any kind is accepted or the inmate is out of the program.

McGhee points out that not all of the inmates come to the Prison Pet Partnership Program ready for the responsibility, so there is a probationary period after they've been hired but before they get their own dog. "Sometimes the probation is extended to work on issues such as patience, tolerance, working with frustration," says McGhee.

McGhee adds that although the change in an inmate after entering the program may not be up to the romantic expectations of outsiders, "You see growth in certain areas," she says. "For example, you might have somebody coming into the program really not able to handle frustrations, either giving up or having little outbursts where you can see the frustration is not being tolerated. With these kinds of things you can watch the women grow through the program, you watch them have successes and learn that a little frustration is okay and this is how we deal with it."

Inmate Patricia Crowl, who has been in the program for three and a half years, agrees, "Patience is a big one. We have rules to work here and one of the number one rules is never hit the dog. You learn a lot, and I figure a lot of that can be used in life skills in your own life," she pauses and laughs, "especially patience." Although Crowl's release date is not until 2009, she's upbeat and optimistic. "It's real rewarding," she says of the Prison Pet Partnership Program. "I've done quite well since I've been in the program as far as even self esteem. It teaches you a lot about responsibility and it builds your self-confidence when you're given the responsibility of taking care of dogs." Although she's trained several dogs in the past, Crowl now works in the program office, explaining, "I got into it so that I could see what the other end is like, if I want to own my own kennel when I get out. Let me learn all of the aspects and then that way I can do my own someday."

Brigette Romero has been in the program only since December of 2001, but she's clear on why she chose to be there, "I wanted vocational experience, to inter-

act with the dogs, and to make a difference in somebody's life by training a dog that can be a service dog." Romero grew up with dogs and was immediately attracted to the program when she found out about it, for both the opportunity to be with the dogs and to help someone, "It's nice that what we do here can help somebody on the 'outs,'" she says, adding that she has a physically disabled grandmother and can relate to the need for the dogs.

To Romero, the benefit of the program for dogs and inmates is clear. "I was here for two and a half years before entering the program and time goes a lot faster; it's time better spent. For me, taking the test was an accomplishment, being able to work with the dogs was an accomplishment, and being trusted with the boarding dogs was another accomplishment." Although she's currently training chow chow mix Wilbur, she's still waiting for a room to open up so she can take him home with her at night.

The Prison Pet Partnership

During my visit, McGhee must leave for a veterinary appointment. It's training time, so Beth Rivard steps in. She sets up an impromptu obstacle course and suggests the women each take several of the dogs through it. The dogs must go up and over an A-frame, open a dryer door, crawl under a chair, jump and sit on the next chair, crawl under another chair, then go through a tunnel, and, finally, lie down on a towel and stay for a short length of time.

Each prisoner takes her own dog through first, with varying success. Despite several problems during each course, none of the women loses her patience, raises her voice, or acts in any way frustrated. Reluctance on the dog's part is greeted by cheerful, jolly voices and tempting treats. I am struck by how calm these women are—all of whom admitted to problems with patience. In all the agility and obedience classes I've participated in and observed, it's rare to see a handler who does not lose some patience—either with herself or her dog. While agility folks can look downright grim after running a course, the inmates are smiling and happy to pet and play with their dogs, even when things didn't go exactly as planned.

One inmate, who is aloof toward me, declining to be interviewed and answering casual questions reluctantly, is like a different person during dog training. As soon as she pulls her dog from the crate, her whole face opens up. "Good dog, good dog!" she says in a loud, jolly voice. She coaxes her dog over the A-frame and shrugs without a hint of exasperation when he balks. Helping him off the A-frame she leads him to an obstacle that she knows he can do, encouraging him through it.

The inmates emphasize how much patience they've gained from the program, but this is just as clear from casual observation. Impatience to have what they want when they want it is often what sets people on the track to incarceration. The women here, like dog trainers everywhere, have

> **The women here, like dog trainers everywhere, have learned that patience is the one great skill in training animals.**

learned that patience is the one great skill in training animals. "I was very impatient before I began this," says Romero. "I wanted it now; now I know it will come when it's time."

The women have also learned the second great key to dog training: the inevitable bond. "Being with the dogs: the bond and the training" is what one inmate involved in the Prison Pet Partnership Program, Colleen Lee, values most from her program participation. "You discover every dog has a personality and I think that's so cool."

More than anything, though, the prisoners learn how to give and give up. They invest heavily of themselves; committing time and work but also love to their relationship with their dogs. And, although they certainly gain from the program, ultimately they're doing it for someone else. "The inmates get a sense of pride but also a satisfaction that they can teach the dogs to do something positive," says Sister Pauline. "I believe that people have to be responsible for what they do, but I also believe that we have to give people an opportunity to change their life. You can't always find in prison that motivation to want to seek something different out because everything looks kind of hopeless." The dog changes all that.

Training scores

1 –shaping behavior (no cue)

2 –rewarding desired behavior (no cue)

3 –dog gives behavior at least 80% of the time (still no cue)

4 –adding cue to behavior

5 –dog gives behavior when cued at least 80% of the time

6 –adding distractions

7 –dog gives behavior when cued at least 80% of the time, with distractions present

8 –dog always gives behavior – behavior is learned

"I think they garner a lot of meaning from this experience," says McGhee. "There are some great industries here at the prison but they're not necessarily making such a big difference in a person's and an animal's life; and their own."

Crowl values the opportunity to give something back, "They always say that when you come to prison you want to give back to the community," she says. "That's not just a saying, that's true for most people in here, it's something we have goals of doing. This is a great accomplishment for the community." When a service dog is placed with a recipient, no matter who trains it, "it makes you cry," she adds.

When an inmate is training a dog, that dog lives and breathes her. They spend the day together and then return to the inmate's unit to spend the night together. Like all dog-handler teams, the bond becomes intense. Throughout their time together, the women learn to love and trust their furry companions and are able to have a bit of normalcy in a place that is clearly not normal. But there comes a point that each dog either graduates and goes to his recipient or is released from the program and goes to a new family. When that happens, the women here are doubly torn: not only do they lose the dog they've come to adore but they are also alone again. There's a great deal to be said for having a dog by your side each night, and not having him is painful. "The inmates aren't really allowed to have physical contact; they're not allowed to hug or have that really necessary human contact," says McGhee. "They get that from the dogs; they pet and love them, and although they're not supposed to, have them on the bed with them. With all the things that come with it, it doesn't cover up that giving up the dog is really hard. It's a tearful experience and there's a lot of anticipatory grief that goes with it, especially with the first one."

"It's especially hard because in many ways they're so alone here," adds McGhee. Over time, the prisoners learn to accept that the dogs, ultimately, are not theirs. After losing their first dog, many of the inmates say "I'm never doing this again; I can't do this again," according to McGhee, but "they always want another dog. Always."

"It's sad, but I know they're going somewhere so I kind of keep that little block up," says veteran trainer Lee. "I love them but I know they're leaving. You miss them a lot but you know they're better off."

> *Adjusting to loss and not using it as an excuse to act out or self-destruct is a vital part of what these women are learning and what Sister Pauline had in mind.*

Letting the dog go is part of the program; learning to love and then learning to lose. Adjusting to loss and not using it as an excuse to act out or self-destruct is a vital part of what these women are learning and what Sister Pauline had in mind. All of these women must learn to focus on the people their dogs are going to help rather than on themselves. "For me, the whole focus in the program is teaching the inmates how to become other-centered," says Sister Pauline.

The dogs in the Prison Pet Partnership Program repay their rescue two-fold. While they are destined for a life of service work, their most important work may happen while they are still at the prison. As the women teach the dogs, the dogs teach the women. One prisoner tells me her sentence seemed very long before she entered the program; now, through the inspiration of the dogs, there's light at the end of the tunnel. As Colleen Lee says, looking at several more years of prison time to go, "it makes it bearable."

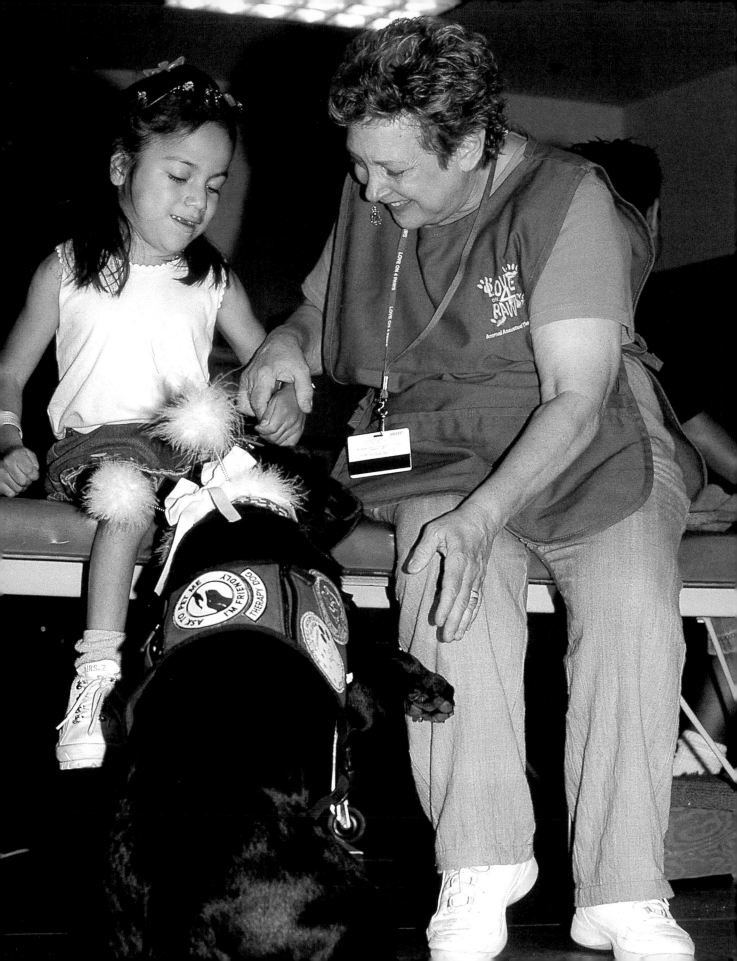

CHAPTER 8

THERAPY DOGS

Dogs provide therapy for people through a number of disciplines. Among them are animal-assisted therapy (AAT) in which the dogs are actually involved in rehabilitative therapy such as being brushed by a stroke patient who is relearning his or her fine motor skills and animal-assisted activities in which the dogs simply visit patients at a hospital or the residents of a nursing home and allow themselves to be petted. Therapy dogs might also demonstrate agility techniques or other activities for the patients. In literacy therapy, a child reads a book out loud to a dog. The idea behind it is that the dog is nonjudgmental and provides motivation. There is also disaster, or post-trauma therapy, wherein dogs are brought to sites following a natural or human-made disaster such as a hurricane or fire to help comfort the victims.

When I first got my dog Desi, I was a volunteer spending time with a developmentally disabled man living in an institution. I thought it would be a good idea to bring Desi with me on my next visit, and it turns out it was. For the next six years, Harry and Desi were fast friends. Our visits followed Harry from the institution through several group homes and only ended when Desi and I moved to California several years ago. Things have changed dramatically in the world of therapy dogs since Desi and I, with no certification and no training, walked into a room of developmentally disabled adults.

Working Dogs

Although the idea of using therapy dogs was started by people with a casual interest in volunteering, it's progressed dramatically in a short time. The use of therapy dogs got its start from volunteers bringing dogs or cats when visiting patients in hospitals or residents in nursing homes. They quickly realized that the animals affected people dramatically. They also realized that there was a lot of room for mistakes when randomly introducing dogs into clinical settings. Many of the dogs were untrained, and often dogs and cats from local animal shelters were used. A bite or a communicable disease could wipe out the use of therapy dogs all together. As a result, several organizations, including Therapy Dogs International, Inc., (TDI) and the Delta Society, began overseeing the use of therapy dogs by providing guidelines for training and certification. The use of therapy dogs developed from an informal hobby to a respected job in many of the nation's hospitals, nursing homes, and other mental and physical treatment facilities.

Established in 1977, the Delta Society initially devoted itself to researching and promoting the human-animal bond. Scholarly research sponsored by the Delta Society focused on the health (physical and mental) benefits that humans gain from close relationships with animals. By the 1990s, the Delta Society added a new role to its repertoire, that of oversight organization for therapy dog–human teams, which they call the Pet Partners Program. "The Delta Society started with education, advocating the animal-human bond," says vice president of program operations, Nancy Dapper. "As the field has developed, human health workers have gotten involved. The 1990s are really the decade that began to resonate with people."

Since the Pet Partners Program was established in 1990, over 5,400 Pet Partners Program teams have been certified throughout the country. Many regional therapy dog organizations require Pet Partners Program certification through the Delta Society or similar certification through TDI, as well as their own training and certification. For example, in Northeast Ohio, K-9's for Compassion requires new teams to visit with an experienced mentor team at least eight times before they can visit on their own.

To become a Pet Partners Program member, the human part of the team must take a one-day workshop, or telecourse. He or she is then eligible for the team evaluation where both dog and human demonstrate a number of skills, including basic commands and showing comfort with loud noises. The dogs are judged on their

Therapy Dogs

temperament and the humans on their ability to read and direct the dogs. Dogs are certified as complex or basic: complex dogs are able to work with high-stress populations such as day-care centers for abused children, where there is likely to be a lot of probing fingers and horseplay. Basic dogs are more appropriate for one-on-one therapy such as visiting one person at a time in a nursing home.

Once certified, therapy dog teams can visit hospitals, nursing homes, or another facility requesting therapy dog visitors. The certified team may contact a facility directly to arrange visitations, or it may work with a regional therapy dog organization to arrange visits through an established program. A Delta Society Pet Partners Program team is required to wear an identifying vest or badge whenever at work and is insured under Delta's insurance policy.

> **The use of therapy dogs got its start from volunteers bringing dogs or cats when visiting patients in hospitals or residents in nursing homes.**

Animal-assisted activities are the most common of the dog therapies. Teams can function in a variety of ways. Some visit hospitals or nursing homes once or twice a month to provide residents a change of routine and others regularly participate in programs such as those designed to help at-risk teenagers develop empathy and patience for other people and animals.

Many therapy dog teams are like that of K-9's for Compassion director Katie Squibbs and her four-year-old standard poodle, Vickie. Squibbs, who is a veterinary technician, knew about the benefits of the human-animal bond and was inspired to get involved in therapy after helping her parents adopt a paralyzed dachshund, Munchkin. Prior to adoption, Munchkin had visited a nursing home weekly, and her rescue group required the new caretakers to continue the visitations. Squibbs thought it was a great idea, but she also thought there should be more to it than just showing up. She was concerned about the lack of certification and health clearances required for therapy dogs going into nursing homes. After contacting the Delta Society and working with an Akron, Ohio, therapy dog organization, she started K-9's for Compassion.

Squibbs points out that each dog in the program has a population she serves best. Vickie, Squibbs's poodle, is popular with women, while a boxer mix may be more popular with the guys. The dogs, too, seem to take to certain people. "Vickie really thrives with cancer patients so we spend a lot of time on the oncology floor,"

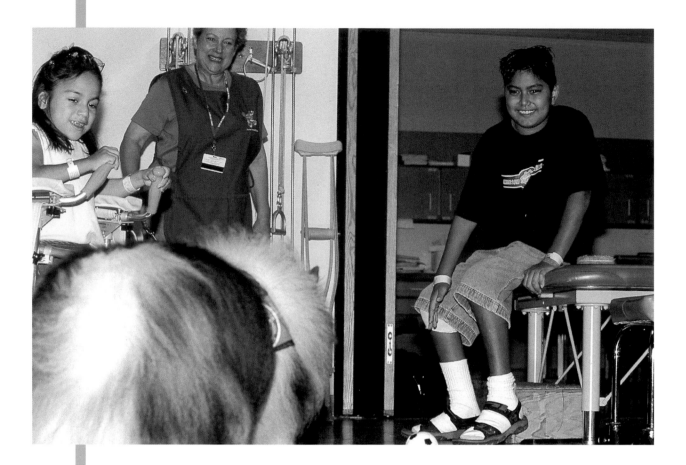

says Squibbs. "Sometimes I put her in a bed and she won't want to leave. I don't know what she's picking up on, but she has a calmness to her."

Munchkin, who continues to work in nursing homes, connects with that community. "She's had people in nursing homes talk who haven't spoken in years. She takes people out of that clinical setting." Squibbs adds that the therapy dogs seem to provide a connection for even those patients with severe dementia. "Alzheimer patients can remember dogs' names from week to week even when they don't remember their own names," says Squibbs. "They also remember back to pets they had as children."

Therapy work, especially with geriatric patients, can be both heartwarming and heartbreaking. "We go to a lot of funerals," says Squibbs. The satisfaction of helping patients and families, as well as the joy their dogs get from therapy work, more than makes up for it. "Recently we had a special request from the cardiac floor by a family that was very into animals," says Squibbs. "I went in with Vickie and put her in the bed and the patient, Frank, just lit up. He'd had a golden retriever, so another volunteer with a golden retriever and I took turns visiting him over the next four days. On the last day it was very obvious that Frank was becoming sicker. I had my camera with me and took some pictures of him with the dogs. He died the next day. We went to the funeral with the dogs and when Frank's wife saw us she hugged us and the dogs and told us this was just the thing she needed."

Although animal-assisted therapy is an innovative concept, it is quickly taking hold in hospitals and rehabilitation facilities throughout the country.

Beth Franklin, a dog handler and executive director of Hand-in-Paw, Inc., in Birmingham, Alabama, has four dogs, and they all volunteer with different populations: Jessica, a toy poodle, prefers to work with children; Maggie, a shih tzu, responds to depressed teens; Isabelle, a sheltie, has a calming effect on autistic children; and standard poodle Val likes rehab. Hand-in-Paw, Inc., is careful about its teams' placement. "The skill of the handler and animal should match the needs of the facility," says Franklin. Hand-in-Paw, Inc., teams are involved in animal assisted activities, visiting children in medical facilities, and literacy programs for children who are struggling to read. It also works closely with at-risk youth, including juvenile offenders and children living in a Salvation Army teen center.

In a 12-week program for teens, Hand-in-Paw, Inc., has several formal goals, including helping the kids to devise ways to handle stress and to understand and verbalize emotions. "Some kids come in not even knowing what an emotion is," says Franklin. The kids learn the satisfaction of sharing and learning and also learn to empathize with both the dogs and other people. The hope is that learning compassion for animals translates to feeling compassion for other people. "They come out learning how to be better adults and parents," says Franklin, explaining that the dogs are often compared to children to help the kids understand their affect on others. "For the last exercise, they go to a nursing home with us. For some of these kids it is their first opportunity to give back."

The program has had successes, both big and small. Franklin is particularly proud of one girl who graduated from the program four years ago and is now returning to work for Hand-in-Paw, Inc., and another boy who has gone through three sessions of the program and has just been hired to work as a group leader.

The kids are especially interested when handlers tell them the stories of their dogs: 60 percent of them are from rescues or shelters. Often this prompts them to talk about abandonment, physical abuse, and drug abuse in their own lives.

As for the dogs, says Squibbs, "They enjoy themselves and that should be first and foremost. When you pull out their uniform they're excited and they're more alive. They seem to know there's a difference between being at home and being at a job. They're much better at tuning into emotions than we are."

Like many working dog handlers, Squibbs is convinced that dogs thrive on work, "I really think all dogs need some sort of job: they like normalcy and guidance; it makes them happier pets."

Although animal-assisted therapy is an innovative concept, it is quickly taking hold in hospitals and rehabilitation facilities throughout the country. In AAT, a dog assists with a person's physical rehabilitation: She may stand still for a patient to brush her, fetch a thrown ball, or shake a person's hand. A dog can also help to steady a person who is trying to walk or just be a soft back for someone to reach out and touch. Physical therapy often involves a great deal of repetitive movement; adapting the movements to grooming or petting a dog can break up the monotony and give the exercises more meaning.

Other dog-related therapies can include buckling and unbuckling collars and vests rather than using a traditional dress board. Maureen Flaherty is an occupational therapist and head of the dog therapy program, PAWS, at Carondelet St. Joseph's Hospital, in Tucson, Arizona. She speaks of one volunteer who brings a whole wardrobe of hair clips and scrunchies that patients can use to dress her black-and-white spaniel mix, Josie. "She's like an animated Barbie," jokes Flaherty.

"Every patient has goals that can be adapted to include an animal," says Flaherty. She stresses that AAT requires four bodies to be present: the therapist, the patient, the handler, and the dog; each has a role and it's not possible for the therapist to be both handler and therapist.

Flaherty points out that rehab medicine has changed vastly during the last 20 years. While hospitals once worked with stroke patients for up to four or five months, helping them to transition smoothly back to the home environment, patients are now in the hospital receiving intensive rehab for only about three weeks. There's an emphasis on basic needs rather than integration back into society and functional activities. "Dogs help to bridge the gap," says Flaherty.

Flaherty started training her own dog, a Welsh corgi named Iggy, for therapy work several years ago. When she made an out-of-state move, she decided to look for work integrating her two passions: occupational therapy and dog training. When she pitched the program to St. Joseph's, Iggy served as her demo dog.

Although the program has been in operation for only one year, initial reviews are positive. Flaherty thinks that operating the AAT program

> **Disaster therapy dogs have worked on-site in the wake of school shootings, tornadoes, and terrorist attacks.**

from within the hospital rather than from outside helps to keep the program cohesive and allows the hospital to maintain quality control. She emphasizes that this is an advanced level of volunteer work and is not appropriate for therapy teams just starting out. All of the 12 teams now working at St. Joseph's were experienced volunteers, and even so, Flaherty estimates that only half are really up to the level they should be. "The dogs should be able to retrieve, catch, do tricks, and the handlers must be able to train them," says Flaherty. A really good AAT dog is active and ready to go, but she must also be well trained and have an off switch—a combination that is sometimes difficult to find.

Flaherty explains that the quality of the program depends on the patients "getting" it. Because patients are often tired and frustrated, it's important they see the value and added benefit of the dogs. Ideally, she says, "they see it [PAWS] as an opportunity to practice but also as something fun to do. We've definitely had examples of patients where we haven't been able to find a hook; sometimes using the dogs is the only thing that can get them out of their rooms."

Animal-assisted rehab therapy can also help patients with pets deal with their new disabilities once they return home. Filling a food bowl or lifting a bag of dog food can be difficult; using the animals in rehab helps a patient make the transition into independent life.

An unanticipated aspect of the program has Flaherty particularly excited. One St. Joseph's volunteer, who uses a wheelchair, has a dog who serves as both a service dog and therapy dog. "It's a real benefit for patients to see what the dog can do for her," says Flaherty. The volunteer's presence has already inspired two or three patients to make the initial efforts toward getting a service dog. "I'm really interested in the use of service dogs in this capacity."

Although Flaherty's mind races ahead to what she'd like to do with the program, she's also pragmatic and is working diligently to make sure that therapists, administrators, and patients are all getting what they need. Her goal, she says, "Is creating more of an awareness in the community of what's possible, but also what's required."

Although therapy dogs were a tough sell for hospitals and other health facilities in the late 1980s and early 1990s, the certification offered through the Delta Society and TDI have gone a long way in reassuring facilities that the dogs are well trained, appropriate, and useful. Many facilities that initially accept therapy dog teams grudgingly become die-hard supporters after seeing the affect they have on the patients.

A new type of therapy provided by some therapy dog teams is in the area of literacy. The idea behind it is that a child struggling to read learns more quickly and is more comfortable when reading out loud to a dog. In 1999, the Intermountain Therapy Animals (ITA) of Salt Lake City, Utah, formalized the use of dogs as literacy aids. "We weren't the first to think up using dogs for literacy, just the first to articulate it," says executive director Kathy Klotz.

The Intermountain Therapy Animals' literacy program, Reading Education Assistance Dogs (R.E.A.D.), has inspired numerous other therapy dog groups to incorporate the program into their volunteer work and has received a good deal of media attention. Dog literacy programs have appealed to the public, probably because it makes so much sense. Once you make the leap, it isn't a difficult concept to grasp. A child who is struggling with reading sits with a dog and the dog's handler and reads a story. It works because the dog is nonjudgmental, but at the same time the child isn't just reading out loud by him or herself. When kids struggle with reading, it's rarely just a learning issue but a social and emotional one as well. Klotz relates that one little boy commented to a volunteer, "It's easier to read with a dog because it won't make fun of you and say *ha, ha*."

Dogs who thrive at this type of work are older, passive types who don't mind sitting with their head in a warm lap for an extended period of time. "We don't have any dogs do it who don't want to. This is good for older dogs and the lazier variety," says Klotz. The handler is there only to support the dog, not to be a tutor or to interject. If a child is struggling with a word, the handler may ask him or her to explain it to Fido; if the child can't, the handler may suggest looking it up in a dictionary. All of the comments come through the dog and are solicited by the child. "You can do so much by projecting through the dog," says Klotz.

One child works with one team throughout a year, which builds confidence. The achievements of these children can be measured using standardized reading tests, but teachers often note that the skills creep into other areas. Other kids think they're cool because they have a dog, and this leads to better socializing and ultimately better school performance.

> **Dogs who thrive at this type of work are older, passive types who don't mind sitting with their head in a warm lap for an extended period of time.**

While the program is currently implemented in six public Salt Lake City elementary schools, the R.E.A.D. program also conducts a four-week library program during the summer to help students whose skills slip during the summer session. The R.E.A.D. program is also looking for ways to implement dogs into preschools and Head Start programs.

Klotz, who just recently retired her 12-year-old Australian shepherd, Foster, because of sight problems, comments, "You really miss it. When Foster saw his bits of uniform, oh, boy, no other dog could get near it—he was excited to go. We tell handlers to look for that level of excitement."

Volunteers are often struck by how seriously the kids take the dogs. Even children who initially find the concept silly quickly become invested in reading to a dog. Klotz relates that one boy confided in a teacher that he had scared a dog.

Concerned, she asked how. "I read him a ghost story," he told her soberly. Another girl, who'd never read an entire book before, was startled when she turned the last page. "She gasped," says Klotz, she was so surprised to have finished a book. "Finishing the book was a real ego boost for her… Something happens and pretty soon they're looking forward to the reading experience."

Dogs can be a cathartic or comforting presence after a trauma or disaster. They allow victims, the families of victims, and aid workers a chance to get outside of themselves. Disaster therapy dogs have worked on-site in the wake of school shootings, tornadoes, and terrorist attacks.

The events of September 11, 2001, served to promote the use of therapy dogs much in the way they did SAR dogs. Before the tragedy occurred, the American Red Cross had never used therapy dogs in disaster situations and was nonplussed when handlers called to volunteer. However, a Delta Society and American Society for the Prevention of Cruelty to Animals (ASPCA) representative, Debbie Freundlich, received so many calls from the 80 Pet Partners Program teams in the New York area, that she helped coordinate their presence at the Family Assistance Center set up on Pier 94 in the weeks following the attacks. From September 25, 2001, until the center closed in January 2002, therapy dog teams were there. The teams were asked not to approach grieving families but instead to wait for the families to approach them. At first the teams hovered on the peripheries of the room, but it didn't take long before families responded to the dogs' presence.

> **Dogs can be a cathartic or comforting presence after a trauma or disaster. They allow victims, the families of victims, and aid workers a chance to get outside of themselves.**

Cate Pontoni was one of the many handlers who ultimately spent time at the Family Assistance Center. She and her basset hound, Molly, had been doing therapy work at United Cerebral Palsy (UCP) in Manhattan for the previous year. An apartment dweller in midtown Manhattan, Pontoni didn't want to be alone the afternoon of September 11, so she left her apartment to visit her work partner uptown. "I left work and got Molly and from the second we hit the street, people would come up and pet Molly—they were just drawn to her like a magnet." Some people even thanked Pontoni for Molly's presence. Pontoni was amazed by the dog's effect on people and thought there had to be something they could do together. Pontoni,

Therapy Dogs

like many other dog handlers, called the Red Cross, only to be turned down. Then she called Freundlich, setting in motion an almost four-month commitment.

In the beginning, Pontoni and Molly visited the pier three times per week: Tuesday, Thursday, and Saturday. After the pier was closed on the weekends, they visited twice a week, all the time continuing their biweekly visits to the UCP. Pontoni was pleased but not surprised by how well Molly adjusted to the size, chaos, and stress of the environment. "If there was any dog who was made to do this, it was Molly," she says. After spending two hours at the pier, Pontoni had to force Molly to leave. Exhausted by the time they returned home, Molly would climb onto her bed and fall asleep within five minutes.

The therapy dogs felt strangely comfortable in a place that was stressful to most people. This was proof for the handlers that the dogs knew they were needed.

Working Dogs

Freundlich points out that the therapy dog handlers did an excellent job reading their dogs and determining what situations the dogs were comfortable in and when they'd been there long enough. "The handlers were wonderful," says Freundlich. "They really understood what was expected of them and were able to read their dogs as a result of their training and experience."

At the pier, Molly and Pontoni comforted wives and husbands, entertained children, and distracted frustrated World Trade Center employees. "Probably 60 percent of the people we talked to were families of victims and 40 percent were people out of work," says Pontoni. Even pier relief workers sought the solace of the dogs. They too needed comfort and a minute or two of normalcy after hours of dealing with the loss and frustration of victims' relatives. "After fifteen minutes with the dogs, they could go back to work calm," says Pontoni.

What affected Pontoni most was seeing Molly's effect on the victims' survivors; seeing how Molly could help someone deep in grief laugh or help someone open up about their experiences. "There was a heaviness about the people that you could feel," she says. One woman, who was crying when she came up to pet Molly, slowly began to smile and then to laugh. She turned to Pontoni and said, "I thought I'd never smile again, and your dog just made me laugh."

More than six months after the closure of the relief center, Pontoni spoke about her experiences there with difficulty. As she started to tell me about the one time that she almost broke down, she paused the interview to collect herself. Half crying, she recalled a woman who approached Molly wearing a button photo of her husband on her shirt. She knelt in front of the dog, petted her, and then pointed to the photo, "Molly, this is Luis, he was my husband; he loved dogs. Luis, this is Molly."

When the family assistance center began escorting victims' relatives to the site on ferries, Molly and Pontoni were among the few teams invited to accompany them. The ferry was small, says Pontoni, and it was Molly's first time on a boat. The basset hound was shaking with fear when they got on, but as soon as someone approached, seeking solace from Molly, her own fear was forgotten. Once she knew she was on duty, she never quavered.

It's no leap to understand why therapy dogs are affective. Anyone who's ever had a pet, be it dog or cat, knows the comfort that simply stroking her fur can bring. After a difficult day, sitting on the couch with your dog nestled next to you is one of

Therapy Dogs

the most comforting things there is. Most dog people have stories to tell about being comforted by their pets during times of loss or just day-to-day frustrations. Dogs also act as a bridge between people. "If I didn't know it before, I knew it then," says Pontoni of Molly's work at the pier. "Dogs can do what no human can sometimes; what more can you say? They help."

Anecdotes alone can serve to convince even the most hardened skeptic of the benefits of therapy dogs. Still, thanks to researchers there is proof that dogs affect human healing, both physically and emotionally. Dogs lower blood pressure and cholesterol, and they decrease the risk of heart attack. We're healthier and less lonely when dogs are in our lives; older adults with pets have been shown to live longer and are in better physical condition.

> *Our pets make us feel good about ourselves and allow us to be strong when we need to be, and weak when we want to be.*

Our pets make us feel good about ourselves and allow us to be strong when we need to be, and weak when we want to be. They help us to reach out and be with one another, but also to be confident when we're alone.

When I met Harry 10 years ago, he talked incessantly of a long-dead canine companion named Sheba. Harry collected white stuffed dogs that looked like the white shepherd, and called every dog he met Sheba. For years, Desi was Sheba to Harry. "Hi Sheba!" he'd greet her as we arrived. I knew Harry enjoyed the visits with Desi, but I never knew how much until one day, years after we began visiting him, he looked Desi straight in the eye and said in sudden recognition, "Desi!"

Dogs might not work miracles, but they do seem to touch something. You know they won't laugh if you stumble over a word, react in shock from a burned or scarred face, or fumble for the right words of sympathy. They're just there, and they're soft and empathetic in a unique way that we can't always be with one another.

CHAPTER 9

SLED DOGS

A sled dog musher is a particular type of person: she is willing
to work long hours in the sled dog sport, then work long hours to support the sport. Mushers
must live somewhere rural and cold because the dogs need space and snow. And mushers must
love the dark because that's when most of their training is done. They can't mind dog hair or
barking or scooping poop. Nor can they dislike travel or long car rides or stays in cheap motels.
Most of all, though, good mushers must love dogs. I mean really love dogs. Because most mushers have at least 12 dogs—and that's a small kennel.

When I talk to musher Karen Damoth-Yaeger, she's home from her 8:00A.M.-to-5:00P.M. job
as a public health nurse in Sisters, Oregon, done with cleaning the kennels and exercising the dogs,
and right in the middle of preparing dinner for her 17 dogs, and for herself and her husband.

She laughs when I ask if I'm disturbing her and explains that she's wearing a telephone head-
set and continuing their meal preparations as we speak. She adds that after we're done, she still
has two hours of work to do on her side business, making dog-training collars, and, like most
nights, is looking forward to six hours of sleep. She goes to bed at 11:00 each night, rises at 5:00
in the morning to exercise her dogs, then drives a half hour to get to work by 8:00 A.M.—another
liability of the rural life and another sacrifice for her dogs. I ask her when her husband sees her.
"Not often," she laughs. Then, seriously, "He's very patient."

Working Dogs

Throughout our two-hour-plus conversation, I hear Damoth-Yaeger's nightly ministrations: pots rattling, food pouring into bowls, the rustling of chains at the dog houses, doors slamming, and the whine of the dogs, excited at her approach. I start to form an image of Damoth-Yaeger: this woman sounds a lot like her dogs.

Sled dogs are runners. If you've ever welcomed a Siberian husky into your home, you know that. They are escape artists and have a genetic makeup that

prompts them to seek adventure. Sledding participants, both dogs and mushers, must be driven. Mushing takes brute strength, and it takes finesse and dedication.

Although there are some teams still used for transportation in remote areas in Alaska, most sled dog teams are now used purely for sport. But don't call mushing a hobby; mushers get prickly when that term is used. The dogs, they say, need care full-time; it's not just a recreational activity. Sport doesn't even really describe what the mushers and dogs do because sled dog racing ekes into every part of a musher's life. To Damoth-Yaeger, mushing isn't a sport, "it's an addiction." She says that eventually the dogs become the focus of your life, even during the off-season. "They need care year round. The dogs are there all the time."

And, regardless of how much their handlers may love them, sled dogs aren't your normal kind of pet. They live in packs and want nothing more than to pull. It's rare for sled dogs to live inside, even with those mushers who don't philosophically oppose it, there are usually just too many dogs, and the handlers say the dogs generally don't care to stay inside.

Most sled teams are made up of Siberian huskies or Alaskan huskies. Alaskan malamutes, while powerful, are not considered fast enough to race, at least if you expect to win. Siberian huskies have been bred as sled dogs for hundreds of years,

Sled Dogs

although they were not used for racing until examples of the breed were brought to Alaska from Siberia in the early 1900s. Alaskan huskies are not actually purebred dogs but a mix of dogs used by a particular breeder to create the perfect sled dog. According to lore, these dogs have been used for thousands of years by native Alaskans for transportation. They may have descended originally from wolves and are a mix of almost any speedy breed, including setters and sighthounds. According to mushers, some modern Alaskan huskies are beginning to look decidedly greyhoundlike.

Alaskan huskies are the dogs of choice for most competitive sled dog teams, although there are the purists, like Damoth-Yaeger, who are committed to the use of Siberian huskies. "I just like a purebred dog," she says.

Many mushers begin their sledding careers with Siberians but move to Alaskan huskies to become more competitive. "I switched to Alaskan huskies in 1981 or 1982 to be faster, more competitive," says musher Lin Neumann, who has been involved in sledding for almost thirty years.

Advised by her doctor to start an exercise regimen, Neumann purchased a Siberian husky from an Alaskan breeder. She named her new puppy Sonja, after ice skating champion Sonja Henning, and began training, "She would dream at night and her legs would run, I thought *Oh my God, this is something dogs need to do.*" Then, Neumann went to a sled dog race and was hooked. "I remember what the light was like, what the snow was like, the dogs, the winter lights, the trees, everything, and I thought, *that's for me.*" Shortly thereafter, Neumann bought another dog and ran a two-dog team at a local race. She ran a six-dog team 12 years later at the same race and won the class, "I got pretty serious," she admits.

> *Many mushers begin their sledding careers with Siberians but move to Alaskan huskies to become more competitive.*

Now with 12 Alaskan huskies and two Border collies, Neumann's dogs dictate her life. "I'm on their schedule," she says, explaining that she rises at 6:40 A.M. each day to feed them hot juice, a mixture of dog food and hot water, and then trains, exercises, or readies the dogs for a race, depending on the season. When the dogs take their midday nap, so does she. She and her husband live rurally, both so that they can legally keep their menagerie of 14 dogs and also so the dogs have space to run and play in a 3-acre fenced area.

Working Dogs

Both Neumann and Damoth-Yaeger keep their dogs in individual doghouses with a tether that does not allow them to reach the dog on either side of them. Although there are many detractors to the sled dog housing setup, mushers defend its use. "This way everyone has their own space," says Neumann. She points out, however, that while her Alaskan huskies don't mind being tethered, the Border collies wouldn't tolerate it; "They're inside dogs." Breeding and training accounts for a sled dog's comfort with the tether arrangement: as pack dogs they want to be close to their brethren, but they're also independent enough not to want to be too close. As puppies, Neumann's dogs are given treats when they are tethered, which helps them adjust to it. Both Neumann and Damoth-Yaeger have large fenced exercise areas for the dogs to play and interact in. Not all sled dog handlers have this setup though, and critics of sled dog racing argue that it is cruel to keep dogs without the opportunity for exercise and socialization outside of sledding.

Damoth-Yaeger and Neumann are softer touches than most mushers. Two of Damoth-Yaeger's retired dogs sleep in the house, and most nights one or two of the other dogs come in as well. There's no system, she says, "They come in because they look at me and say *tonight's the night I want to.*" Unlike many mushers, Damoth-Yaeger trains all her dogs for "house time," although some of the dogs choose never to come inside. Both Damoth-Yaeger and Neumann also bathe and obedience train their dogs, again, something of a rarity among sled dog handlers.

> **Although the sled dogs of today usually aren't saving the lives of remote villages or providing everyday transportation, they take their jobs no less seriously.**

A good musher is aware of what his or her dogs are feeling, and although a musher works with more than 10 dogs, the bond must be foremost. The dogs, especially the lead dog, must be well trained and able to take verbal directions from the musher.

In northern Oregon, where both Damoth-Yaeger and Neumann live, the training season runs from October through April, although there is snow on the ground only from mid-December to mid-March. When there is no snow on the ground, mushers train by hooking the dogs up to all-terrain vehicles (ATV) and running them on dirt. During the summer, both mushers and dogs take a break.

Damoth-Yaeger trains six hours a day on both Saturday and Sunday as well as after work on two weekdays, adding to her already hectic schedule. Neumann trains

Sled Dogs

three to five times a week. Both cut training down to two days a week during the race season, when they are racing most Saturdays and often traveling to get there.

Although Neumann mentored Damoth-Yaeger when she first entered the sled dog world, the women have differing philosophies when it comes to training. Damoth-Yaeger runs a 12-dog string in training, "That way all the dogs get the same conditioning and it takes less time." Neumann, on the other hand, trains with two 4-dog strings so that she can monitor them more easily, "I can't see every dog when 12 are hooked up," she says.

In the Northwest, mushers run 4-, 6-, and 8-dog teams, although in other areas, including Alaska, larger teams can be run as well, up to 18- or 22-dog teams. Damoth-Yaeger adds that there are both sprints and distance races, although the Northwest's 15- to 25-mile distance races are scoffed at by mushers in Alaska;

Working Dogs

home of the 1,049-plus-mile Iditarod Trail International Sled Dog Race.

The granddaddy of all sled dog races, the Iditarod is supposedly inspired by an event that illustrates just how important sled dogs were, and still can be, to those who live in Alaska's remote and often hostile environs. The original Iditarod Trail ran from

Seward to Nome and was heavily traveled by gold rushers seeking their fortune in Alaska. Before the establishment of air service, dog sleds were essentially the only way to get from one town to another. By 1925, the sled dog team was losing its status to airplanes, but when a diphtheria epidemic threatened Nome, there were no airplanes capable of ferrying the vaccine from Anchorage through treacherous winter weather. So a relay of dog teams sped the vaccine the 700 miles to Nome in six days, delivering it in time and saving the town from hundreds of deaths. Although the relay did happen, critics say the idea that the Iditarod commemorates the serum run is just part of Iditarod boosterism. Many critics of the race point out that the serum run was done in relays, so no dog actually ran the entire 700 miles, unlike the modern Iditarod. Such a grueling race is hard on the animals; to date over one hundred dogs have died during the Iditarod.

Although the sled dogs of today usually aren't saving the lives of remote villages or providing everyday transportation, they take their jobs no less seriously. When at a race, says Damoth-Yaeger, the dogs are quiet "until the first dog gets hooked into the line, then the whole truck explodes." Bystanders have described a sled dog race as overwhelmingly noisy with hundreds of sled dogs barking at once. Although it's annoying to most, for a musher it is heavenly. "The sound of those dogs getting so excited is just music," says Damoth-Yaeger. Damoth-Yaeger invites detractors of the sport to watch her train or race her dogs. "I don't make them pull, I let them pull," she says. Adding, "Siberians are instinctively bred to be sled dogs: to live in a pack, to be out and travel, to pull. When we let them do that, we're making them more complete." For these dogs, running is their lives. They live and die to pull a sled.

Neumann concurs, assuring me, "If I had my coveralls on and got out the harnesses, we could not speak because it would be bedlam." She adds, "My dogs will run until they drop; they love it."

They both point out that for Siberian huskies and Alaskan huskies, not running them is unfair. Dogs who are bred for sledding are often agitated and unfulfilled when kept only as companions. Siberian owners often complain that their dogs are out of control, and Neumann points out that even her well-exercised dogs rip at their houses if they're not exercised for a day. Neumann, who is a professional trainer as well as a musher, often encourages Siberian owners to get involved in sledding or another pulling activity when their dogs act up, "It gives them something to do; they're so satisfied when they run."

Sledding is an exact science: of course, you need a dog, a musher, and a sled, but there are also certain niches dogs fill and specific commands that mushers use. Sled dog teams have several

> **Dogs who are bred for sledding are often agitated and unfulfilled when kept only as companions.**

components: lead dogs, swing dogs, wheel dogs, and team dogs, as well as the sled and the musher. Everyone on the team knows his position and knows what to do and when to do it. The musher gives commands to the lead dog who leads the team to follow the commands. Occasionally, a musher runs two lead dogs who run next to one another. The two swing dogs are directly behind the lead dog and help guide the team through turns. The two wheel dogs are directly in front of the sled and keep it from tipping or hitting obstacles. The rest of the dogs are team dogs. In general, all the dogs on a team are trained to take on the other roles when necessary.

The musher uses some basic terms when commanding the team, including *gee* for right, *haw* for left, *on by* for passing or going straight, and *whoa* to stop or slow. To command the dogs to go, the musher may say *hike* or *let's go* or make a *tchh* sound. He or she does not normally use *mush*, as it's considered too soft a word. Neumann explains that a musher must be able to read his or her dogs and be able to communicate with them. Especially important, she says, is communicating with your lead dog so that he doesn't look back at you, and helping your lead dog through rough spots. A team can encounter all kinds of obstacles on a trail, including wildlife, downed trees, and loose dogs. A good musher talks his or her dogs through difficulties and keeps them inspired. "My job is to make them want it," says Damoth-Yaeger.

Both Neumann and Damoth-Yaeger train their dogs with a positive reward system, using treats and verbal praise. In addition, Damoth-Yaeger uses a half-check collar, which she makes, that is essentially a quick-release choke chain for leash corrections. She adds, however, that the use of voice is generally all she needs as far as corrections go. Neumann limits any physical corrections to fighting, "The only behavior that's bad is fighting," she says. "Then you find out that I am very grumpy."

> **A team can encounter all kinds of obstacles on a trail, including wildlife, downed trees, and loose dogs.**

Fighting, in general, is not a big problem with either Neumann or Damoth-Yaeger's teams, "I breed for it," says Damoth-Yaeger. "I only select dogs with gregarious personalities. They all get along because they have to." Neumann adds that she has a three-strikes policy, "Third strike, you're out; it's to the vets for neutering."

Neither Neumann nor Damoth-Yaeger sees any reason to force a dog to pull, "This is doggy drugs," says Damoth-Yaeger. "When they're hooked up, their eyes glaze over." She adds, "The goal is to understand the dog. If you try to mold a dog to be what it is not, you will be unhappy and the dog will be unhappy. People talk about breaking pups to harness, but I don't break my dogs to anything, I train them."

Neumann adds, "The dogs' motivation to run is to be free and happy." When a dog is left behind, it feels like it has done something wrong."

Being a musher is not a sport that can be taken lightly. The costs of feeding 10-plus dogs are exorbitant, and add to that the cost of the sled, ATV, doghouses, veterinary bills, travel, and racing entry fees. Damoth-Yaeger says she tries not to add it up. Even when they win, it's rare for sled dog racers on the level of Damoth-Yaeger and Neumann to earn back even 20 percent of their investment. They really must do it for the love of it. Damoth-Yaeger explains that although having 17 dogs may seem excessive, it's necessary to running a full team.

As with all working dogs, there comes a time when the sled dogs must retire. "They let me know when they're ready," says Neumann, adding that she's had dogs continue racing into their teens. Says Damoth-Yaeger, "They can do it as long as

Sled Dogs

their mind and body allows them to." She adds that retired dogs can continue to work as mentors for the other dogs, "they're valued for what they can teach."

"Dogs who retire with me live out their full life with me," says Damoth-Yaeger. While she has 12 racing dogs, she has an additional 4 who are fully retired and 1 who is semiretired. Cirrus, a 13-year-old male, "comes back with a glow and a smile," after running with the younger dogs. "You see on his face how proud he is for what he has to give; no one could mistake him for thinking he's just an old dog now." Neumann adds that one of her dogs, who became depressed after retirement, has become an indoor dog, "I allowed him in at night to sleep by the fire." She teaches him to use his brains in other ways, including doing obedience.

It's important to remember that Neumann and Damoth-Yaeger don't represent every musher. In Alaska, where competition is fierce, there are many accounts of dogs being culled from litters because they are not the best of the best. These dogs may be humanely euthanized, or they may be shot or beaten to death—either way, it's a policy that reflects badly on the sport in general. In addition, not all sled dog kennels are equal; while Neumann has a 3-acre fenced area for her dogs to run, some mushers keep their dogs tethered almost twenty-four hours a day. Like any work a dog does, there are good handlers and bad.

What is it that draws a musher to sled dog racing? For some it is the dogs, for others it's the thrill of the race, for most it is a combination of factors. "I do it for the satisfaction and pleasure of being with the dogs," says Damoth-Yaeger. Although racing has been described as 90 percent boredom and 10 percent sheer terror, "Eighty percent of the time there is no other place that I would put myself at that moment. Everything else in the world is gone except for that trail and that dog team. You become enveloped in this unit that you're part of."

Neumann concentrates sledding to one moment: "There is bedlam, and when you unhook the line, the snow hook, there is quiet, and you just fly. It's smooth and it's wonderful. I love to see the shadow of the dog team on the snow. There is nothing else like it on the planet; that's why we keep doing it."

CHAPTER 10

ANIMAL ACTORS

Animal trainer Stacy Basil and her husband, trainer Tom Gunderson, live on a ranch about an hour northeast of Los Angeles. The Vasquez Rocks, film site of such TV and cinematic westerns as *Wild Wild West* and the *Legend of the Lone Ranger*, can be seen from their gated estate.

Within the ranch's gates, a dozen canine stars live a life of pampered luxury. There's Fly, a Border collie last seen as Nana in the Cuba Gooding Jr. movie *Snow Dogs*, and up in the kennels avoiding the heat is one of her *Snow Dogs* costars, a shaggy Siberian husky. There's also Linus, a pushy French bulldog who first appeared in *102 Dalmatians* and has been working ever since; his most recent movie is *Bringing Down the House* with Steve Martin and Queen Latifah. Basil says that having a French bulldog is like having a trained piglet in the house and comments, "If Linus could talk, he'd say, 'You aren't the boss of me.' " Linus quickly proves Basil's point by squirming his way to the front of the pack and occasionally snarling at and generally intimidating his housemates. As Basil moves through the house and grounds, a pack of dogs follow her, all seeking her attention and, perhaps, a snack from the bait bag she carries with her.

Both Basil and Gunderson work for Gary Gerot's respected Birds and Animals training company. While Gunderson sticks mostly to exotics and reptiles, Basil works with dogs. "Dogs are my heart and soul," she says. "It's something that's developed over the years."

Basil admits that some trainers think her overwhelming affection for her dogs is a little kooky, but she doesn't care, "I have 12 dogs and they're like my kids and I'm like their mom—they live with me and they think I'm it." Whatever horror stories we've heard about animal trainers are thrown out the window when you see Basil interact with her dogs.

Hollywood animals haven't always lived the good life, however, and trainers are quick to point that out. "As an animal trainer I have to live down what trainers in the 1930s and 1940s did—killing and abusing animals just to get a shot," says trainer and owner of Critters of the Cinema, Rob Bloch. Although there were good and bad trainers then, as there are now, there was no overseeing body in the early part of the century to ensure that animals on movie sets were not mistreated. That changed when a horse was deliberately run off a cliff to its death in the 1939 film *Jesse James.* Responding to a public outcry, the AHA, which had worked to protect children and animals since 1877, opened a Los Angeles office to establish its Film and Television Unit to advocate for the safety of movie animals.

> **Movie dogs are now trained with an eye toward positive rewards and attention to the dogs' health and safety.**

For the most part, trainers welcome the observers from AHA on sets because their presence allows the trainer to tell the director when the dog needs to stop working without fear of recriminations, "When I'm ready to pull the plug, it's nice to have someone to back me up," says Bloch. "The problem for most trainers is that they're worried that if you say no to the director they won't hire you again." When an AHA representative is on the set, an animal trainer can ask the rep to talk to the director. The AHA representative also monitors that the trainers are keeping their dogs safe and comfortable.

"AHA makes a balance between the nuts out there that think nothing sentient should be used for films, with the nutty director who wants to run a horse off a cliff and kill it for the value of his movie," says Dave McMillan, who owns animal-training company Worldwide Animals. "Without them we'd be up against it sometimes."

"We're the ones that intercede," agrees Karen Rosa, communications manager for the AHA Film and Television Unit. "They have no power over us because we're not getting paid by them. The director won't argue with us. The trainer, on the other hand, may be worried about that job and the next job and being labeled as difficult. To have somebody neutral like us to be calling the perimeters saves a lot of aggravation."

Since *Jesse James* there've been changes to both the film industry and animal training in general. As with all types of working dogs, movie dogs are now trained with an eye toward positive rewards and attention to the dogs' health and safety. "The world of animal training has such a stigma," says Basil. "People have no idea the advancements that have been made."

"There's variation in any animal industry; look at the difference in breeders," says McMillan. "You've got everything from puppy mills to conscientious breeders that are very cautious. You've got people in here to make a quick buck, and you have people that understand dogs are their living. I think it's an anomaly for people to not have much respect for their animals. If an animal looks bad it's not going to work; if it's cowed, it's not going to work. You have to take care of them for them to work."

Although emphasis is on positive reward-based training, McMillan points out that training requires a spectrum of tools "from leash corrections to a high-pitched 'good dog!'—you have to use the continuum. Animals understand a dominant/submissive world, but that doesn't mean you don't have to give them all kinds of love and affection."

Back at Basil and Gunderson's ranch, Fly, aka Nana, cheerfully performs tricks for us with a little prompting from Basil and her bait bag. "Bother him," directs Basil as Fly pokes her head between Tom's legs, then paws at his leg. She lies down and sits pretty, her paws crossed neatly in front of her. Fly takes a break in the shade for a quick moment, maneuvering her butt into scratch range, then hurries off to find a plastic hot dog covered with dirt,

which she carries with her proudly until something else grabs her attention.

Basil laughs and explains that in *Snow Dogs*, Fly's character, Nana, was the only dog who liked Cuba Gooding Jr.'s character, so she was taught to imitate some of his habits, including cracking his neck. Basil gives her the command and Fly obliges, shaking her head from one side to another just as she did in the film.

When watching a movie, it's easy to forget that the dogs are really dogs; they are anthropomorphized, and that's how we like it. I sort of expect Fly to give me a Nanalike wink. It's important to realize that actors act but animals react, says Basil. "You can't tell a dog her motivation but that's what people want to see." Basil describes a scene in *Homeward Bound* in which the dog had to bump into a fire hydrant; the trick wasn't getting the dog to walk into the hydrant (which was foam), but getting her to look surprised. "That's one of the things I'm very proud of," she says. Although she's not proud enough to tell me how she did it; like a magician, I suppose, a good trainer never reveals his or her secrets.

According to Bloch, it's often less about training than knowing the animal. "In Hollywood they don't just want the dog to walk into the room, they want the dog to walk into the room happy. Sometimes you really have to know the inner workings of the dog's mind—especially if you have to make the dog look afraid because you have to scold the animal to make him look flat. You have to have a good relationship with the animal. I may do two or three takes and then say, 'Guys, that's enough, because now the dog's starting to take it seriously.' "

When you get a feeling for how the animal reacts to certain things you can pull these emotions from the animal, explains Bloch. "That's the really fun and challenging part of this job: getting the animal to be happy when there's no reason to be happy or pulling them out of an air-conditioned truck and getting them to look hot and tired."

Sometimes, however, dogs are just fickle. Once, when working on *Laverne & Shirley*, McMillan had to borrow a whippet on the day of the shoot. On the drive to the set, McMillan said the dog's name and gave him a treat every time he looked at him. By the time they arrived, the dog knew where the treats were coming from. Noticing the dog's rapt attention of McMillan, one of the show's stars exclaimed, "Oh, how long have you had him? Look how he looks at you!"

Technically, not all the dogs who live with Basil are hers. Birds and Animals owns 10 of them, while only 2 are her pets. This setup is not uncommon with movie dogs; a company may own 100 dogs, with 40 living on the company's compound, another 40 living with various trainers, and an additional 20 scattered among families throughout the Southern California area. The production companies pay the animal-training companies to rent the dogs and the animal training companies pay the trainer for training the dog. It's a somewhat complicated system, but it seems to work.

To complicate it even further, the many animal-training companies in California may borrow dogs or other animals from one another when they're hired to be the

trainer but don't have the "right" dog on payroll. For example, Birds and Animals is hired to do a movie, but the director wants a Newfoundland. If Birds and Animals doesn't have a Newfoundland, it can either buy one, or if it knows there is a well-trained Newfoundland owned by another animal-training company, it can rent the animal from that company. "Some of our competitors are our best business," laughs McMillan, explaining that the owner of the animal gets two-thirds of the fee, while the contact gets one-third.

Sometimes a trainer doesn't have the right dog and can't find a previously trained dog for a specific movie, so he or she must find one at a shelter, purchase a dog from a breeder, or even borrow the right dog from a family. For big productions with a lot of animals, trainers usually need to adopt dogs from a shelter or purchase them from breeders. For *Snow Dogs*, for example, Basil searched the U.S. and Canada for Siberian huskies, buying or rescuing 45 in all. In addition, directors can make capricious demands, asking for a rare breed that happens to catch his or her fancy. For example, one trainer rolls his eyes over a director who insisted on using an Anatolian shepherd in a recent movie (read, *Kate & Leopold*) despite the fact that there were no trained Anatolian shepherds in the business, and the director probably wouldn't know an Anatolian shepherd if she bit him in the ass.

Animal Actors

Once a shoot is over, new homes must be found for many of the dogs or, if a home can't be found or they are especially promising actors, they stay with their trainers. For that reason, trainers will tell you that an investment in a dog is lifelong. Good trainers never send dogs back to animal shelters once they're adopted, even if they turn out to be uninterested in working. "If it was a computer that broke I'd throw it in the trash," says Bloch, "but live animals, I don't think so." He adds that he has five or six dogs living in his compound who no longer work. For example, 14-year-old golden retriever Duncan is now mostly a pet, living in the house and living out his golden years. "Duncan doesn't work anymore unless I get a call for an older dog and only then if it's not going to be too difficult for him," says Bloch.

Basil adds, "We retire the animals once they get old or start to show signs that it's no longer fun. Dogs at 9 or 10 start to get a little arthritic and that's when they stop working. In retirement they still get to go on set, that's what they deserve."

When dogs don't work out for one reason or another, animal training companies usually try to find them homes rather than have them living in the kennels. "I may get a dog who just isn't enjoying it, so I find him a home," explains Bloch. "I would not want to do with my life what I don't want to do; why would I make somebody else do it?"

"It's part of our responsibility to the animals," says Bloch, "to take the best darn care you can from cradle to grave, as they say." He adds that he's set up a trust for his animals in the event that something happens to him. "I've got two hundred animals, and the money has to be here to maintain those animals until they're no longer around."

Some dogs, trainers say, aren't cut out for a working life, while others thrive on it. McMillan even opted for a trade in one situation, "I had a trainer whose dad had a really high-energy dog who he was having a lot of trouble with. At that time I had a dog who was the only dog I've had that simply did not like to work. He had a good look and he'd get hired but he'd punish you on the set, cuddle up to a female actress and say *I'm with her.* We switched and they love him, 'Oh, he's such a great pet,' and that's what he wanted to be." At least half of the dogs used in the entertainment industry come from shelters, and some say it's more like 75 percent. According to AHA's Rosa, "Trainers

> **When watching a movie, it's easy to forget that the dogs are really dogs; they're anthropomorphized, and that is how we like it.**

are the largest unsung rescue groups in the country. The truth is, they don't dispose of them and they're very careful to adopt them out to people that they think will care for them. The dogs are better trained and easier to adopt out when they have movie credits. It's a win-win situation."

McMillan explains that trainers turn to shelters for several reasons: it's less expensive to adopt a dog than to buy one; most movie dogs are random-bred, valued for their "every dog" look; and you save a life. Purebred dogs are found at shelters, when possible, or bought from breeders or private individuals.

Basil adds that she always tries rescues and shelters before turning to a breeder, and says, emphatically, "All our animals are neutered."

When McMillan searches for a dog at a shelter, he looks for a number of things, "A lot of things you can't quantify, but their responsiveness to bait, their attitude in that horrible situation that they're in—if they're resilient enough to deal with the kennel environment. I also look for ball drive or something you can get a handle on that will make it easier to train them. You're also looking for a look; if it's just a plain black dog, you're not going to pick it." McMillan adds that while the ideal look for a movie dog changes, "Right now it is tan and white with facial markings, and those clear, 'pit bully' eyes." Often the most vital clue to a dog's aptitude for work is just a spark in her eye, says McMillan, "because that means their minds are active."

Good trainers never send dogs back to animal shelters once they're adopted, even if they turn out to be uninterested in working.

Every trainer has had an animal who has touched him or her more than the others. Even McMillan, who shrugs off the idea of bonding with his working animals, admits that. "The first animals you work with you fall in love with," he says. "My case was an elephant and when I left that job I cried; I still think about her. But you learn to toughen up. You've got to keep just a little bit of distance, but sometimes you can't help yourself."

McMillan bonded particularly well with a dog named Buster, a beagle. "The dog who stands out in my mind just died last year, and that was a tremendous dog who I really miss. He's got a commercial out right now and every time I see it I get a feeling. Buster was a tan and white beagle; he started as a seven-week-old puppy on *The Wonder Years*. He was a character and he was an honest worker—he threw

Animal Actors

little stuff in; he'd do something on his own. The commercial is the one with the kids running around the backyard with the dog—it's like looking at your kid that died or something."

Bloch recalls that his first dog was a soft-coated wheaten terrier mix named Friday, whom he adopted from the Carson Animal Shelter. "Friday turned out to be an unbelievable animal, just one of those unique animals that after a couple years of working, all of a sudden a light bulb went on in his head and he really, really understood what we were doing. Usually when you're showing a dog a trick, the dog's looking in your face, but he would look at my hands to see what I was showing him and then look up at me as if to say, *I think I got it*. People would just stand back and watch me work with him; once they forgot to roll the camera because they were so busy watching us."

"With Friday I did probably the most difficult and rewarding job I've ever done with one animal in one day," says Bloch. "We had to work in heavy rain machines. The dog had to be outside in the rain and the girl was on the phone with her back to the glass sliding door where the dog was. She was talking to her friend and her parents were trying to call her to bring the dog out of the rain, but they didn't have call waiting. The dog was out in the rain and we had to have him do all kinds of antics to get the girl's attention. He was standing up scratching the door, dancing in circles, had to walk through the shot on his hind legs holding an umbrella in his mouth—that was a fun thing to train, that was something else—then he had to come back in the other direction in a rowboat with a yellow slicker on. Then, at the end of the commercial, when they break away for the final sales pitch and come back for the final tag, the dog comes up from below wearing a snorkel and mask."

Working Dogs

For many outside the film industry, the idea of animal training leaves a bad taste. After hearing the rumors of electrified aluminum making animals dance and cotton being stuffed in their mouths so they look like they're talking, it wasn't a stretch to expect an adversarial relationship between the AHA and animal trainers, and maybe I would have seen one had I not gone through AHA for my interviews; I don't know. I do know that the animals I met at Stacy Basil's ranch seemed to be as happy and content as my own, and, if you can apply the philosophy about all working dogs to movie dogs, they are probably a lot happier than they would be only as pets.

If there is one concern I have, it is that many movie animals do live on large compounds in kennels. Bloch argues that dogs only know what they know; they can't imagine a different life than living in a kennel if they've never lived elsewhere. He also points out that the kennel runs are large, his are 50 feet by 6 feet, and that most dogs live with another dog, so they're not socially isolated. The dogs at his ranch, 15 to 20 at a time, are turned out in the large exercise areas and get to romp and play to their delight. And, of course, they're also trained at least a few times weekly and get to go on set. When they are working, they are meticulously bathed and groomed and there's nothing more exciting for a working dog than getting to go to work. "As soon as the dogs hear the rattle of the choke chain and the rattle of the bait bag, it's *yee haw*," laughs Bloch.

In addition to my concerns with large kennels is the fact that not all animal trainers are as good as the ones I spoke to, something these trainers readily agree with. Like anything, there's good and bad. Although the AHA can keep bad trainers and overzealous directors from injuring an animal on set, they have no jurisdiction over their lives off the set.

> **At least half of the dogs used in the entertainment industry come from shelters, and some say it's more like 75 percent.**

Bloch adds, just as with us, work isn't always perfect. "Most of the dogs enjoy it most of the time. When you have to do something 50 or 60 times, then no, but it's your responsibility to make the dog enjoy it. And sometimes you just have to say, 'I don't care, you need to get out there and do it; you have to work today.'" Bloch's dogs work about 40 or 50 days in a year, so the times that they are working, he expects them to finish the job. Movie dogs

Animal Actors

appear to like what they do; when they don't like it, they don't do it for long.

Many movie dogs were not successful as companions or in their previous jobs. They had too much energy or they were unhappy with their lot in life. Fly, Basil's super-affectionate Border collie, came to Basil from a dairy farm, aggressive and neurotic. The dairy farmer told Basil he couldn't even get a collar on her without her biting him. There's no doubt Fly's celebrity lifestyle is a better fit.

When McMillan goes out to the kennels to get a dog for a job, it's a cacophony of sound, he says. "All the dogs are thinking, *Pick me, pick me!* They're like a bunch of young actors trying to get a job!"

CHAPTER 11

DETECTION DOGS

In the past few years, we've all become accustomed to the use of dogs in law enforcement. We see dogs when we disembark from airplanes, cross borders, or even when we leave cruise ships. Dogs are used by the United States Department of Agriculture (USDA), U.S. Customs, the Transportation Security Administration (TSA), and the U.S. military to detect everything from narcotics to vegetables to explosives. They're also used by local police and fire departments to find drugs and currency and to determine if a fire was accidental or caused by arson. All of these agencies have come to realize that the dog is a reliable, mobile, and objective means to finding almost anything someone wants to hide.

The TSA has created a strong program over the past 30 years using dogs to protect airlines and passengers from terrorist and criminal threats by screening bags and departing airplanes for explosives. Since the terrorist attacks of September 11, Dave Kontny, manager of the Explosives Detection Canine Team Program, or TSA Canine Program, explains, "Everyone's looking for dogs to do a multitude of things."

For any sniffing job a dog does, he is trained to detect specific smells and then alert on the smells. The dog must discriminate among many smells to find the specific one his handler is after. Any dog used for detection work can be trained on any of the smells; it doesn't take one type of dog to sniff out explosives or another type for fruit, although different agencies do use different breeds for various reasons. Small-sized dogs and dogs with gentle dispositions are considered most appropriate when working in public, while larger, sharper dogs might be used in cargo settings. Ultimately, all that matters is what smells a dog has been exposed to and trained to detect. Since dogs have something to the tune of 200,000 more olfactory receptors than we do, even a Pomeranian can do a better job of finding a hidden substance than a human can.

U.S. Customs officer Danny Turner uses the analogy of a hamburger to describe what a detection dog does: "It's like having a hamburger and you have the bun that smells and the lettuce and tomato and the meat and the cheese and the ketchup—all of these have individual odors. The dog is able to discriminate. If we're training him to look for sesame seeds he can discount the bun, the meat, and everything else. He might want the meat, but he'll discount it because he's trained and he knows what he's working for and there's no point to alerting on it." A detection dog can smell all the individual ingredients that go into the hamburger as well, including the type of wheat in the bun or the individual spices in the ketchup. And he can smell the residual scent of the hamburger for up to a week after it's been removed.

Depending on what the dog is searching for, he may do a passive or an aggressive alert. A passive alert is usually sitting and maybe using his paw or nose to indicate the direction of the smell's source when the handler asks him to pinpoint the source or says, "Show me." An aggressive alert can include barking and scratching at the source. For obvious reasons, dogs who work in public or dogs working with explosives always use passive alerts. Although aggressive alerts were once the norm, many agencies are switching to the passive alert for public relations and cargo safety.

Detection Dogs

In Guam, the USDA's Wildlife Services utilizes Jack Russell terriers—for their sense of smell, prey drive, and small size—to seek out brown snakes, which have proven destructive to wildlife on this island. The mission here is to prevent the brown snake from making it to other islands such as Hawaii and the Micronesian Islands where they could wreak havoc on indigenous wildlife and pose a health threat to humans. "The Jack Russell terriers were originally trained to go after the snake," says Wildlife Services' Mike Pitzler. "That was a problem in the public's eyes—having a dog rip apart a snake in front of their eyes. Now, the dogs' training is passive. They sit and put a paw in the direction of the snake, and the handler catches it."

The TSA Canine Program, then under the Federal Aviation Administration (FAA), was started in 1972 when an explosives dog detected a bomb on a TWA airplane just 12 minutes before it was set to go off. Since then, the dogs have been ever-present components of most major airports. Kontny himself came to the FAA from the Department of Defense (DoD) after TWA Flight 800 exploded over the coast of Long Island, New York, in 1996. The TSA took over the program from the FAA after September 11, 2001.

Kontny, who worked his way through the ranks starting out as a dog handler, is able to provide the transportation administration with a unique perspective. "Dogs sometimes get a bad reputation for doing something they shouldn't be doing," explains Kontny. Part of his job is to explain the dogs' abilities and needs to airport and government officials so that the dogs are utilized in the best possible ways without being second-guessed. When airport or airline officials don't understand the capabilities of the dogs, the dogs may not be used effectively or they may be used for jobs for which they are not adequately trained. As a former handler, Kontny

> **Since dogs have something to the tune of 200,000 more olfactory receptors than we do, even a Pomeranian can do a better job of finding a hidden substance than a human can.**

also understands the effectiveness and inevitability of the dog-handler bond. "The bond is essential," he says. "If you don't have the bond, you don't have a good team."

The TSA Canine Program is operated in cooperation with local and/or airport police departments. The TSA pays for both the dog and the training, as well as partially reimbursing the local police departments for the handler's salary and the dog's expenses, including food and veterinary costs. The TSA Canine Program also works closely with the DoD; training takes place at Lackland Air Force Base, in San Antonio, Texas, the same facility in which military dogs are trained. The dogs, who enter the program at about one and a half to two years old, receive several weeks of cursory training, but they get most of their training during the 11-week team training. "The handlers and dogs teach each other," says Kontny. "The handlers bring that dog from its infancy in training to being fully trained. When dogs were push-button trained [trained without their handlers], the teams didn't know what to do when they encountered problems."

All of the dogs, usually sporting breeds such as Labs and Chesapeake Bay retrievers, are trained on a reward system, utilizing whatever the dog determines he wants. Although the dogs traditionally were purchased from private breeders in the U.S. or Europe, the TSA Canine Program initiated a breeding program in 2000 due to unreliable sources and an expanded need for dogs.

Like all detection dogs, the TSA's dogs are playing a game; a combination of drive, training, experience, and eagerness to please dictate how well they play. By the end of 2003, the TSA plans to have 350 dog teams in 82 airports. Every dog deployed by the TSA is rigorously tested and goes through annual recertification, which takes three to four days.

As Kontny points out, the dogs are trained so well because, "We can't evacuate an airplane at 30,000 feet." With an explosives dog, there are no second chances. As the bomb squad community, police departments, airports, and public continue to be educated about detection dogs, Kontny sees their use only rising. The dogs are mobile, accurate, and they appeal to the American people in a way that equipment can't.

The U.S. Customs canine program was started in 1970, when a study showed that dogs could be trained to detect marijuana, hashish, heroin, and cocaine.

He describes an incident in the St. Louis airport shortly after September 11, 2001, when passengers began applauding as an explosives detection canine team entered the terminal; the applause followed the team as it walked through the entire airport. "People have a different respect for dogs than equipment," says Kontny. "It's a comfort level. In order for us to maintain that comfort level, we need to make sure standards are high."

Detection Dogs

Kontny mentions that reporters are often disappointed to find out that the TSA Canine Program had implemented a rapid-growth plan prior to September 11. He's quick to point out that the FAA has worked extensively with detection dogs for many years, and that their use is no knee-jerk reaction to the events of 2001. For several years the program has anticipated a growing interest and need for detection dogs. Kontny expresses concern about opportunists in the aftermath of the terrorist attacks. Although he accedes that some new dog-training businesses are trying to provide a service and are working under the same strict guidelines as the TSA Canine Program, others are simply looking for a way to make a quick buck. His fear is that uninformed airports or airlines will hire dogs through less-than-scrupulous operations: undermining the use of dogs in explosives detection as well as opening themselves up to an inevitable tragedy.

In Los Angeles, California, U.S. Customs dogs are being used to find drugs in cargo shipments coming into The Port of Los Angeles as well as on passengers disembarking from cruise ships. The U.S. Customs canine program was started in 1970, when a study showed that dogs could be trained to detect marijuana, hashish, heroin, and cocaine. U.S. Customs began using the dogs to search cars, ships, airplanes, cargo, and passengers entering the U.S. by air and sea, or crossing the Canadian or Mexican borders. Since then, the dogs' uses have been extended to finding currency as well as an ever-increasing selection of illegal narcotics, including methamphetamine, opium, and ecstasy. The program is currently being expanded to include explosives detection.

On a gray June morning at the Port of Los Angeles, passengers are ending a weekend cruise to Mexico. Sunburned and hungover, couples exit the ship with over-sized sombreros and miniature guitars in hand. Parents corral their children, and a few groups of girlfriends excitedly recount their travels. As the passengers disembark, they are directed through one door, and then moving in a U-shape they are sent back through an adjoining door. In the room to which they're directed wait Customs officer Danny Turner and his partner, drug dog Mugsy, a yellow Lab. Mugsy is wagging his tail in anticipation. It's clear he's used to this procedure and looks forward to it. While they wait, Turner plays vigorously with Mugsy, rubbing his sides and cuffing his muzzle affectionately. As the first passengers come through the door, however, Turner and Mugsy are all business.

One of the biggest advantages of using detection dogs is that they are unbiased.

Directed by Turner, Mugsy walks briskly up and down the line of passengers, occasionally pausing to sniff the air or to nuzzle his nose against a pocket or bag. Turner keeps the inspection upbeat and jokey, in contrast to his more formal behavior when we first met a few hours before. "Keep it movin' folks. Nice hat; yes, it's a dog, How was your trip? Good job, good job!" He explains later that it's part of his job to keep passengers comfortable during the process.

Many of the passengers are startled to see the dog coming toward them, but calm as Mugsy quickly eases past. Suddenly, Mugsy pauses to sniff one passenger. As the man tries to continue toward the second door, Mugsy spins and pulls, and Turner drops his leash. Mugsy runs through the line of passengers to continue sniffing at the man intently, his nose glued to the man's pocket and tail wagging high in a stiff, intent sway. Turner approaches, "Please step out of the line," he instructs the man. The man nervously follows Turner and reaches into his pocket. Another customs agent nods to Turner, "Training aid!" he yells, and the passenger pulls a tube-shaped package from his pocket, which a Customs agent retrieves, thanking him. The passenger, a bit embarrassed over the scene hurries back into line and continues out the door. Turner pulls a carefully folded white towel from the back of his pants and throws it to Mugsy, "Good job, Mugsy, good job!" he says, tugging at the towel now between Mugsy's teeth. The two play an intense game of tug for a minute or two before Turner puts the towel back into the waistband of his pants, and Mugsy, appearing proud of himself and invigorated, returns to Turner's side.

Mugsy has found one of the several training aids hidden with passengers on each ship. The training aids, which consist of synthesized narcotic odor rather than the real

Detection Dogs

thing, serve both to reinforce Mugsy's training and to test his competency. For U.S. Customs dogs, receiving the towel is their ultimate reward; any dog who loses interest in the towel is washed from the system. Each day, Turner carefully folds and tapes a white hand towel into a firm tube before starting their shift.

Unlike some other detection dogs, U.S. Customs dogs don't choose their toy or reward; for them, it's the towel or nothing. Although, Turner points out, the physical and verbal praise is just as much a part of it, and the towel reward is alternated with what these handlers call praise offs, when a dog receives only physical and verbal praise instead of the towel. Turner laughs that the first time he did a praise off with Mugsy, the dog was dumbfounded. "I've never seen a dog react like that," says Turner. "He was shocked." Still, Mugsy quickly figured out that the towels and praise offs were all part of the game, and when they find another training aid a short while later, Mugsy seems just as pleased to receive a vigorous rub down and verbal

affirmations. Every dog is different, says Turner, describing a dog he worked with temporarily a few weeks previously. "This dog was so aloof, but he had such drive." Uninterested in the praise Turner meted out, "he'd release the towel and go right back to work without a command—he was rewarding himself." For some dogs, the work drive is so strong, the work in itself is the reward.

The room where Mugsy is working is small and airless. It's

becoming a hot, humid day, and he's working hard. Turner takes him to the truck parked outside for regular breaks, offering the Lab a drink of water and a chance to cool off. Turner scoffs at the idea that Mugsy might need any additional exercise than his work, "These dogs are exhausted at the end of the day," he says.

Turner procured Mugsy from the Orange County Humane Society in 1998. Mugsy was screened before leaving the shelter. Turner looked at his size, age, breed, temperament, and, most of all, drive for the towel. "We throw the towel under a car," says Turner. Whether the dog is interested enough to go after it dictates his acceptance into the program. "You can't teach a dog to like the towel."

Once adopted, most dogs go to the national training center, the Canine Enforcement Training Center (CETC), in Front Royal, Virginia. It was summer when Mugsy was adopted, however, and the airlines were not shipping animals due to the heat. After Mugsy languished in a kennel for almost a month, Turner, who did not have a dog at the time, received special permission to train Mugsy himself. Although training at the academy usually takes 12 to 15 weeks, Turner had Mugsy on the ground in 4 weeks. Once certified, the two became an official team and have worked together ever since.

> **While the dog is responsible for finding the drugs, the handler is responsible for the health and welfare of the dog.**

Watching them work, their rapport is obvious, "You become familiar with your dog," says Turner. "Dogs have quirks just like people have quirks, and you learn them over time. On the flip side," he adds with a laugh, "the dog usually figures the handler out before the handler figures the dog out."

Turner explains that much of what makes an effective team is being able to read your dog and his different behaviors and alerts. While one behavior may be indistinguishable from another to an outsider, the handler easily interprets each behavior. "The dog responds to different smells, including animal smells and food," says Turner. "You learn what the dog looks like when he detects narcotics; there are certain physical characteristics you see. When he's on another smell, there are some things that you don't see. At the same time," Turner adds, "you don't want to discount what the dog's going after. Narcotics can be concealed by using anything and everything to mask its smell, but the dog will disregard the other odors." Turner describes drugs found hidden in laundry detergent or food items or baked into ceramic pottery. Sometimes a dog alerts and the agent doesn't find a thing, "But you don't know where the person has been, so I don't discount the dog," says Turner. For example, the cruise ship has a partying atmosphere, and passengers disembarking may have been smoking marijuana or in a room where it was smoked during the trip. The dogs will sometimes alert on a bag with dirty laundry, where smoke has permeated clothing, or on a bag in which mari-

Detection Dogs

juana was brought onto the ship. Occasionally, the dogs will alert to prescription medications, as well.

Although U.S. Customs is looking for the big smuggler, there is a zero-tolerance policy; anyone found with the smallest amount of a drug is subject to an automatic $5,000 fine.

Detection dogs can screen bags, passengers, cargo, and vehicles more quickly and more effectively than can humans, but one of the biggest advantages of using detection dogs is that they are unbiased. A human Customs officer makes judgments about people and is unlikely to, for example, suspect a four-year-old child of carrying a backpack full of drugs. "Unfortunately," says Turner, "that happens." The dog doesn't discriminate. "Mugsy is trained for specific odors and that's what he's looking for." Good handlers know that when a well-trained, experienced dog makes an alert, chances are something is or was there, no matter how little sense it makes.

"There was one guy that the dog alerted to that swore up and down that he didn't have anything." A cursory search turned up nothing, and it seemed like he was telling the truth. Nevertheless, he was referred for a secondary search based on the dog's very solid alert. "Going through his wallet, in among the pictures and business cards, was a tiny brown disk no bigger than a nickel," says Turner. "He had a little piece of 15-year-old hash that he didn't even remember was there,

and the dog still got him." Turner uses this story to illustrate why officers trust their dogs so much, "You never second-guess the dog because you don't know. That guy didn't even know."

Another time, Turner was doing a training exercise at the airport with another handler's dog. As they walked back to the office, they passed some passengers going through Customs. Although the dog was not under a search command, "All of a sudden he ran to the left and started searching the line. He sat in front of this guy and the whole line was looking except for this guy. He ended up having a block of hash in his pocket."

While the dog is responsible for finding the drugs, the handler is responsible for the health and welfare of the dog. It's clear Turner takes this seriously. As passengers continue to disembark from the cruise ship for over an hour, Turner rests and waters Mugsy often, and he puts a great deal of energy into keeping the dog focused and interested in the game, praising him effusively when he alerts and playing with and petting him whenever there are pauses. "I suppose you could work a dog without any physical and verbal praise, but it would give the impression that you don't really care about what the dog is doing," says Turner. "We feed off of verbal praise and so do the dogs." The relationship between Mugsy and Turner seems a hard one for him to articulate, "You're always told it's not a pet, but you are responsible for the health and welfare of your dog. Without the bond, your dog wouldn't work for you very long; it's the same if you had a human partner."

At the time that we meet, Turner is considering leaving his job at U.S. Customs. That means giving Mugsy up to another handler. Although Mugsy, like all U.S. government owned dogs, lives in a kennel, he and Turner spend eight hours a day, five days a week together, far more time than most pet owners spend with their animal companions. Leaving will be a difficult transition and clearly not one Turner relishes discussing. "Somebody's going to end up with a good dog," he says at first, then adds, "It's difficult, but it's not the first dog I've lost. I'm not going to say I'm used to it because you never get used it, it just becomes a little easier to handle."

There's no doubt Turner's proud of Mugsy; he points out a service award pin on his uniform, saying, "That's from an operation he worked on where they made the largest seizure of ecstasy in the world—700 pounds." He adds, petting Mugsy as he speaks, "He's doing a lot of work out there. If he could write and drive, I'd be out of a job."

Across town at the Los Angeles International Airport (LAX), a group of beagles are assembled for training. Outfitted in their green USDA vests, these dogs look far too cute for work, but work they do. In counterbalance to the puppylike dogs sitting primly next to them, the Beagle Brigade handlers are all business in their black-and-white uniforms.

Detection Dogs

The Beagle Brigade falls under the command of the USDA's Animal and Plant Health Inspection Service (APHIS). The beagles and the APHIS Plant Protection and Quarantine (PPQ) officers work to intercept any contraband fruit, meat, or other agricultural product before it accidentally or purposely enters the country. Meat can carry diseases that could be spread to American livestock, while fruit and vegetables can be contaminated with pests that could decimate our crops. The PPQ's mission is to keep these pests away from American agriculture. Although many passengers flippantly opt not to declare a piece of fruit, thinking, *it's just an apple,* it's a lot more than an apple to the USDA. As one Beagle Brigade handler tells me, "My dog is saving the world."

The PPQ officers make about two million seizures each year, of those, the Beagle Brigade detect about seventy-five thousand. Although they can't check every bag that enters the country, they'd like to.

Photographer Keith May and I are lucky enough to see a training session, where the dogs are looking for a variety of items, including pork, mangoes, and citrus fruit. But first they must get past us. Upon our entrance to the room, Keith is immediately set upon by a pack of beagles, all sniffing at his camera bag. As one after another sits in alert, then paws at the bag, Keith sheepishly pulls out an apple. One handler looks at Keith in disgust and shakes her head, "Don't tell me you brought fruit in here!" Keith, anointed Apple Man throughout our half-day visit, is a true fruit eater and his bag carries enough residual apple scent from years of fruit transportation to garner the beagles' attention until we leave.

For the Beagle Brigade handlers, part of the job is determining whether a dog is alerting on residual odor, the smell that an item leaves even after it is removed from a bag or pocket. When a dog alerts on a bag without any contraband agricultural items, the handler will ask the owner of the bag if it had held any fruit in the last week, "Apples, oranges, bananas?" Once prompted, most people affirm that it had, "Oh yeah, I carry my lunch in here everyday."

As with the U.S. Customs dogs, the Beagle Brigade dogs live in kennels outside their work areas; the LAX beagles are all housed in a special area in a private kennel off-site. Also like the U.S. Customs dogs, most of the beagles are adopted from shelters or rescues. Shelter workers across the country are instructed to contact the Beagle Brigade if they receive any beagles with a strong work drive. The agency uses beagles for a number of reasons, but chief among them is their approachability. Passengers aren't afraid of a beagle and feel less intimidated than they would with a large German shepherd or rottweiler sniffing around their bags. The PPQ teams used in cargo can be any breed because they are not working with the public. Beagles are also valued for their excellent sense of smell and small size; they're able to wiggle through passengers and bags without being obtrusive. As PPQ officer Chevy Dyson says, "Sometime we're so fast, we've been in there, sniffed their bags and are three people down before people notice—we're in and out."

> **When a shelter or private individual contacts the Beagle Brigade with a potential beagle, one of the officers visits the dog, testing him both for temperament and drive.**

When a shelter or private individual contacts the Beagle Brigade with a potential beagle, one of the officers visits the dog, testing him both for temperament and drive. "We like really friendly dogs," says Diana Verity one of three western region program coordinators. They're also screened for any health problems. Once the dog is procured for the program, he goes to the PPQ's Orlando, Florida, training center for a 10-day quarantine and then begins a five-week protocol training, where he is trained on five basic odors, which differ depending on the port, or pathway, he will be assigned. Verity explains that a dog assigned to LAX will be trained for different smells than a dog at the Mexico–U.S. border or one at the Seattle-Tacoma International Airport (Sea-Tac), outside Seattle.

In the training process, about three-fourths of the dogs procured are weeded out, generally for a lack of drive. Dogs who do not make it are adopted by good homes. Once the dogs' preliminary training is complete, they are matched with an incoming handler for an additional 10-week training program. Beagle Brigade han-

Detection Dogs

dlers go through both a 10-week officer's training as well as the dog training school. During dog school, a handler may work with several dogs as the trainers shift dogs and handlers, trying to determine the best match. There are only four students in each session, so the trainers get to know the students and dogs well. Sometimes the matches aren't always clear at first but almost always work surprisingly well. "I was matched with Hal, although I was quiet and he needed a lot of voice," says Verity. "At first I felt really silly but it taught me, and it turned out to be a good match. The trainers know what they're doing; they picked me because I'm patient, and Hal needed a lot of patience."

Beagle Brigades have formal training two times per week throughout the working life of the dog, but they are always training whenever they are on the floor. A confirmed alert means pay—a treat. These guys work for food, and being typical beagles, they can't get enough of it. Verity laughs that they have to keep the beagles on a strict diet to ensure they don't "end up like sausages. People think they're skinny but they're at optimum weight. They're just used to seeing fat beagles," she says.

As they work, the beagles continue to learn smells, "It's like a vocabulary," explains Verity. By retirement, some dogs know up to 50 smells, many quite unusual. Saroya Waite's dog, Brutus, works in the post office one day a week and has learned some particularly interesting odors, including fresh ginger.

The dogs don't only alert to odors they know, sometimes they react to an odor simply because it is alarming or interesting to them. Brutus, for example, recently found an elephant's trunk when working the post office. Although PPQ is not looking for endangered species, they work closely with other agencies, such as U.S. Fish & Wildlife Service, and they turn these types of finds over to them. Handlers pay (reward) their dogs for these finds so that if they come across this strange odor again, they'll alert to it. "We look for the alert but also unusual behavior," says Verity. "There might be something to it."

The dogs may not do a classic alert when they've discovered a new and unusual odor, but because the handlers know their dogs so well, they know how to read their behavior. Verity describes one incident when a dog simply wouldn't go near a bag, acting almost afraid of it. The handler investigated and found smuggled human body parts hidden within. Verity's dog, Hal, even found a monkey hidden in a passenger's bra. "She'd given the monkey a sedative and smuggled it in her shirt," Verity explains. "When she came off the plane, Hal was very interested in her. He was jumping up on her, which was very strange because they're trained not to. He just wouldn't leave her alone, and another dog did the same. Customs searched her and found the monkey." Verity laughs, "Usually we're finding fruit."

After several years of working together, the handler and dog become a strong team; while the dog does the sniffing, the handler needs to be able to read the dog's moods and behaviors as well as his alerts. "I know when he's not working," explains Dyson, referring to her dog, General. "I'll pull him out and talk to him. If he's mad at me, he'll [ignore] me; you've got to learn how to work though that. For example," Dyson continues, "with passenger dogs, I've learned if I let him go sniff the cage, say hello, he will work for me. If I don't, he will not work. It's easier to comply. Why should I fight that? You want the dog to be willing to work; I don't want my dog to work because he's scared of me or I'm forcing him to."

Handlers also stress the need to communicate their pleasure with the dogs through verbal and physical praise as well as with treats. "I make him feel that I'm pleased; when we're walking, we're talking," says Waite of Brutus. "When he looks at me, he knows I'm happy. I make sure that he knows that this is the best thing he's doing for me today. I don't want him sad; I want to make sure he's feeling good before he goes on the floor." As with all detection dog handlers, the beagle handlers emphasize the bond they share with their animal. "The bond is the biggest issue," says Waite. "You bond with your dog, you got smooth sailing."

The dogs also need to have an extremely strong work drive; the desire to find the contraband and play the game. "If you watch him on the floor, he is always looking," says Waite. "Without his jacket, with his jacket on, if we're going to the car; he will catch a passenger on the way to the car to make sure he's getting paid." Dyson adds that although passengers often try to pet the dogs or even pick them up, her dog "could care less what they're doing. He's in work mode; he just ignores them."

All of the handlers are keenly aware of not overworking their dogs and letting them have a chance to be dogs. "I make sure he gets downtime," says Dyson. "We play tug-of-war or take a long break. I let him have his doggy time too." Handlers also have to look out for the dogs' safety on the floor; harried passengers often do not pay attention and can drop a heavy bag onto or push a cart into a dog.

Detection Dogs

It's vital the dog be excited and happy to work; when a dog decides he no longer wants to work, he is no longer effective. "When I pick him up, he's excited," says Waite of Brutus. "He tiptoes, it's a pitter-patter move. For him, it's time to play. They like the game, *This is it—I'm going to get treats for this!*"

Once a dog chooses to stop working, he is retired. "We don't push it because it's counterproductive to push a dog," explains Verity. After they're 7 years old, the beagles are health screened more often, but many work up until 9 or 10. Once they are retired, the handlers have first option to adopt them. "I'll most definitely [adopt] Brutus!" says Waite. "Nobody gets my dog; that's *my dog*. Most of the handlers keep their dogs, you bond with that dog—that's my man." Dyson also stresses that General will eventually come home with her, "That's my child; that's my baby. They're like your kids. I know he's my work dog and when it's time to work, we work, but I'm attached to him."

While Verity is philosophical about giving up a dog if a handler leaves the Beagle Brigade, pointing out, "these aren't pets, they're our partners," she's no less sentimental than Waite and Dyson about Hal with whom she's worked for almost seven years. "Everyone's said they want my dog but that would be like giving up my child. After six years, eight hours a day, five days a week . . .your dog only has eyes for you."

As the beagles and their handlers work, it's clear that both dog and human know their job. Wearing his green vest with Protecting American Agriculture printed on one side and Agriculture's Beagle Brigade printed on the other, Brutus sits in front of a woman with several bags, almost grinnin with pleasure. This is his favorite part; he knows there's something there, and so does the passenger, who frowns in displeasure as Waite asks her to open the bags. There it is, a plastic-sealed gift box of fresh ginger. Brutus receives his well-earned treat, and after Waite marks the woman's declaration card, they move on—they've saved the world again.

CHAPTER 12

POLICE DOGS

Jerry, an excitable Belgian Malinois with what can only be called a canine grin, is lying on his back, looking for belly rubs. Even on the ground, he is wagging his tail so hard—that is, what's left of it—his whole body sways. "We had to amputate it," says his handler, police officer Bill Kift, a little sheepishly, "He wagged it so hard it kept getting injured."

Although there's a public image of canine cops being fierce and even vicious, meet most of these fearsome hounds away from work and they're as gentle as your own four-legged companion. Bill Kift of the Long Beach, California, police department should know. He owns three current and retired canine cops: Jerry and Nero, both patrol dogs, and Lucy, a bloodhound.

Police dogs have several duties: there are detection dogs, who search for suspects or victims and sniff out drugs or explosives; and there are patrol dogs, who accompany their human handlers when they pursue and subdue suspects, respond to 911 calls, and disperse crowds, among countless other duties. Most police dogs are cross-trained in both detection and patrol work, although bloodhounds are trained exclusively to track human scent.

Kift's bloodhound, Lucy, for example, will look for a victim one day and a suspect another. When she's on a trail she's "one-minded," says Kift. Once on scent, Lucy can follow a trail for hours, nose to the ground without a chance of distraction. Her sense of smell is so discriminating that she can visit an arson scene and smell the traces of a human's touch on a container of

accelerant—sifting past the smells of charcoal, accelerant chemicals, and other humans.

Patrol/detection dogs can find drugs in a car that has been pulled over or pursue a suspect into a dark building; they are also trained in bite work, meaning they subdue suspects through the use of force. "The public thinks these dogs are vicious, but they're just playing the game," says Kift of police dogs. As with all working dogs, police dogs are taught that their work is the ultimate in fun, plus they get the extra bonus of a treat, toy, or praise if they do it right.

Patrol dogs who train for bite work see the protective sleeve that the pretend victim wears as the reward. It's hard to imagine that attacking the arm of a suspect is a game, but think of it this way: Jerry is being trained for bite work, and a volunteer playing the suspect is wearing a big, heavy sleeve on his arm. When Jerry is commanded to bite the "arm," the suspect pulls away, and Jerry pulls back. This back-

and-forth pulling frenzy, punctuated by some excited growling, continues until Kift calls him off. Sound familiar? The bite work police dogs do isn't all that different from the tug games our own dogs play.

Gary White, a master patrolman and dog handler for the Raytown, Missouri, police department, reiterates that canine cops aren't always as fierce as they appear. As an example, he discloses that the crazed-looking rottweiler shown in the opening credits of the TV show *Cops* was his canine partner, Knitro. "We were called out in the middle of the night for a search and didn't know *Cops* was filming," says White. "Knitro grabs a duffel bag from the car and is growling and pulling on it, so the sound guy sticks his mike in Knitro's face. He sees this big furry thing and bites the mike!" Although the footage makes him look ferocious, in fact Knitro had just found a new favorite toy.

Unlike the military, whose dogs live in kennels, most police departments are so keen to keep dogs from becoming vicious that they insist the dogs live with their human partners. "Living with the handler adds to the dog's stability," explains Sgt. David "Lou" Ferland, a former Portsmouth, New Hampshire, canine officer and current head trainer at the regional police academy. His own dog, Dragon, now retired, has always been an inside dog and part of the family.

Canine police officers in the Kansas City area are always encouraged to bring their dogs home, says White. "Dogs work just as well when kept in the home, and they bond better. They also bond with the family." This is something that White thinks is so important that he insists on speaking with a potential handler's family before he or she enters the canine program.

White explains that his first two canine partners, Midnight and Knitro (both retired), were family pets before becoming police dogs. Midnight, a black Lab, was his daughter's dog

> **Meet most of these fearsome hounds away from work and they're as gentle as your own four-legged companion.**

before White trained her for detection work. Rottweiler Knitro then became his daughter's dog until several years later when he too became a police dog, doing both detection and patrol work. Still, Knitro's heart always belonged to White's daughter. "She's grown, but he still looks for the yellow school bus at the end of the day and pouts if she doesn't visit with him when she comes over," White laughs. He recounts one decidedly unmachismo moment in Knitro's early life, "We had a Dog's

Day festival and she dressed him up as a ballerina with a little tutu on. They took second place, but Knitro was really shamed about it."

Police dogs are owned by their handlers rather than by the city or county for which they work. Handlers are expected to buy their own dogs, which can cost as much as $6,000. Fortunately, most police departments have strong citizen support groups that cover some or all of the costs a dog handler incurs. Some groups even fund the dog's retirement, a big boon to handlers, who, like Kift and White, often have one or two retired dogs as well as a working dog, and, perhaps, a pet dog.

> **As with all working dogs, police dogs are taught that their work is the ultimate in fun.**

The Long Beach K-9 Officers Association, Inc., is a community group that is especially supportive. Handlers pay the first $3,000 toward buying their first dog, and nothing else thereafter. The group pays anything above the $3,000 for the cost of the dog, the cost of any additional or future dogs, the equipment a dog team needs, food, kenneling, and veterinary bills.

The public's interest in canine cop programs is both a benefit and a detriment, according to handlers. Police departments often assume that citizens will pick up the bill. "Police dogs are always an underfunded program," says Ferland. When citizen groups don't cover the necessary costs, they are left to the handlers themselves. "It would be nice if [the police department] had a retirement for [police dogs], says White, who has two retired dogs and one working dog in his home. He adds, "The canine unit is a low-cost program for the reward. I'd like to see a dog in every patrol car."

Police dogs more than compensate for their expense. Ferland points out, "Canine cops are the cops [that] cops call." When patrolmen are stumped or in danger, they call the K-9 unit. For this reason, canine teams are often at the highest risk and incur more danger than other police officers. According to Ferland, "For most officers there is a 1-in-1,700 chance they'll be involved in a gunfight; for a dog handler it is a 1-in-100 chance." Canine teams are on point, meaning they're the ones going into the dark building or bushes after an armed suspect. Kift concurs, describing a recent afternoon when he and Jerry responded to a call about a man shooting at people on the freeway, "When we arrived, everyone was waiting for the dog; 'The guy with the gun's down there.' " White adds that canine teams are always on hot, or dangerous, calls and agrees approximately with Ferland's numbers. He adds that a police

Police Dogs

dog's day is much like her human counterpart's: "sheer boredom to sheer terror."

Kift adds that the bloodhounds are usually called in when the police are at a dead end. To complicate matters, they're often not thought of until hours after a crime scene is discovered, making the trail harder to follow. "A lot of times when they call the bloodhounds they know nothing; for example, finding a body in a dumpster with no head," says Kift.

While canine teams are more often on point, the presence of a dog does work to diffuse potentially dangerous situations. "Knitro kept things from escalating," says White. Suspects simply didn't fight White when Knitro was present. He points out that although police departments are wary of using dogs for crowd control because of the history of using dogs against civil rights and peace activists in the 1960s, introducing a dog into a volatile situation can subdue parties without any further escalation. "There

was one situation when a group of people were being very hostile and the cops couldn't control it. I brought the dog and just had him lie there and it diffused it."

"Nine out of ten times the suspect will come out once the dog starts barking," adds Ferland. The presence of the dog often leads suspects to simply give up, even when the dog isn't let out of the car. The presence of the dog diminishes the likelihood of a suspect fighting arrest. "No rounds have come my way when I've had a dog," says Ferland. "The dog is a powerful deterrent."

In addition to acting as a deterrent, the dogs respond when their handlers are threatened or harmed. Ferland, who has had two patrol dogs, Kasha, who died several years ago, and Dragon, who is now retired from patrol work and used only in training demos, recalls one incident in particular. "Dragon saved my life. A suspect was hiding in a drainage ditch; he came after me with a

knife, and Dragon took him to his knees before I could even pull my gun."

"I know that Knitro was always there for me and the same with Kilo [his current dog]," says White. "Once, Knitro was in the car kennel and a suspect grabbed a package of dope to run with it. We had to wrestle the guy, and when I got back to the car I found that Knitro had destroyed the kennel trying to get out, *Someone was going to hurt Dad.* A dog will lay down its life for you without being asked. I know my dog is not going to hesitate." Illustrative of how close the bonds between officers and their dogs are, most police dog handlers consider their dogs their partners—as much as a human partner could be.

The bond between handlers and their dogs stems from years of training and working together. Training for a police dog is nonstop. The initial training can take anywhere from six months for a patrol and/or detection dog to a year for a bloodhound. Throughout the working life of a police dog, however, training is a daily task that both reinforces the dog's skills and the bond between the handler and the dog. Most police departments dedicate one day a week to team training, and handlers generally train their dogs for at least fifteen minutes every day.

Police dogs who do detection work are trained for either an aggressive or passive alert. A passive alert is generally sitting or pointing with a nose or paw, while an aggressive alert involves scratching, barking, or digging when a find is made. Dogs trained to detect explosives are always trained with a passive alert. When tracking people, dogs do a passive alert until the handler gives them a signal to bite. This is important because all police dogs go after both good and bad guys. "We did one search for a 16-year-old autistic boy who had run away naked on a freezing cold night," says Ferland. "When Kasha found him, he ran up to me and gave me a hug

that brought me close to tears." He adds that it's this type of scenario that mandates the dogs be trained to bite only when given a specific command. Kasha could have misinterpreted the hug as a threatening gesture or attack.

Canine handlers also send their dogs into places where it is not safe enough for themselves to go such as into a building where an armed suspect is hiding. "We'll wait at the door, securing the building until we hear the dog barking," says Ferland. In this instance, dogs are sent in with a bite command, but each section of the building is verbally cleared for bystanders before the dog is released.

In the past, police dogs were largely trained in the military model, with mostly negative corrective training. Modern police dogs, however, are more likely to be trained through a positive reward system, with only light leash or verbal corrections. There are some handlers who still use harsh leash and verbal commands, or remote control shock collars, but in general the trend is moving toward reward-based training. "Every discipline has a reward system," says Kift, "be it the sleeve, ball, or food." In police work, dogs generally choose what their reward will be, "We want to find what thrills this dog," says Ferland. All three of White's dogs, for example, have different rewards: Kilo works for a Kong when tracking and a plastic pipe for narcotics work; Knitro loves a rolled-up jute toy; and Midnight is a typical Lab who works for food.

"We take a dog who wants to find a rabbit and we say if you really want to please me, why don't you find this person instead. Then we'll get a goody and have some fun," says Ferland. "The dogs like playing these games, and they like the work. They have a great life; if anyone believes in reincarnation, I'd like to come back as a police dog."

Ferland points out that dogs won't work for just food or a toy, "The bond is the only way to work the dog. You've got to be a goofy person; you can't be stern." Despite a cop's often-machismo image, a canine handler needs to be willing to get on the ground and play with his or her dog and use a fun, jolly voice. Ferland laughs, "Sometimes we have to teach a handler how to be goofy with his dog."

Handlers say that the bond with their dogs is the key to a successful team. "My dogs have been the best partners I've ever had," says White. "You get so bonded with these guys; you spend more time with them than you do your own family."

"It's hard for people to understand the bond that officers have with their dogs," adds White, but it's this bond that allows the officers to have utter confidence in their dogs in every aspect of their work, and which keeps the partnership working smoothly.

> **Most police dog handlers consider their dogs their partners—as much as a human partner could be.**

"You've got to love your dog," says Ferland. "If you don't have the bond, you're not going to stay in dogs. They're not machines." He emphasizes that the relationship grows as a team works together, and sometimes it takes several years before a team reaches its high point, "The best teams are the ones that have been together for more than three years."

"With patrol dogs it's all about the bond, bloodhounds will work for anyone," explains Kift. He adds that it's the reading of the bloodhound that is really impor-

Police Dogs

tant; something that takes years to perfect. As a bloodhound handler, an officer must completely trust his or her dog and depend on the accuracy of her alert. The handler also must be able to accurately interpret what the bloodhound is finding. "With the bloodhound I have to testify, so I have to trust what she's saying. It's almost scary."

Based on Lucy's finds and Kift's ability to determine what her behavior is com-

municating, the conditions of a search may change dramatically. Kift cites one example when Lucy was trailing a missing six-year-old girl and the trail ended abruptly, "I had to tell the FBI that a six-year-old girl has gone into a car. Now she's not missing, she's abducted; we have a crime now." Kift knows all too well that misinterpreting Lucy's signals can be life or death for a victim, "Sometimes I feel burdened."

These are true working dogs, and it's no exaggeration when their handlers say they live to work, "Nero knew when I was going to work," says Kift of his German shepherd dog. "He loved to work; if he saw me in uniform he was like, *Where's the car?*" He adds with a laugh, "Lucy's not all that excited to go to work, I have to beg her to get in the car. She's a total prima donna."

"Dragon always got excited to go to work," says Ferland. "Even now, when he's on vacation, he's a monster. He's a working dog and he's not bred to sit around in front of the TV."

As much as police officers depend on their dogs, the dogs depend on their partners for their care. Canine officers worry constantly about their dogs' health and safety. Although some dogs wear bulletproof vests, the biggest risks they face don't come from guns. Police dogs have a high incidence of cancer, which White suspects has to do with their exposure to toxic and carcinogenic chemicals in drug labs as well as pesticides used in lawns. Dogs also face other on-the-job hazards. Kift's Nero had a tendon sliced when he ran through a piece of plate glass in a backyard, and both Ferland's dogs, Kasha and Dragon, had on-the-job injuries, Kasha fell through a ceiling, and Dragon cut himself jumping over a barbed wire fence.

The most common hazard for police working dogs, however, is heat. Knitro's one injury was heatstroke after training on a hot day. Almost all squad cars are now

equipped with a so-called Hot Dog system. This system connects to the car windows and horn, sometimes even the alarm. If the temperature in the car goes above a certain point, the system activates, lowering the windows and sounding the horn and alarm. White urges all police officers to use them, even above bulletproof vests. He argues that bulletproof vests don't protect where dogs are usually shot and you can buy three heat systems for the price of one vest. "Heat is the biggest killer of police dogs," he says.

As with all officers, there comes a time when a police dog must give up her badge. Most police dogs are retired when they become elderly or have a health problem that necessitates it. The transition is difficult for both handler and dog. "I was in tears when Nero retired," says Kift. "They always say your first dog is your best dog."

It's extremely rare for a police dog handler not to keep his or her retired dog. "I've never known a cop to give up his dog," says Ferland. "We owe them that much." He adds, however, most police dogs don't live long after retirement, "They're not happy being at home, so we usually let them work until they can't do it anymore."

White is not uncommon in having two retirees; Midnight and Knitro are both still living with him. "They eat and watch the animal channel," laughs White. "I'm glad it worked out this way because they get to enjoy retirement. A lot of times we work dogs until they don't get to enjoy retirement; it's nice to be able to spoil them." He adds that despite Knitro's comfortable retirement life, he and Kilo don't get along, "Knitro's pissed off that Kilo took his place." Out of deference for Knitro, White has never let Knitro see Kilo get into the squad car.

Retired Nero is also jealous when Lucy and Jerry go to work, "I give him a treat to distract him," says Kift. "Nero always liked the work, all these dogs do—they live for it." He agrees that many dogs don't last long after retirement because it is the work that keeps them going.

If retirement is hard on officers and dogs, it's the dog's death that the officer truly has to experience alone. "The happiest day in my life is the day I start with a new dog," says Ferland, "the saddest is the day I put it down. It's a terrible, terrible moment." White, knowing that Knitro's days are waning is dreading when that day finally comes, "It's hard to think about Knitro having to go. He was the best partner I ever had."

One Missouri canine handler died within a week of his dog's death. The ashes of dog and officer were buried together. "We have burials for police dogs and hundreds of cops show up," says White. "People ask why are you doing that for a dog, and we tell them it's because he's a police officer."

According to canine officers, a police dog's work never ends. These dogs serve to protect their partners and other officers in the field but work just as hard to protect all citizens. They find lost children and dementia patients but also keep dangerous situations from escalating out of control, reducing the times in which an officer must pull his or her weapon. "I can recall my dog, but I can't recall a bullet," says Ferland.

Police dogs are also extremely useful public relations tools, as I see the day I meet with Kift and his dogs. As Lucy sniffs her surroundings, she immediately captures the attention of children playing in the park. "Can I pet her?" several chil-

> **Although some dogs wear bulletproof vests, the biggest risks they face don't come from guns.**

dren gleefully ask, approaching Officer Kift with no trepidation. "Dogs show cops on a softer side," says Ferland. "A lot of people approach a canine officer more than they will approach another officer."

Ultimately, say canine officers, their dogs work for them, and they work for their dogs. To Ferland, it's simple, "My dogs were the best partners I ever had in my life; they always looked out for me."

CHAPTER 13

MILITARY DOGS

Dogs have served people in times of war for thousands of years. Some of the first images of dogs depict them in battle scenes or outfitted for combat. As with hunting, dogs have proven inseparable from humans in warfare. As long ago as 1352 B.C., the Egyptians used dogs in battle, as did many other early civilizations, including ancient Greece and Persia. The Romans brought war dogs to a new and fearsome level, equipping large mastiff-type dogs with deadly barbed collars. Today, dogs are used in a variety of military capacities: as sentry dogs guarding army depots and bases; as patrol and scout dogs, searching for enemy soldiers or missing comrades; and as explosive detectors.

Despite this long history, the use of military dogs is still hotly contested for many reasons. Among them is the fact that military dogs are often used for work deemed unsafe for humans and the often poor treatment inflicted upon them—not only by the enemy but also by the country they are serving. The U.S. military, for example, keeps military dogs in kennels throughout their lives and, until 2000, uniformly euthanized them when they could no longer perform their duties. In addition, dogs are used on all sides of conflicts, not always in ethical ways. In Nazi Germany, for example, dogs were used extensively in concentration camps to subdue prisoners.

Although dogs have served in almost every European conflict in recorded history, the formal use of military dogs is fairly new to the U.S. There were dogs present during every American war since the Revolution, but they were generally mascots or companions. During the Civil War, many soldiers brought their faithful canine friends into battle with them—for their company more than anything else. Still, these companion war dogs probably did serve in unofficial guard duties, just as our own dogs do in everyday life.

Even in World War II, the U.S. didn't immediately endorse the use of war dogs. The only U.S. military dogs at the time war broke out were sled dogs in Alaska and a handful of sentry dogs in the California Coast Artillery. Shortly after the attack on Pearl Harbor, a group of U.S. dog fanciers formed the organization Dogs for Defense, encouraging Americans to donate their dogs to the war effort. While Dogs for Defense began as both procurement and training for the K-9 Corps, training was quickly taken over by the Army Quartermaster Corps Remount Branch, while Dogs for Defense maintained its procurement function.

According to Luther Hanson, curator for the U.S. Army Quartermaster Museum, many Americans felt it was their patriotic duty to donate the family dog if no one else in the family could enlist, thinking *I'm too old, my wife can't go, and my children are too young, so I'll send Fido.* Under the quartermasters, who serve in the supply-side of the military, military dogs were trained and deployed first as sentry dogs and later as patrol dogs. All dogs started out with the rank of private first class but could gain the rank of sergeant; some dogs actually outranked their handlers by the end of the war. According to Hanson, dogs were also given medals and honors for extraordinary military feats, although that policy was overturned at some point during the war.

By the summer of 1942, the military was convinced of the potential for military dogs and put out an order to train dogs for four categories of work: sentry, patrol, mine detection, and messenger work. By the fall of 1942, the quartermasters were procuring and training dogs for the navy, marines, and coast guard.

In 1944, after several years of trial and error, the quartermasters were procuring dogs only between the ages of one and three and from only seven breeds (or mixes thereof): Alaskan malamute, collie, Doberman pinscher, German shepherd, Eskimo dog, Belgian sheepdog, and Siberian husky. About ten thousand dogs were put into service in all, while another ten thousand were procured but failed their training.

Military dogs were present in every amphibious landing in the Pacific, as well as several in Europe, according to Hanson. Some of the most famous of the World War II dogs were the marines' so-called devil dogs. The devil dogs are usually

Military Dogs

depicted as Doberman pinschers but also numbered German shepherds, Labs, and other breeds among their rank. The devil dogs were used extensively in combat in the Pacific Theater, about one thousand in all. On the island of Guam, where 25 devil dogs served and died, there is a large sculpture of a military Doberman pinscher in memoriam.

Among the dogs most famous for their heroic actions during World War II was Chips, a mixed breed who served first in northern Africa and then in Sicily. Although he fought in eight campaigns, it was his capture of a machine gun nest in Sicily that he is heralded for. Folklore about Chips asserts that when he later served as a sentry for General Eisenhower, Chips nipped him in the hand to the delight of low-ranking soldiers everywhere.

Shortly after the attack on Pearl Harbor, a group of U.S. dog fanciers formed the organization Dogs for Defense, encouraging Americans to donate their dogs to the war effort.

Hanson points out, however, all of the dogs deployed were heroes to their handlers and the men who served with them. "It's estimated that between eight and nine thousand lives were saved by dogs during World War II," says Hanson, adding that that's probably a low estimate, given that much of a dog's work was preventive. "The dogs could tell when there was a booby trap and the handler could sense in the dog *there's something wrong here.*"

He adds that soldiers have always had a "battle buddy"; the two soldiers eat and sleep together and watch over each other. "That's how it was with the dogs. The dog was depending 100 percent on the handler and the handler was depending on the dog to keep him alive."

One story that his former boss, Sergeant John Cargill, told Hanson, exemplifies just how useful the World War II dogs were. "The war was over and Sgt. Cargill was assigned to going out in the islands to find Japanese soldiers. He had leaflets to give them [explaining that the war was over]. He found a Japanese officer and walked up and handed him a leaflet. The officer drew down to pull out a weapon—to kill Cargill or himself. A dog handler was six feet away and the dog jumped up and literally ripped the man's arm out of the socket."

When the war ended, dogs who could be returned to their original owners were sent home—three thousand dogs were discharged and returned to their homes.

Working Dogs

Before returning to their families, the dogs went through a rigorous "reeducation" program in which they were taught to accept strangers and play gently with children and other animals. Few complaints followed their repatriation, and many families praised their dog's good manners on their return home. "The quartermasters got in

touch with the families and said the war is over, Fido is coming home," recounts Hanson. "The dog was literally delivered to their house." Although most of the dog handlers from World War II have died, Hanson often hears from their children, "They always tell me about the bond their dads had with the dogs."

After World War II ended, the dog program began years of transition, moving from the quartermasters to the U.S. Army Military Police (MP) Corps, and then, ultimately, landing with the air force in 1957. Probably due to the multiple shifts in administration, dogs were not used extensively in the Korean War, less than one thousand in all.

During this transition, the attitude toward war dogs changed dramatically. Concerned about the lack of appropriate dogs and the logistical problems with "borrowing" dogs from families, post–World War II policy was to purchase dogs outright. Dogs were reclassified as military equipment. This philosophical shift dictated the use of military dogs for the next 50 years.

The next stop for military dogs was Vietnam. The Vietnam War brought the largest overseas deployment of U.S. military dogs in history, about four thousand in total. It also brought a stunning disregard for the welfare of the dogs who served so well. According to most estimates, the dogs in Vietnam saved at least ten thousand lives. They were considered such a threat by the Vietcong that there was a bounty placed on the head of both dogs and dog handlers.

Only two hundred of the dogs sent to Vietnam were brought home. The rest were euthanized or given to the South Vietnamese. Although the official explana-

Military Dogs

tion from the U.S. military was that the dogs could not be brought home due to a disease dubbed the Vietnam dog disease, collaborating proof of widespread infectious disease was never provided. According to the Vietnam Dog Handler's Association, the World Health Organization denies any knowledge of the so-called Vietnam dog disease. Air force officials now say that the dogs were turned over to the South Vietnamese under their agreement to continue assistance after pulling U.S. troops out. There is no official record of the dogs' fates after the fall of Saigon.

Colonel Larry Carpenter, director of the Department of Defense's military working dog veterinary hospital, at the Lackland Air Force Base dog training center, comments that the Vietnam War was a different time. "I know that there were substantial concerns about the dogs that did not return from Vietnam. There were medical and diplomatic reasons for that. Part of it was that as the U.S. involvement in the war decreased, the Vietnamese picked up those responsibilities. They had their own program and they received some of the dogs that were there near the end. It's 30 years later and I represent a program that I don't think resembles that much. I understand [Vietnam dog handlers'] resentment and emotional response. There just isn't much I can do about it."

> **All dogs started out with the rank of private first class but could gain the rank of sergeant; some dogs actually outranked their handlers by the end of the war.**

In Vietnam, dogs served with the air force, navy, army, and marines. They worked as scouts, sentries, and combat trackers. Most of the dogs who served were German shepherds, although there were also 58 Labs who served with combat tracking teams.

When Charlie Cargo was drafted in 1970, he didn't even know there were military dogs. When he left Vietnam over a year later, his experiences as a dog handler had changed his life. Nineteen years old when he shipped out, Cargo landed in a world he was totally unprepared for. "Basic training is just what it says," says Cargo dryly, "very basic." After a month in Vietnam, however, Cargo was an experienced infantryman. Many of the men he deployed with had already been sent home injured.

When a canine handler made a pitch for scout dog handlers, Cargo figured he might as well give it a shot: his family raised German shepherds (his mother owned six dogs during the time he was in Vietnam—four being puppies that she couldn't bear to part with). He also had the sense that he was marked for misfortune—injury or death felt inevitable. A dog, he figured, might better his odds. This, despite the popular and correct perception that scout dog handlers pulled particularly dangerous duty walking point (walking ahead of the rest of the soldiers). The day after Cargo volunteered to be a dog handler, he received his transfer orders and was gone. "It was the fastest I've ever seen anything happen in the military," says Cargo.

Cargo was now a member of the 48th Scout Dog Platoon, stationed in Chu Lai. When he arrived at the dog training center, he was surprised that he was allowed to choose his own dog—a rarity for dog handlers. He walked through the kennels, raising a cacophony of barking and howling

> **Only two hundred of the dogs sent to Vietnam were brought home. The rest were euthanized or given to the South Vietnamese.**

from the dogs. When he reached the end of the kennel, however, Cargo stopped and waited, then turned around. All of the dogs had turned away from him except for one: a black-and-tan German shepherd named Wolf. After two weeks of training and three or four missions with another handler, Cargo and Wolf were on their own. Wolf and Cargo were inseparable for the next year, the longest year of Cargo's life.

Cargo and Wolf, like thousands of other canine teams deployed in Vietnam, completely relied upon one another. Wolf depended on Cargo for his food and affection; Cargo depended on Wolf for his life. Together, they served on one hundred missions, marching for endless hours through hot, humid jungles, some so thick there was no difference between day and night.

Cargo quickly learned to depend on Wolf and to trust his instincts over his own. "They'd tell us 'You walk exactly where your dog walks, no matter what you think. You're dumb, the dog's smart.'" Almost immediately he found out how true those words were. On one of their first missions, Wolf and Cargo encountered a log almost a foot off the ground. Wolf jumped over it and tried to keep going, but Cargo held him back. The log was high and difficult to navigate, so he decided to go around it. He'd barely stepped around the log when his foot slipped into a waist-high hole. Unharmed but stunned, Cargo brushed away the debris covering the hole and found a sharpened pongee stick, which he'd barely missed stepping on. The stick came so close that it slid up inside his pant leg, ripping the fabric. Explaining that the Vietcong urinated on the sticks before covering the traps, Cargo says that

Military Dogs

had he'd stepped on it, he'd have been out of duty from the sure infection. "That would have been the end of it." After Cargo slipped into the hole, "Wolf just turns around and comes back and looks at me," laughs Cargo. "After that, I stepped over anything he stepped over. You never realized how much the dogs knew over there until something like that happened."

On another mission, Wolf again saved Cargo as well as the lives of the men in the unit they were with. "We followed Wolf into a streambed and he went up the other side. When he came up to the top, Wolf stops and everyone is stopped on the sides of the riverbed. Everyone was getting mad so I called him back and he stopped again. When I tried to walk he moved and took his body and stepped in front of me. I tried again and he clamped on to my hand, every time I tried to move he bit harder." Cargo finally stopped and Wolf released him. He looked closer and just a few feet ahead was a trip wire hooked up to an artillery shell, a big artillery shell. "I thought, *I will never second-guess this dog again,*" says Cargo.

In addition to point and patrol dogs, Vietnam War dogs also served as sentries, guarding army bases and munition sites. A sentry dog handler in the 981st U.S. Army Military Police Corps, Arthur "Pete" Peterson landed the job when his unit requested 12 volunteers who weren't afraid of dogs. He raised his hand and "it ended up being a blessing in disguise."

Peterson had two dogs in Vietnam. The first was King, but he and Peterson "weren't communicating," so he requested another and got Fritz. When Fritz and Peterson were united, the bond was immediate. "He was a fantastic dog," says Peterson. "He could work off leash if I wanted him to and his alerts were always accurate, no second-guessing anything he'd indicate. He was a dog who I'd put my complete trust and faith in."

Working Dogs

Peterson recalls that in dog training school it was said that intelligence runs down the leash. But in his experience, it was the opposite. Sentry dog teams usually worked alone and at night. Once on duty, a sentry and his dog often didn't see another person until morning. As Peterson describes it, "It was usually either too dark to see or too light to hide." No matter the conditions, it was terrifying and lonely.

Another sentry dog handler, Ernie Ayala of the 212th MP describes sentry duty as, "every cliché, every movie you ever saw, where someone would sneak up and choke 'em or kills an entire squad. It all goes through your mind when you're on sentry duty." Like Peterson, Ayala took great comfort from his dog, Heidi, "I'd just look at her head and it would tell you what was out there."

When Ayala was initially assigned Heidi, he balked at the petite German shepherd, "All the other guys were getting big dogs." He relented, however, when told she'd be euthanized if he didn't take her; he never regretted it. "She saved me three times, twice she saved me from snakes, and once she alerted me to a black panther," says Ayala. Recounting one of the snakes, Ayala says, "I can't believe how fast she reacted. She darted across me, and I just saw the snake jump into the air and saw its yellow belly."

Another sentry dog team, Steve Janke and his dog Kobuc, worked to protect the vast perimeter of the Cam Ranh Bay Air Base. Cam Ranh, Janke explains, was the largest U.S. military base in Vietnam, and sentries were placed 10–12 miles away from the center of the base. When they went on duty, each sentry team was dropped off at intervals along the natural perimeter. "They'd just drop you off in the middle of nowhere," says Janke. "But with the dog, you always felt you had an edge."

May 23, 1971, still stands out among the other endless nights for Janke. "I had a post in a clear area about 100 yards outside of a field staging area, where we stored fuel, jet fuel. Kobuc hit an alert [alerted to an enemy presence] farther out. Then the fellow next to me, his dog hit an alert. We followed the alert out, then Kobuc turned me around and I was able to see a dozen enemy soldiers trying to penetrate the area. They threw a satchel charge [an explosive] at Kobuc and me and knocked us to the ground. The next day we ran a sweep and found a campsite with weapons."

Janke remembers other alerts with Kobuc when they were on sentry duty far from other posts, "Other times he'd alert and there would be standoffs. When you're all alone you have to sweep the area by yourselves. You get old very fast in war."

For Vietnam War sentries, the remoteness of their posts meant that much of their time was spent alone with their dogs. The dogs served as fellow soldiers in every way, from protecting the human soldiers to keeping them company and comforted when they were lonely or afraid. "I

> **In addition to point and patrol dogs, Vietnam War dogs also served as sentries, guarding army bases and munition sites.**

talked to Kobuc about everything and anything; I read my mail to him," says Janke. "You develop a really close bond to the animal in that situation."

One way in which dogs were used in Vietnam received little attention but for the men who served with them. Their contribution is indisputable.

At the beginning of the Vietnam War, a small contingent of U.S. soldiers was sent to the British Jungle Warfare School, in Malaysia, to learn to be combat trackers. The combat tracking teams (CTT) consisted of four or five men and one dog, instead of the usual team of one dog and one handler. They were also unusual in that their missions were classified until 1968. The British government did not publicly acknowledge training U.S. soldiers until several years ago. The CTT used Labs rather than German shepherds because the dogs needed to be good trackers but didn't need to be aggressive. The original tracking Labs had been utilized by the British in Malaysia and were purchased by the U.S. military. Some had even been decorated already for their earlier service to Britain.

The CTT's duties were three-fold: to seek and destroy enemy troops, to clear areas from enemy troops, and to find and rescue "friendlies." Each man on a team had a specific role. There was the team commander, the visual tracker, the dog handler, the cover man, and the radioman. The team commander led the team on missions, making decisions based on the input of each team member. The visual tracker examined the terrain for signs of footsteps or other disturbances. The dog handler worked the dog, watching his behaviors and alerts and interpreting them. The cover man served as the dog handler's eyes because his attention had to be solely on the dog he was handling. The radioman was responsible for radio communications between the team and outside units. Sometimes the team only consisted of four human members, with the radioman also serving as the cover man.

John Dupla served as a combat tracker in the First Cavalry Division from June 1967 to June 1968. Trained at the Jungle Warfare School, Dupla was a visual tracker, although he took over as a dog handler for three months during his tour of duty.

Because they worked as a team, every man in the CTT had to trust the dog as much as the handler. The handler read the dog, and the team commander made a decision based on the dog's input and the visual tracker's input. Once it was determined that the dog would search, a harness was placed on the dog, and the dog walked over an area until he got a scent. Then the handler would tell him to seek on. No one in the team could second-guess the dog's alert, or it would not have worked. "The dog became part of the team," says Dupla, "When a dog alerted by sitting, as far as the trackers were concerned. . . that's it, buddy."

Dupla adds that pivotal decisions were based on the dogs' alerts, "One time Lucky alerted so we said we wouldn't go any farther. They called in an air strike based on that dog's alert, and we sat on a hilltop watching and thinking *do you know how much money that dog just spent?* The next morning they did find evidence of enemy troops in that area."

Although there were four or five men on every team and several dogs were transferred among teams, this did not dissipate the affection and respect the team members had for the dogs. "That was when I first came to the realization that dogs have personalities," says Dupla. "Some of the dogs worked better with some team members than others, but you'd get close to your dogs." Of the four dogs Dupla worked with in Vietnam, he remembers them all distinctly. "Bruce was neurotic," says Dupla. "Sambo was the meanest, but he was a real good dog. Lucky," whom Dupla handled, "was the old man and laid-back; Shadow was the athlete—that dog could jump out of the back end of a transport truck."

Dupla also remembers what happened to each of them, "Sambo took a hit and was wounded, as was his handler," says Dupla, adding that Sambo was ultimately euthanized. "Lucky wound up with 'tracker dog disease' " and was also put down. "Shadow broke away from his handler and attacked the enemy and they killed him. Bruce was diagnosed as

> **The CTT used Labs rather than German shepherds because the dogs needed to be good trackers but didn't need to be aggressive.**

being dysfunctional and the team commander was ordered to euthanize him. It's the only order he fictionalized in his career and he retired as a colonel. The commander took him as a pet and Bruce had free reign of the compound until the end of the war when he found some missionaries and gave Bruce to them." No one knows what became of Bruce, but Dupla hopes he wasn't killed or abandoned in Vietnam. As with the German shepherds who served, few Labs made it stateside.

Working Dogs

The only ones Dupla knows of were two who a general took home as pets.

We can only imagine what these dogs meant to the young men in Vietnam. Most of them were under 21 and away from home for the first time. Maybe a few months or years out of high school, they'd been plucked from the normalcy of their suburban subdivisions or brownstone apartments and plunked down into the middle of a war, a world away from home.

> *We can only imagine what these dogs meant to the young men in Vietnam. Most of them were under 21 and away from home for the first time.*

For many dog handlers, the war was spent largely alone but for their dogs. Sentry dog handlers were essentially alone with their dogs at night, sometimes left at positions miles away from other sentries. Scout dog handlers switched units by mission, sometimes in one place for a week, other times with a unit for only a couple hours. They might have returned to the unit several times throughout the war, or they might have never returned again. "Scout dog handlers were the odd men out," says Cargo. "You didn't have close friends because you went where the people were having the worst time." No matter what their job, the soldiers who came in contact with the dogs learned to rely on them implicitly. Experience quickly taught them that their best chances at returning home safely came with having the dogs at their sides.

Their dogs were with them in battle, and they were with them in rest, as well. They worked together and they played together—I haven't spoken to a dog handler who didn't tell me that his dog was his best friend in Vietnam. What many of the handlers seem to remember best about their dogs are the times when the animals allowed them to be normal, allowed them to do things that had nothing to do with war. Dupla remembers taking the Labs to a river to swim, while Janke recalls a monthly beach run. "We'd let them run in the ocean, not working, just playing. But all too quickly it was back to the war," he says.

"You relied on your dog for everything," says Cargo. "When you got letters from home you'd read to him. My mother would always send dog treats…When I was off I'd take my dog everywhere; I did everything I could with him… Once, I wrote to my mother and told her about the old collar Wolf had. She mailed him a choke chain. He was so proud of that new chain; he knew someone cared about him."

Leaving a dog was the hardest thing a dog handler had to do. Cargo tried everything under the sun to have Wolf sent home with him. When that didn't work, he

Military Dogs

applied for an extension but was turned down. "In my mind, I already had it all planned, right down to where he was going to sleep," says Cargo. When he finally had to turn Wolf over, "You could have shot me and I wouldn't have felt as bad."

Dog school taught Vietnam dog handlers to get close to their dogs but not too close. According to the soldiers, that was impossible. "It's like he becomes a brother, a member of your family," says Janke. "We had the bonding experience of war together. I still carry his picture in my wallet, that's how I feel about that animal."

When the U.S. completely pulled out of Vietnam, fewer than two hundred war dogs were returned to the U.S. The rest were euthanized or turned over to the South Vietnamese. When Saigon fell in 1975, many handlers believe that the remaining dogs were eaten.

Despite the estimated ten thousand lives the Vietnam War dogs saved, the air force considered the animals to be surplus military equipment. Even those who returned to the U.S. were not retired. Instead, they lived out their lives in kennels and were euthanized when they no longer served a purpose.

Many of the Vietnam dog handlers have researched the fates of their dogs, looking for some kind of closure. Whether motivated by guilt or anger, just knowing seems to help. Heidi died from a canine disease a year and a half after Ayala left her. "I felt some closure when I found out. I was happy she didn't get killed," he says. Kobuc was turned over to the South Vietnamese. "I just hope he died before Saigon fell in 1975," says Janke. "When I left Vietnam, I picked a night to say good-bye to Kobuc. I had a conversation with him and gave him a hug; I thanked him for keeping me alive."

Peterson never found out what happened to Fritz, adding that he still feels guilty for never saying a proper good-bye to the dog he calls his lifeblood. "For everything he did for me, I felt like I could've done more for him when I left."

Working Dogs

Thirty years later and after extensive research, Cargo learned that Wolf was one of the few dogs shipped back to the U.S. The dog was diagnosed with testicular cancer upon his return to the States and neutered, but in 1978 he was diagnosed with lymphoma and euthanized. Despite Cargo and his family's extensive efforts to track down Wolf after Cargo was discharged, the military never informed the family that Wolf was returned to the U.S. or that he was ill.

Much as the Vietnam vets were swept under the carpet, so too were their dogs. Returning home under a cloud of shame and resentment, many of the handlers tried to block the war and the dogs out of their minds for years. Ayala vividly recalls talking to a young woman at a party soon after his return. Upon finding out he was a veteran, she asked, "How did it feel killing innocent women and babies?" Connecting with the Vietnam Dog Handler Association 20 years later finally helped him to process his experiences as a soldier and handler in the war.

For many Vietnam dog handlers, true closure came when the documentary *War Dogs* was released, just as many vets reacted intensely when *Platoon* came out. The dog handlers finally saw their stories acknowledged. The film not only resonated with dog handlers but with Americans at large. That the dogs served so loyally and selflessly and were simply discarded when their use was up shocked viewers and provided an impetus to finally acknowledge the achievements of both dogs and handlers.

It's impossible to separate the horror of the dogs being abandoned from the pain the soldiers felt leaving their dogs. Through the story of these dogs, somehow, we can understand something of what American soldiers went through in Vietnam and the immeasurable comfort they gained from their dogs.

Military Dogs

The profits from *War Dogs* have gone to a war dog memorial fund. Since the film was released, two Vietnam war dog memorials have been established, one in Washington, D.C., and one in Riverside, California. To this date, the military refuses to allow a war dog memorial in a national cemetery, stating that its presence would be disrespectful to the men buried there. Cargo disagrees, "Every soldier in there had a dog watching over them."

Although the Vietnam War ended almost 30 years ago, the air force has not drastically altered its treatment and philosophical outlook on military dogs. The vast majority of military dogs live in kennels for their entire lives. Until 2000, military dogs were uniformly euthanized when they could no longer do their jobs. American citizens, horrified by the abandonment of the Vietnam dogs as well as the treatment of current dogs, applied pressure to the U.S. government to change this. On November 6, 2000, Congressman Roscoe G. Bartlett, R-Maryland, introduced a bill requiring that the air force retire military dogs to appropriate homes when possible. The bill, now Public Law 106-446, was approved unanimously.

> **Dog school taught Vietnam dog handlers to get close to their dogs but not too close. According to the soldiers, that was impossible.**

According to Colonel Carpenter, during the first year there were 33 adoptions of retired military dogs and an additional 23 dogs transferred to police departments. He adds that the program is growing each year. The adoption process is lengthy: the dog is screened for terminal or debilitating medical conditions and is tested to determine his level of aggressiveness. He's then closely matched with an adopter who can provide a secure environment for the dog. Nonmilitary families can adopt the dogs, although handlers are given first priority. "We've had very little negative feedback on the program," says Carpenter. "We take the screening process very seriously. Now that the program is up and on its feet, if one of these dogs was involved in a serious bite it would call the whole process into question. I think everybody sees this as a winning situation."

Although the lives of military dogs are still not ideal in any working dog advocate's mind, the passage of Public Law 106-446 is encouraging. It's the first step toward seeing these dogs as the soldiers they are, rather than equipment that can be casually discarded when its purpose is served.

CHAPTER 14

DISASTER SEARCH AND RESCUE

The use of disaster SAR dogs was largely unknown in the U.S. until the 1980s. At the time of the Oklahoma City bombing, in 1995, there were only about 15 Federal Emergency Management Agency (FEMA)–certified dogs in the country. Interest in disaster SAR dogs has grown, however, since they proved their mettle in the notorious bombing. There are now about 113 FEMA-certified teams in the U.S.; that's progress, although the agency's goal is 300.

Disaster SAR teams are largely volunteer, and participation is expensive. Handlers estimate they spend three to five thousand dollars of their own money each year in training, certifying, and deploying their dogs. The FEMA certifies the dogs at two levels: basic and advanced. It generally takes at least two years of training before a dog is tested at the basic level and another three months to two years for advanced. Once certified on either level, teams must recertify every two years.

When preparing for the basic test, handlers usually train their dogs every day in obedience, directional commands (sending the dog to locations away from the handler, much like a hunting dog handler does), and agility. Then, depending on the local SAR organization with which they're affiliated, they may have group training one or two times a week.

In group training, dogs learn to search out the smell of human beings. Most groups follow a basic principle of building upon foundation blocks. First the dog learns to bark for a toy, then the

handler runs away with the toy and the dog runs to him or her, barks, and gets the toy. Gradually, handlers progress to running to a hidden area—many groups use what they call a bark box, which is a wooden box with guillotine-type door that the handler gets into—and then getting the dog to bark for them. The dog barks, the handler appears and gives the toy. Eventually, the handler runs somewhere the dog can't see and the dog has to use her nose to find the person and the toy. From there, dog and handler move on to the rubble pile. Everything is done in tiny steps, and the toy is always there as a reward for the dog once she finds the hidden person.

Disaster dogs alert their handlers by barking at the site where they pinpoint the victim. Some dogs also scratch at the site. Cadaver-trained dogs usually lie down to indicate a dead body. Even dogs who are not trained for cadaver search indicate when they find a cadaver versus a live body. Handlers do expose the dogs to the smell of a cadaver so they are not distracted by it during an actual search. Through careful observation of the dogs, handlers know when a dog is indicating a cadaver based on body posture or tail movement. Some dogs spend extra time at a spot where there is a cadaver, sniffing deeply and perhaps wagging their tail down low rather than up high. Other dogs urinate on the spot or try to roll in it.

Being able to read their dogs is paramount for dog handlers. It's important to know how your dog reacts when she smells animals or other distractions as well as a cadaver. A good handler can tell almost exactly what a dog has found just by watching her. Because of that, handlers emphasize the value of a strong bond with their dogs. Many have their dogs with them 24 hours a day, seven days a week.

In San Diego, at the defunct Point Loma Naval Station, FEMA task forces from around Southern California are converging to train as a team. With aban-

doned and mid-demolition buildings covering the grounds, these task forces are able to set up several stations, allowing the dogs to search in different environments: a rubble pile, an emptied swimming pool, a dark building, and the splintered remains of what appears to have been a workshop of some kind. Gary Smith stands facing a giant pile of cement rubble with his black Lab, Kelly, at his side. He checks the wind by releasing a bit of talcum powder, then directs Kelly to search the rubble for the volunteer who is hidden beneath debris. She quickly ascends the rubble pile, her nose in the air, sniffing for the scent of the hidden person. She ambles past the volunteer's hiding space until the wind brings his scent her way, then she turns quickly and makes a beeline to him. She barks until Smith climbs to her location, stopping only when he offers her a toy and plenty of praise.

Working Dogs

Meanwhile, Ron Weckbacher's Border collie, Manny, nimbly picks his way through twisted metal and violently strewn boards in a destroyed workshop. Agility is the Border collie's specialty, and he makes it seems effortless even as boards and rebar sway under his weight. His tail wags fiercely as he searches, and it's clear that his job is his passion. Watching Manny gives the tiniest sense of what it is to watch him in a real disaster. Take this and times it by a thousand, take it and times it by a hundred thousand, then maybe you'll have a picture of what this dog can do.

Handlers constantly train their dogs to respond reliably to commands and to handle all types of environments and obstructions. Besides training on rubble piles, groups use recycling plants and other smelly areas. "My job," says National Disaster Search Dog Foundation (NDSDF) handler Ron Weckbacher, "is to show Manny as many different looks and as many different environments as is possible." Handlers also introduce the dogs to ladders and jungle gyms. Children's playgrounds, rather than dog agility equipment, are put into use because they more realistically simulate real-world conditions. An advanced FEMA dog is comfortable walking up and down almost vertical ladders, walking over open-metal grates, and up open-backed stairs. Their pads are toughened to withstand working on rough concrete and they are nimble enough to work their way among splintered wood, broken glass, and carved-up metal.

To ensure SAR dogs don't freeze up when they search in a new environment, handlers constantly train their dogs in new places, sometimes driving three hours just to do a training session. As Debra Tosch, a handler with the NDSDF in Ojai, California, describes it, "If I teach you to sit in someone's chair and then I bring you another chair, you're going to say 'oh, that's a chair' and sit in it. A dog doesn't do that. You have to show them that chair and teach them again, and then teach them at the next chair. So by generalizing, by the time they've got their certification the dogs know a chair is a chair is a chair and a search is a search is a search, no matter where you're at."

Most handlers train their dogs with a combination of positive and corrective training, although food is rarely used outside of obedience and directional training. A dog's toy reward may be a squeaky toy, a Kong, a Frisbee, or even a length of fire hose. Some handlers allow the dog to pick the toy she is most enthused about; other handlers dictate the toy. Because toys are such an intrinsic part of SAR work, these dogs must be highly play- and toy-driven animals. Dogs who do not have a strong toy drive rarely do well in disaster work. The goal is to make searching the most fun, most rewarding thing the dog can do, with the toy and play being the culmination of it all. "Generally it's positive because we want the dogs to really enjoy what they're doing," says Jane David, a handler with Northwest Disaster Search Dogs, in northwest Washington. "It's work but it's really fun work for them. It's not really play because they have to do things we ask them to do, they can't do whatever they want. But for them, it's pretty much a big game when they search for someone."

Corrective training may be a leash and collar correction or a verbal correction. Some groups use a remote training collar, commonly known as a shock collar, although this practice is somewhat controversial. In general, the training is focused on positive toy rewards simply because, as any handler will tell you, you can't force a dog to search, she has to do it because she loves it. "When I let my dog go, she wants to go bad," says David. "Kita lives to run up there on the rubble and find somebody. She's not doing it to please me, she's only doing it to please herself."

> **Their pads are toughened to withstand working on rough concrete and they are nimble enough to work their way among splintered wood, broken glass, and carved-up metal.**

Consistent praise is key, however, even if that means praising your dog for finding a dead body when the family is nearby. If a dog makes a find and is not praised, her ability to search in the future is compromised. "You need to praise your dog," says Northwest Disaster Search Dogs handler A. J. Frank. He pauses and then adds with a wry laugh, "but only if you want it to keep working." He acknowledges that sensitivity can be an issue when family members are close to a disaster scene, especially when the dog alerts on a cadaver rather than a living person. "You take out your toy and you praise your dog," says Frank. "You don't yell and scream and jump all over the place, but still the dog's going to get its praise and its toy."

To get a dog with a good nose, strong toy drive, and willingness to please, disaster SAR handlers often use Labs and golden retrievers. Other working breeds with a strong drive are also put into service, including German shepherds, cattle dogs, and Border collies. That said, the right dog of any breed or breed mix can make an excellent disaster search dog. There are Doberman pinschers, rottweilers, rat terriers, and mixes of all kinds involved in disaster SAR work.

There are 27 disaster SAR task forces in the country. Each has four dog teams, and each position is four deep, meaning that there are four teams for each team position so that each group of four teams can be deployed in succession during a long-term deployment. In the case of the World Trade Center, each team served for nine days and was then replaced by a new, fresh team. Task forces generally have approximately 60 positions, including the four dog teams. At four deep, each task force ideally has 240 members. National Urban Search and Rescue (US&R) Response System task forces are sent in waves, each serving about nine days at a disaster. For a smaller disaster such as a building collapse or mudslide, only one wave from a few US&R task forces, probably local, are sent. For a major disaster such as the World Trade Center attack, multiple waves from almost every task force in the country are sent to look for survivors and recover bodies. Although the system is primarily focused upon rescuing survivors, the Oklahoma City bombing proved that the system can also be utilized to recover bodies—something that has affected the way deployments occur and has put into question whether dogs should be trained only on live victims. Most victims recovered in major disasters are dead.

Controversy is a word that comes up often in conversations with dog handlers. Maybe that's no surprise, given the nature of disaster work. Unlike most jobs, if you don't do your job on the pile, people do die. If you can't trust your dog or the people around you don't trust your dog, people can die. Disasters are unexpected and even the best-laid plans are not always carried out. Although experienced handlers tell me there can be a "nice disaster," one where the system functions properly, this is not always the case.

At the World Trade Center, many of the dead were those with disaster leadership experience, including Chief of Department Peter J. Ganci Jr. and First Deputy

Disaster Search and Rescue

Commissioner William Feehan, both of the New York Fire Department, and countless other assistant chiefs, and battalion and division chiefs. In response to the loss of the fire department leadership, a quickly devised power structure was put into place.

Inexperience, factionalism, and mismanagement can all lead to gaps in a disaster-response system. When the local city does not understand or appreciate the importance of integrating FEMA into the rescue and recovery effort, things can go awry. In the case of most disasters, the city agencies respond first and FEMA task forces respond anywhere from a day to several days later. There may also be miscommunication within task forces themselves. Because most dog handlers are civilians, emergency personnel sometimes dismiss the teams' ability to contribute to the search. "The search team managers have to understand more about what the capabilities of the system are," says veteran handler Bruce Spears of the Northwest Disaster Search Dogs. "Canine [teams] need to be a closer part of task force teams rather than emergency officials saying, 'Oh, they're just damn civilians and they don't know what they're doing,'—which happens quite a bit. If people were to come out and watch our evaluation process, I think it would impress the hell out of them."

Although handlers were wary of being quoted about the World Trade Center effort, there were reports of dogs being diverted from search areas even when they were giving live or cadaver alerts. And there was a tendency for nonemergency city officials to make decisions about the use of dogs based on what handlers perceive as erroneous information. One handler confided that when he and his dog arrived on the pile on the night of the September 13, 2001, "There was an area [where] my dog gave me an alert, just like [he does] in a test, and we were called off of that area

because of issues that are way beyond what I want to talk about."

In the traditional search mode, SAR dogs search the entire disaster area for human scent. When a dog gives a live or cadaver alert, a second dog is brought in to back up the first. Once two dogs alert on an area, often a camera is brought in to search the area. If a person or body is discovered, the process of extricating him or her begins. At the World Trade Center, dogs were brought in only when other searchers suspected there might be a body or a person. When a void was uncovered or the workers smelled what they thought might be human remains, SAR dogs were brought in to search the specific area or pinpoint the source of the smell.

Other handlers were disappointed by the way in which dogs were deployed at the World Trade Center. Dog teams train daily for years on the off chance that a disaster will occur. All handlers know there is a good likelihood that they will never be deployed during their dog's working life. Because of the way task forces are deployed, only four handlers from each task force are sent in each wave. That means that qualified advanced teams may not be sent from one task force because that task force has many advanced teams while another task force with fewer teams may send less-qualified basic teams.

In the case of the World Trade Center, although there were dozens of FEMA-certified teams deployed, many FEMA-certified dogs did not make it to New York. Because there was a need for more dog teams than FEMA deployed, there were many dog teams working that were not FEMA-certified or even trained for disaster search work. Although handlers don't question the desire to help, they argue that having uncertified teams on the pile is a safety risk for dogs and handlers and also under-mines the system. "Get off the pile because you're screwing up the search and rescue system," says NDSDF handler Seth Peacock to handlers who are not FEMA-certified. "You have no business being out here because even if the dogs go over that area, we can't say that it's been cleared." With any search, what dogs don't find is as important as what they do find. By clearing one area, searchers can go on to the next.

> **Although handlers don't question the desire to help, they argue that having uncertified teams on the pile is a safety risk for dogs and handlers and also undermines the system.**

Some teams have dropped out of disaster SAR work since September 11, dis-appointed at the way the system functioned. Although one confides, "maybe we wouldn't feel the same way if we had been deployed." The aftermath of a disaster often leads to fallout among SAR handlers, especially when they are not certified.

After the Oklahoma City bombing, few non-FEMA certified dog teams stayed involved in SAR. Bruce Spears went to Oklahoma City a week after his German shep-herd, Hunter, was certified. "It was baptism by fire. Hunter was the only certified dog who went with the Washington task force and the only dog who's continued to work with the task force after Oklahoma City. If you look at all the teams that went to Oklahoma City, there was a very high dropout rate of teams that were not certified."

Spears attributes the high dropout rate to several factors. "It's the level of dedi-cation that it took to get certification; you had to think about what you were doing more, you had a better relationship with the dog, and a better idea of what you were doing. Anyone who went to Oklahoma City and says it did not change them is lying, but the handlers who were certified had less posttraumatic problems than handlers that were not certified."

The stress, tension, and drive to do their best can lead to conflicting philoso-

phies among disaster SAR groups. There are arguments over whether dogs should be trained to alert on both live and dead victims. Some believe that training a dog for cadaver detection makes them less motivated to find live victims and believe that if a dog is sent on a cadaver search she will not alert on a live victim she happens upon. Others argue that the system has proven that cadaver training keeps a search going long after there is any chance of victims being found alive. Because most of the situations dogs are sent on will largely involve cadavers, they believe it is better to teach a distinct alert rather than relying only on the dog's body posturing, as most handlers do now.

Training methods are also disputed: coercive, inductive, or a combination? Treat, toy, praise, or self-rewards? How often should a dog train, and who should do the training: volunteers or professionals, civilians or firefighters?

One group, NDSDF, has bucked the system by using a training program for disaster dogs modeled after assistance dog training. Dogs are either adopted from shelters and rescue groups at about a year old, or raised by foster families. At one year, they're sent to professional dog trainer Pluis Davern at Sundowner Kennels for a six-month training period. They're then placed with their handlers, usually firefighters, who may or may not have experience with SAR dogs. As with assistance dog schools, the handlers do an in-house week's training at Davern's, then get considerable follow-up over the next several months. The NDSDF dogs are expected to train at least two times weekly as a group and daily individually. The group has produced 26 FEMA-certified dog teams, something of a national record. Although there are several non-firefighters involved in the NDSDF, they must pay for the six-month training at Sundowner Kennels, while firefighters receive the dogs for free.

Some handlers question the longevity of the NDSDF program. They dispute the use of push-button dogs who arrive at their handlers' completely trained and argue that without going through the process of training the dog, a handler is less able to deal with problems when they arise. There are also questions about the long-term viability of a SAR dog program that depends upon professional emergency personnel. The argument is that firefighters receive bonuses for participating in the program, whether that means pay, time off, or increased opportunities for promotion. Being a SAR dog handler is all about commitment, say some, and unless the focus is completely on the dog and the mission, handlers don't last. The NDSFD contends that its dogs are certified far more quickly than average disaster dogs; that rigorous follow-up addresses any training problems that a handler may have with his or her dog, and that participants are rigorously screened.

> **The stress, tension, and drive to do their best can lead to conflicting philosophies among disaster SAR groups.**

What SAR handlers don't argue about is what they're doing it for: to them it's all about providing the victims the best chance for survival and working with their dogs. "I always approach it with the idea that if it were me or my wife or my son, I would want the best team out there and that's how we train. We want to make sure if there are live people we give them the best possibility of being found," says Weckbacher.

Steve Powell and his rottweiler Bronte were one of the first SAR teams on the site at Oklahoma City. They had been involved with wilderness SAR for several years and in their work together, Powell and Bronte had found murder victims and even a dead baby killed in a hurricane. Nothing, however, prepared them for what they would find in Oklahoma City.

Powell lived only an hour's drive from the city and when he heard the news, he loaded Bronte into the car and set out. They arrived with the city in chaos. What Powell saw when he entered the building was beyond description. Wires and beams hung into nowhere, jagged bits of glass, concrete, drywall, and smashed office equipment were everywhere. Walking was precarious, there were sudden chasms, and no light except the light they had with them. "It was extremely loud—the elevator alarms were going off," says Powell. "Bronte was usually like a torpedo, that day he was like a cat."

When Bronte alerted, Powell was told Bronte had found four people alive; later, he was told three had died and only one was still living. That person was 15-year-old Brandy Liggins, the last living victim to be found in the Alfred P. Murrah Federal Building. "I saw things that day that no human being should see," says Powell, who quit working SAR after Oklahoma City. "We watched them wheel her out. To this day, I would swear she was a white girl in a frilly red dress. In fact, she was a black girl covered in plaster dust and blood. There are some things the human mind just can't accept."

> *Being a SAR dog handler is all about commitment, say some, and unless the focus is completely on the dog and the mission, handlers don't last.*

Other handlers were inspired by the events at Oklahoma City to recommit to disaster search. Wilma Melville was deployed with her black Lab, Murphy. When she returned to Ojai, California, she started NDSDF. Bruce Spears became increasingly active in Northwest Disaster Search Dogs; he is a FEMA evalu-ator and teaches disaster search workshops. "I was inspired to do better," says Spears. "I knew after that where I wanted the standards to be."

The amazing thing is that when Manny or another SAR dog searches the largest search site it is no different than a small practice session. To him, it is a game. It doesn't quite fit with our romantic notions of search dogs, but there it is. The dogs don't care if there is someone dead or alive as long as they get their toy at the end. The dogs don't get depressed when they don't find live humans; they get frustrated because they are not getting their toy. It's just the same as if you were to make a dog sit and get rewarded 10 times a day every day, and then one day you were to make her sit 40 times with no reward; she'd lose interest.

"I think people get confused and say that the dogs are depressed because they're not finding something," says David. "What's happening is the dog gets frustrated because they're sent out on live search commands and never get a reward. Plus, the handler starts to get depressed and they pick up on that. The dogs them-

Disaster Search and Rescue

selves, it sounds harsh, but to them it doesn't make any difference if there were dead people or live people as long as they get a reward."

During a SAR mission when live victims are not being found, handlers keep up the dogs' drive by doing runaways when they return to their lodging each night: another handler with a toy hides and the dog is sent on a search.

A SAR dog is essentially no different from a hunting dog or a narcotics detection dog, only SAR dogs are looking for people. That's not to say they're robots; they aren't. They can be stressed or frustrated and are sometimes imperfect. They can also be heavily affected by the mood and tone of their handlers, who recognize that to be a good handler they have to put their emotions aside. "You don't want to do that while you're there," says handler Peacock of his emotions at the World Trade Center. "That's for later." Since SAR dogs do pick up on what their handlers are feeling, the handlers must work to make the search feel like a game, even when it's not.

Being deployed to a disaster is the culmination of years of training and sacrifice. When they arrived at the World Trade Center, most of the handlers were apprehensive as they approached the site. Because only a few handlers continued in SAR after Oklahoma City, many of the handlers had never been deployed at all. Most were overwhelmed by the sheer size of the World Trade Center's Ground Zero. "It's indescribable how big it really was," says David. "Sixteen acres of rubble is just tremendous." The dogs, however, were unfazed, if a little more excited than at a usual training session.

Tosch was deployed to New York with her black Lab, Abby. "When we walked up to the site, the first thing was, gosh, where would you even begin to start? It was just huge; it was everywhere. Is Abby even going to be able to negotiate that? We were asking them to cross these 6-inch I beams with 40-foot drops, and the beams were warped and the metal was moving. But her attitude when I released her for her search was, *Yes! A new playground!*"

David was concerned that her ability to detect her black Lab, Kita's, alerts would be tested by the chaos of the site, "There was so much cadaver scent everywhere, how am I going to know? But the reality was, where the scent was really

strong, that's where she'd stop and focus, as opposed to sniffing everywhere, which was what she was doing all the time."

Janet Linker was amazed by how well her rat terrier, Ricky, did on the rubble site, "They had a lot of the thin sheet metal that was twisted into pretzels, and he'd just trot along it, hopping from beam to beam—he made it look like a piece of cake." She adds that his small size gave him extra maneuverability in getting into holes or crawling under beams.

The World Trade Center rescue effort was the biggest deployment of disaster SAR dogs in American history, and to a one, the FEMA-certified dogs did exactly what they needed to do, say handlers. Of the FEMA-certified dogs who were at the World Trade Center, few, if any, were injured. Although thousands of Americans sent dog booties to protect the SAR dogs' feet, no handler I spoke to used them. "We felt that putting booties on was more risky than going without," says David. "The dogs are used to walking on this stuff and they know how to move on it and hopefully not cut their feet. The thought of having them slip and fall was way more scary than having them cut their feet."

Frank assures me that the only mistakes made on the pile in New York were his own—"handler error," he calls it. "We got to the bottom of an I beam and I said let's go search, and Ohlin didn't want to search anymore. He wanted to stop." Frank got the Lab to continue searching the void, but when they came back to the I beam,

Disaster Search and Rescue

Ohlin balked again. "He didn't want to go up the I beam, he wanted to stop." Frank pressured the dog to continue up the I beam, discounting what the dog was telling him. "It turned out there was a piece of spine."

As much as the endless training allows the dog to focus and do her job in any situation, sometimes the adjustment is harder for the handler. "You'd see the shoes, the clothing, and you'd find a bone periodically," says Weckbacher. "There were a lot of reminders that this was where people worked and this is where people died…Every once in a while you'd sit there and think, this was somebody's shoe—they wore this that day; this was somebody's work that they were working on that day, and now it's all a big mess."

Although few dogs found living victims, many SAR dogs found a number of cadavers and cadaver parts. Finding a living person is always the goal in disaster work, but being able to help a family gain closure on a loved one's death is also rewarding. Generally, when a dog indicated cadaver scent, the handler would mark the spot and go on to something else, so often they didn't know what the dog had alerted on. Linker, however, was told that in one location, Ricky had found a policeman. The next day, two other policemen were found at the same location. Frank's chocolate Lab, Ohlin, also found an intact body.

Like many SAR dogs, Kita was on alert even when not on a search command. On David and Kita's last afternoon at the World Trade Center search site, the Lab found several small pieces of human tissue outside of the search zone. "She was really interested in smelling the large heavy machinery that had been on the pile. She went over and started sniffing and digging in the dirt and found a piece of human tissue." David bagged and marked the tissue and brought it to the fire department. "I looked behind me and there was a priest crossing himself and murmuring a blessing looking at the bag. It just really hit me that this isn't a piece of tissue, that this is someone."

Frank knows too well the value of recovering bodies. He was first introduced to canine SAR by a fellow firefighter, Lieutenant Gregory Shoemaker. In 1995, when four firemen were trapped and killed in the notorious Pang fire, in downtown Seattle, Washington, Frank was among the dog handlers who searched for their bodies; Shoemaker was among the missing.

CHAPTER 15

SEARCH AND RESCUE

Search and rescue dogs search in suburbia and in the wilderness, in water and in avalanches. Their searches involve finding missing people in woods and in housing divisions, underwater, and buried under feet of snow. Teams may be trained to do live or cadaver searches, or both. Dogs who are trained only on live searches also alert to cadavers, as long as they've been exposed to them, although there's some controversy as to whether dogs trained in both will pass over living humans when on a cadaver search. Proponents of training both defend the practice as vehemently as detractors oppose it. As with disaster SAR, there is a fair share of controversy, ranging from differences in training to how dog teams should be deployed to who should cover their costs.

Search and rescue dogs are trained in largely the same way disaster dogs are: repeating runaway exercises with a favorite toy or treat until the dog begins to use his nose to find the missing person. They do not, however, work in the same situations. While disaster SAR dogs are usually deployed in urban areas where buildings have collapsed and where they are contending with shredded metal and glass and chunks of broken concrete, SAR dogs are mostly used in rural or suburban areas. The agility that's so vital in disaster work is less important in other types of SAR. Disaster dogs work in short intense sequences, while SAR dogs must have stamina, sometimes working 5 to 10 hours and hiking long distances.

Working Dogs

Each SAR discipline—wilderness, water, and avalanche—has particular techniques unique to it and dogs tend to favor one over another. For example, wilderness SAR requires a dog with stamina and a willingness to search for long hours over long distances and water searches require a dog who's hard-headed enough to continue to work even when the reward is not immediate.

Unlike disaster SAR, there is no federal agency that certifies all SAR dogs. Dogs are certified in specific disciplines by local and state-level SAR organizations. Training time and expense, however, is comparable to disaster dogs.

Salvation can come through a cup of hot chocolate. When Greg and Joanne Varney were called out on a search for a group of lost hikers, Joanne's golden retriever Hylee had only one thing to go on: a discarded hot-chocolate cup. Hylee sniffed the cup and got a trail almost immediately. A search vehicle was sent ahead to scout in the direction of Hylee's trail and found the group several miles away. When the vehicle returned with the lost hikers aboard, Hylee jumped in and went straight for the lap of one woman: the hot chocolate drinker. When the group left for their hike in the woods outside Seattle, they never imagined that a predilection for hot chocolate would assist in their rescue later that day.

> **Watching a trailing dog work is impressive. After the dog smells the scent item, he sniffs along the ground until he picks up the scent there.**

In wilderness SAR, dogs utilize one of two methods: trailing or air scent. Dogs who trail must get a scent from the missing person through a wallet, an item of clothing, or even a cup. They then try to pick up that trail and follow it to the lost person. Watching a trailing dog work is impressive. After the dog smells the scent item, he sniffs along the ground until he picks up the scent there. Once the trail is established, the dog is off and running, trying to find his reward. Air scent dogs do not need a scent article and find the scent of any person in the vicinity they're asked to search. So, if an air scent dog is commanded to search a 10-acre park, he'll alert on a couple walking or an elderly man sitting on a bench as well as the missing person.

While trailing dogs are more precise, the benefit to air search dogs is their ability to work without a scent article and their speed. Often a trailing dog and an air scent dog are worked in tandem, getting a direction from the trailing dog, allowing the air scent dog to work farther out in the trail's direction.

Search and Rescue

Although trailing dogs may work SAR either in the wilderness or in a town, the technique is the same; only the surface is different. A wilderness dog, unless trained in town, is not as competent on concrete as in a wooded area; and a dog used only in urban areas is less competent at trailing in a wooded area. It's rare for volunteer trailing teams to work only within urban areas. Even if a team lives within a city, it is most likely to be called out on rural searches.

Greg Varney trains with his 16-month-old golden retriever, Trulee, two or three times a week. They started when Trulee was only seven weeks old, and they just recently went on their first search; they found a 16-year-old girl in the woods near her home, shivering and hypothermic but alive.

We meet at a park in Seattle, where Joanne, Greg, and other members of the King County Search Dogs are training. Hidden somewhere in the vicinity is LaFond Davis, a veteran member of Northwest Disaster Search Dogs. The two groups train together often, and several teams are members of both.

Greg gives Trulee a scent, an item of Davis's clothing in a plastic bag, and the dog breathes it in deeply. Once on the trail, Trulee makes a beeline, occasionally distracted by other smells but always coming back to his original trail. Varney explains to me that in trailing, as opposed to tracking, the dog doesn't need to follow the scent exactly, "I'm interested in direction of travel, but I'm not too interested in whether they were on the left side of the trail or the right side of the trail," says Varney. "We just want to know where they went and get to them as quickly as we can."

After following a circuitous path on concrete and grass, around trees and buildings, Trulee begins to show signs of excitement, his tail wagging and his pace quickening. He quickly finds LaFond's hiding place and jumps on her then sits and faces Varney, waiting for his reward. Out comes the Kong, a hard plastic chew toy, and for

a few minutes every bit of Varney's attention is on Trulee. This is what it's all about for all wilderness SAR dogs: the chance for a few minutes of undivided fun with their favorite toy and their favorite person.

The reward of choice differs among wilderness SAR dogs; some handlers let the dogs pick their own, others choose it for the dog. Most handlers use toys, but some use food. Hylee, for instance, is a chow hound. "She works for different things: a Frisbee or big, fuzzy toys," says Greg, "but she works hardest to get food."

On a recent search, Joanne, Greg, and Hylee were called out to search for a woman with Alzheimer's who had wandered away from home. Before they began the search, they spoke with the woman's husband, who related that she loved to look at cars. "We start from the back of the house and Hylee picks up the scent," says Greg. "Down the driveway on to the main drag, makes a turn, and starts going down the road. We go to the next property and there's a driveway and about five cars up there, Hylee's showing all kinds of interest in the cars but there's nothing there. So we go back down to the road, up the road, down another street, up another, and the whole time Hylee's going from side to side, toward a car, toward another car. We turn into a driveway and there's a car in the driveway. Hylee goes up to the car, to the passenger side, to the driver's side, to the trunk, running around the car like crazy. I look inside and the windows are all fogged up, but I see a plaid blanket on the seat and I tap the window. All of a sudden a person sits up and there's a face looking out at me, and there she was." Hylee's reward? "Hylee got to go to Baskin and Robbins and get a cup of vanilla ice cream—that's her really big reward," says Varney.

Other wilderness SAR handlers use anything from gloves to squeaky toys to rubber bumpers. Sue Purvis, a SAR handler in Colorado, laughs that her dog, Tasha's, toy is an oblong rubber bumper that she calls the schlong. When *Smithsonian* magazine did a story about the pair, they wouldn't print the toy's name, Purvis tells me gleefully.

Julie Weibler, another wilderness SAR handler in Colorado, had a cattle dog, Tassie (short for Tasmanian Devil), whose reward was a porcupine squeaky toy. Weibler always assumed that Tassie was more interested in playing than in what she was playing with. "As much as she liked to play, I would've thought it wouldn't matter," says Weibler. "But one time I forgot, and I went to throw a stick and she just watched the stick go flying and sat there and looked at me, *That is not my toy.*"

Weibler's current dog, Zephyr, a German shepherd–cattle dog mix, has a horse who whinnies as his toy. In his case, however, it's not good enough just to play a game of tug or fetch; he wants to be chased. "He pulls his toy out of the pack and then you chase him while he runs with the toy—he loves to do that," says Weibler. "Sometimes it takes time to find what really gets their attention. I know some dogs who don't want to play, they want to be petted and loved."

In general, wilderness SAR dogs are also allowed to choose their own alert, the thought being that the behavior that comes naturally will be the strongest. "I don't believe in forcing an alert," explains Weibler. "I think you get a much stronger alert if you encourage the dog's natural behavior."

Every dog has a different working style; Tassie always carried a stick until she got scent and then when she got scent she dropped the stick and was all business.

Working Dogs

"She'd work the alert in," says Weibler. "She'd do refinds [going back and forth between the handler and the victim] and she would do that to me when she got a strong scent. Then, when she actually got to them she'd jump on me and bark." When Zephyr gets scent, his tail starts to wag in circles, then, when he gets close, his ears go flat and his tail goes low and wags side to side. With almost every dog, the alert for cadaver is different, generally more subdued. The first time Tassie made a find on a cadaver she actually crawled on her belly to it.

Doing wilderness SAR depends on the relationship between the handler and the dog. A handler must take all the information, what the dog's telling him or her, what the terrain and weather are like, the wind direction, and any witness information, and put it all together. Above all, the handler must be able to trust the dog.

On one of Tassie's last missions, Weibler started out in the direction she thought the missing hiker would have gone. "I looked back and there she was, just sitting there, tapping her tail tip. *If you want to know where he is I'll take you there; if you wanna go out there go ahead, but I'll wait for you here…*" Weibler opted to follow Tassie's lead, and the cattle dog took her right to the victim. Unfortunately, the hiker had died of hypothermia.

To handlers, knowing how to watch the dog is about encouraging natural behavior and knowing what is abnormal behavior. Varney points out that knowing when a dog is on task is imperative. "I need to be able to know when he's working and when he's goofing around, when he's taking me for a walk. If he's looking close to the ground and doing short quick moves, he's probably crittering [smelling a wild animal], when he's smelling another dog he leans down and curls up one of his paws so that he's standing on three legs."

All of these observations can make or break a dog's ability to search. While the dog is paying attention to the trail, it's the handler's job to pay attention to the dog.

Of the many SAR disciplines, water is arguably the most difficult. Water searches invariably end with a dead body, so it is hard on the handler and, in a way, hard on the dog. Because the reward is not immediate, water SAR is difficult to teach to the dog, but it is also confusing for animals when their discoveries are invariably greeted with dismay rather than joy. That is why endless training, a stoic handler, and a tough-minded dog are essential.

When I first speak to a water search handler Deb Tirmenstein, she quickly corrects me when I call it water rescue, "It's water recovery," Tirmenstein explains

Search and Rescue

firmly. By the time a water dog is brought in, there is no chance for survival. She adds that training a water recovery dog is frustrating because it is impossible to provide a quick reward for an alert. Even in training, the dog must wait for the "victim" to be brought to the surface before being rewarded. Unlike other SAR disciplines in which the dog finds a victim, alerts, and is almost immediately rewarded with food or a toy as well as a tangible discovery.

In water recovery, dogs generally work either from a boat or the shoreline. Some dogs are allowed to search in the water once they've caught scent, but the majority of handlers discourage it because of safety issues. Most water recoveries are not on placid lakes but rather in swift-moving river currents where a SAR dog in the water could easily lead to another, canine, victim. The alerts vary among water recovery dogs; they may scratch or lick the bottom of the boat, do a classic passive alert on the shoreline, bark, or even paw the water to indicate a discovery.

Just setting up search scenarios is a production; handlers generally start out training on live scuba divers, but eventually the dogs start alerting on the bubbles from the scuba gear, so they need to switch to a "scentillator," where cadaver scent is placed underwater and then forced upward to the water's surface through a generator.

Weibler enjoys doing water searches, even more than wilderness, "I think because it's so challenging, but it's also the most frustrating. All you can say is my dog's alerting; there's scent here. But I can't tell if the person's here or if the scent is pooling here. It's a mystery because I can't get to it because of that water medium."

Handlers may also use scent articles when training for water search, although some handlers think this can be detrimental because it may train the dog to alert on any article in the water. Dogs are conditioned to ignore distractions on the shoreline or on the boat, but during an actual search, precautions are taken to have no divers or other swimmers in the water so the dog does not have false alerts. To help train Zephyr on real recoveries, Weibler often asks the divers to let him sniff at the body while it's still in the water, and then rewards him.

Water search teams may combine work from a boat, from the shoreline, or in the water, depending on the dog's working style, the handler's comfort level, and the body of water. Teams that work on rivers rarely work in the water because of the dangers that come with white water and obstructions, but they may do some shore work to pinpoint an area before getting into a boat. Some river sections are too dangerous even for a boat, so they work only from the shore. On lakes, shore work tends to be inconclusive, so the dog may work from a boat or the water, or start out in a boat with the dog jumping into the water when he gets scent. Each search necessitates a different approach.

"I did a search in Nebraska," says Weibler. "I was walking Zephyr along the shore to get somewhere, and he suddenly alerted, so I started to pay attention to what he was doing. It was a fence line and he did the same thing when we got back. Then, when we got out in the boat, we made the search area longer than that. He's really subtle, not super animated when he's in the boat, licking the bottom to give an alert. He started licking right in line with where he was giving me alerts on shore." Her older dog, Tassie, and another dog then alerted in the same place. They threw out hooks and caught the drowned victim on the first try. "We used shore work, boat work, plus multiple dogs—it was the best water search I've ever been on; it doesn't usually go that well."

The geographical location and type of water also affects the smell of the body, which is another reason handlers train on both live divers and cadaver scent: a drowning victim who is in a glacier-runoff river for fewer than four hours is going to smell fairly similar to a live human being. A cadaver that's been in a warm water lake for a week, however, is going to be well decomposed. Tirmenstein has worked three black Labs in water search. One, Choteau, died at the age of 16, but the other two, Ruby and Fergus, are still hard at work. "Fergus actually made a find one hour after a guy went into the river," she says. "It's not exactly like a live human being, but it's not decomposition scent either. Other times we'll find an abandoned car and there's a long time elapse after death, so I try to cover all the bases."

> **Is the bond more intense for SAR handlers and their dogs than it is for other working dog handlers? They do talk about it more than most.**

Bodies may end up on shore after days of searching the water. Sue Purvis, who has trained in water search as well as wilderness, responded to a water search call last summer. Divers and boats had spent six days dragging the lake with no results. Finally, the sheriff asked Purvis to come out, more than anything to give the family the sense that they were doing everything they could. She got there while it was still dark and no other searchers had arrived. "I let Tasha out of the car to pee and she put her nose in the air, sniffed, and boom! In 45 seconds she ran across a bridge, down the bank, and started barking. I was like, 'What's going on?' " Purvis's husband yelled at her to follow her dog, which she did. "The body was just starting to come up out of the water."

The fact that a dog can even find a body in the water seems to go against everything we know. Even to the handlers, water search is amazing. "Water search is still kind of a mystery to me," says Tirmenstein. "It's so wild to see it. Some of these expanses of water are huge, and to think a dog could find a human in something that big, given those conditions, it blows me away."

Water search takes a special kind of dog; not only does he have to have the excellent olfactory senses and play drive that all SAR dogs have, but he also must be driven enough to accept a lapse between the alert and the reward, friendly toward people, and comfortable in the type of situations most dogs find terrifying. Tirmenstein's dogs, for example, are perfectly happy white-water rafting. "We've done some searches on the Salmon River, which has a lot of white water," says Tirmenstein. "It's a good challenge for them. Some really good search dogs are terrible water dogs because they can't relax in a boat." She adds that the dogs are constantly jostled and lifted in and out of boats, often by people they don't know.

"In a strange way it's like playing a slot machine, sometimes they hit the big jackpot and sometimes they don't, "says Tirmenstein. "We reward like crazy in training, so the times in real life when they don't get rewarded, they deal with it okay. Water search takes a real hard-headed dog because they don't get an immediate reward; they have to want to work for the sake of working." Luckily, she adds, Labs are forgiving, "They're a dog you can make a lot of mistakes with and still end up with a pretty good product—that was good for me in the early times."

Safety is always an issue when it comes to water searches: handlers are cautious that they do not become victims themselves in the process of doing a search. Tirmenstein, for example, does not allow the dogs to do a jump alert because her work is often along mountain streams. She also doesn't let them search in the water, laughing that she would be the next victim, drowning in an attempt to rescue the dogs.

Although all her dogs have been trained in avalanche, wilderness, and tracking, it's water that takes up most of Tirmenstein's time. Living in Montana in an area with many lakes and rivers, Tirmenstein has had times when she and her dogs have gone on as many as seven searches in one month. Although she initially started SAR work in avalanches, she quickly realized that water search was more appropriate. "We trained like crazy for avalanche and never had a use in this area," she says.

Although Tirmenstein's dogs are her pets, she acknowledges that they are working animals at heart. "They want to work; it's work, but to these dogs it's play—it's what they really, really want to do. It's not like you're twisting their tail to make them do it."

> **The fact that a dog can even find a body in the water seems to go against everything we know. Even to the handlers, water search is amazing.**

Having adaptable dogs is a priority when doing searches that are always unpredictable. "Last fall we did a search for two guys who fell out of a canoe. No one knew where they went in, but they found one guy dead near shore and the canoe floating on the lake and gear in various places. It was a hike-in lake so we couldn't bring a boat in. We decided to use the guys' canoe and were pulled by a Jet Ski. It worked. I worked Fergus first and she's digging and squeaking, then Ruby nailed it. They dropped a buoy and used a camera. It took six minutes and they found the body. It was rewarding because the family was there and it was fast; we put an end to it really quickly."

Search and Rescue

Tirmenstein adds that that search stands out for many reasons: "The family was incredible. Every family member filed by the dogs and hugged them and talked to them. It was very emotional. The guy's widow put an ad in the Missoula paper thanking the dogs." Tirmenstein says, "I think my dogs have a secondary role as grief counselors sometimes." On water searches, as opposed to wilderness searches, the family is usually right there throughout. There are even times when the families participate in the search.

Because the family is so close to the search, some handlers struggle with being sensitive to the family's feelings while making sure to reward the dogs. "I discreetly talk to the family first," explains Weibler. "I explain to the family that this is what we will do and this is why we do it. Death can be stressful for the dog as well, so it's even more important to be positive. If you're going to want to continue to use the dog for body recovery, you need to make that a positive experience for it."

Ultimately, water search is like any other type of SAR, it comes down to the handler knowing and trusting the dog. "There's an art to watching the dog's body movement," says Tirmenstein. "I've had a dog come from a full sleep to a full alert. I used to get upset when Choteau would be lying down on the job, but I got so that over the years I totally trusted him. The brain is still going, the nose is still going, but his eyes are closed."

As with all SAR work, avalanche search is motivated by tragedy. For handlers, it's often tragedy close to home. Patti Burnett, the author of *Avalanche! Hasty Search: The Care and Training of Avalanche Search and Rescue Dogs*, has been a part of the Copper Mountain ski patrol, the Summit County Rescue Group, and the Colorado Search and Rescue group since 1980, but it wasn't until a fellow ski patroller died in an avalanche that she turned to handling rescue dogs.

When patroller Mickey Johnston was killed in Graveline Bowl in 1983, his body was found quickly because he wore a beacon. Most of the skiing public, however, does not wear beacons so using an avalanche dog is the next best way to find an avalanche victim. After Johnston's death, his fellow Copper Mountain ski patrollers held a fundraiser, and with the proceeds they bought Hasty, Burnett's first avalanche dog.

They also started an avalanche deployment organization, which operates in cooperation with the local SAR group, the sheriff's office, local ski patrols, and Flight for Life helicopters. If there is a backcountry accident, dispatch is called and the sheriff enacts an avalanche deployment. The helicopter picks up the dog team as well as a snow safety technician and flies them to the area. There, they determine if someone is buried, and, if so, whether it's safe to search.

When Hasty started to slow down in his old age, Burnett bought another golden retriever to eventually replace him. "We'd picked out all kinds of names for our new pup but he was born on the same day that one of our Flight for Life nurses died in a helicopter accident while she was doing SAR. Her name was Sandy Sigman; it seemed only natural that my new partner would be named in her memory." Sandy, now eight, worked alongside Hasty until the older dog retired at age 12 and later died. Sandy is now Burnett's only SAR dog.

Burnett spent a lot of time researching the use of dogs in avalanche SAR. She chose a golden retriever because she wanted a dog who would be good with the public as well as be the right size and build with an excellent nose and strong play drive. "Golden retrievers make great diplomats," explains Burnett, adding that they also use Labs and Australian shepherds. "They also have to be well bonded with their handlers because we need to work the dogs off lead."

A dog who is too small can have difficulty navigating avalanche debris, and small paws can sink into the snow. A dog who is too big may not move as quickly and may have a shorter working life because of stress on his hips and joints. "The desired size is between 40 pounds and 80 pounds," says Burnett. Although most of the dogs the ski patrol uses are purebreds, they have used mixes.

Burnett explains that the Copper Mountain ski patrol quickly gained experience on avalanches, "Summit County, Colorado," where they're located, "has more avalanche fatalities than anywhere else in the U.S." This is partly due to the large number of recreational mountain users, but also because of what Burnett calls "a lousy snow pack." "It's not unusual for Colorado to begin its winter season without much snow. That, combined with cold nights, creates what most people know as sugar snow or what snow safety workers call temperature-gradient snow," she explains. "It doesn't make for a good base for the snows that come afterward. With little support underneath the new layers of snow, avalanches occur and people get in trouble." Victims can be skiers, ice climbers, snowboarders, snowmobile riders, and even motorists, but most of them are caught in avalanches when outside of ski resort bounds. The ski resort itself works hard to maintain the avalanche paths in their bowls to diminish the possibility of guests getting caught in slides.

Right now, Copper Mountain has five dogs in the program, three operational and two in training. There is a primary handler and a secondary handler for each dog; the dog goes home with the primary handler. Burnett explains that although having two handlers can sometimes be problematic, it's necessary when doing avalanche work, where time is of the essence and the primary handler is invariably unavailable when an avalanche actually happens.

The secondary handler is sometimes the spouse or partner of the primary handler. With professional ski patrol avalanche teams, as opposed to volunteers, the secondary handler is usually another ski patroller. Although the dog lives with the primary handler, the dog will go to work with the secondary handler when the primary handler is off duty and stay in the secondary handler's home if the primary handler is out of town. Most of the training is done with the primary handler, but the secondary handler must be familiar enough with the dog to read alerts and other behaviors and to reliably give the dog commands.

By the time SAR is called, most avalanche victims are dead. The one time that a live victim was found by Hasty, Burnett was not immediately on-site, although she did arrive by the time that Hasty, being worked by his secondary handler, Kevin, was alerting on the victim. "She was only buried about 4 feet deep," says Burnett. "It was a witnessed slide and the people on scene were probing in one area. Kevin brought in Hasty and he started digging and alerting at a place that was not exactly where they were probing. They moved the probe stick to where he was sniffing, probed, and got a strike. She was buried for fourteen minutes. She wasn't breathing but had a slight pulse. Sandy, the Flight for Life nurse who later died, intubated her and got her breathing again. It was such a weird thing for me; I was right there at her head as we worked on her and I saw her beautiful eyes open and I saw ice crystals on her pupils as they started to focus. I've been on a bunch of avalanches where people have died, just to see someone alive was…I'll never forget that."

Burnett says that many avalanche SAR teams, including her and Sandy, do wilderness SAR as well, explaining, "There's a lot more wilderness searches than avalanche, and it's nice to find someone who's still alive." She hastens to add that the fact that most avalanche victims are found dead doesn't negate its importance. "Even finding people dead is very important because it brings closure to the family," she says. "There are times when people die in avalanches and the family and friends have to wait until the spring thaw because they're buried so deep or buried in a place that's so dangerous no rescue people can go in there and search for them. How tragic, how awful that their friends and family can't bring any closure to their deaths."

> **As with all SAR work, avalanche search is motivated by tragedy. For handlers, it's often tragedy close to home.**

Although handlers mostly train on live people, avalanche dogs do alert on cadavers, even when that's not specifically trained. As with all SAR disciplines, the live and cadaver alerts are quite different. "The first time a rescue dog is on a search for a dead person, typically the alert is way more subdued. They might just scratch at the snow instead of digging like a steam shovel," says Burnett. "Rather than the tail wagging high in the air, it might be that the tail is tucked between their rear legs with just the tip sticking out."

Burnett uses two different commands: *search* for live, which she always uses in training unless she is implementing articles or cadaver scent; and *slow search* for dead. "We usually start with *search* and then change over to *slow search* after an hour or so." Switching to *slow search* allows the dog to give a more enthusiastic cadaver alert because he knows the scent is going to be different. She's not worried about her dog passing over a living victim in the search for a cadaver, "I'm sure if I give my dog the command for *slow search*, he will find a living victim if there is one."

Avalanche dogs are taught to dig at the scent site, even if he does a bark alert in other SAR disciplines. Digging, handlers believe, allows the dog to pinpoint the victim more accurately. Also, "as they dig, they may find that they're getting closer to the scent and it's here to the left or it's more to the right," says Burnett.

When a dog alerts, the handler flags the area with a wand, a wire with a flag attached that is planted in the snow. The handler tags the flag with Dog Alert and then continues to search while a navigator probes until he or she hits the victim. "Even after a strike we continue to work the dogs because there may be other people who are buried or maybe the dog will have an alert that's stronger than the alert he had initially," explains Burnett. "Maybe the first alert was on the buried person's backpack, so you want to keep him working the entire time until you're sure all the buried people have been found."

For avalanche work, handlers often use a glove as a reward. In training, the glove is placed inside the neck of the subject's jacket. When the dog makes his find, he grabs the glove and the dog and victim play tug. In a real-life scenario, a handler brings other rewards, but often the dog rewards himself by pulling a glove off the victim and playing with it. "Sandy loves that self-rewarding, being able to get that reward directly from the victim," says Burnett. "When we're doing wilderness, he'll grab whatever the subject has, a book or anything else that might be on hand. I always warn our subjects ahead of time."

As with water search, avalanche recoveries are often done with the victim's friends and family close by. "We have to be extremely sensitive," says Burnett. "Sometimes I take the dog to another location. I try to get away from the friends and family immediately because I don't want to miss the opportunity of giving my dog a timely reward. This is the game they've been learning since they were two months old and it would be so detrimental not to reward the dog or to have them feed off of me that this is a sad situation—the dog might think it's a bad thing to find dead bodies."

Burnett adds that not being able to express grief can be detrimental to handlers, as well, so Copper Mountain patrollers are provided stress debriefing after recoveries, "Dogs will sense the sadness and react to it, but when we handlers hide it from our dogs, we will have to deal with it later."

As with all working dogs, the key to a successful team lies in the strength of the bond between dog and handler and the passion both have for the job; even the secondary handler must establish that bond to work the dog reliably. "I retired Hasty a few years before he died," Burnett tells me. "About a month before he died, I took him up the hill one last time and we did our group picture with the whole ski patrol. He was like a young pup again, to go up there and be with everybody. These dogs have the greatest life. When Sandy gets off the chairlift at the top of the mountain in the morning, he just runs up to the ridge and puts his nose straight into the wind and stands there, as if to say, *I'm the king of the mountain; this is my mountain.*"

Is the bond more intense for SAR handlers and their dogs than it is for other working dog handlers? They do talk about it more than most. Like police and war dog handlers, who go into dangerous and stressful situations with their dog partners, SAR dogs become something like war buddies to their handlers. "I think the bond that develops between a SAR handler and dog is second to none," says Burnett.

Trusting what the dog is telling the handler is key to the work SAR teams do. Handlers know that the time and trust they put into their dogs is exactly what they'll get out of their dogs—to reliably interpret their dogs' alerts and behaviors, they must be completely confident of their skills. Handlers say that interpreting their dogs for law enforcement or families is especially difficult because outsiders rarely understand or trust the dogs' skills as well as the handlers do. Weibler describes a search at a local city lake when Tassie ran straight from the car and jumped off the ledge into the lake, alerting. The divers who were working the site didn't believe Tassie's alert because they'd already done numerous searches in that area. The body surfaced at the exact location the next morning.

Weibler adds that although SAR teams don't always face the kind of danger a police dog team does, there are instances when dogs have literally saved handlers' lives. "We were looking for a 12-year-old girl at night, and a dog stepped in front of a handler. When the handler tried to move, the dog would not let her. It turned out there was a cliff there and the girl had fallen in that spot."

Although most examples of the intense relationship between dog and handler aren't as dramatic, that makes it no less real. "The dog's trusting that you're not going to put them in a bad situation, and you're trusting the dog that it's working," says Weibler.

"The real bond comes in when you're stressed out, the dog's stressed out, there's nothing out there, and you're still working," says Purvis. Being able to read your dog and believe what your dog is telling you is the essential work of a SAR handler. "When 15 sheriff's officers are looking at you and you say that your dog says there's nothing here, that's a huge statement."

BEYOND WORKING DOGS

CHAPTER 16

FINDING A JOB FOR YOUR DOG

If a dog was ever looking for a job, it was Sunshine. Her weekdays in the city were spent devising schemes to run away or steal food. Over the years, we reinforced our fence by putting boards under it, chicken wire over it, and patches everywhere Sunshine created a new opening. Our kitchen cupboards had childproof locks, yet she still found her way into boxes of cookies and bags of trash. Desperately seeking a job, she'd created her own: food forager. When she inevitably escaped from our house, she'd return home with loaves of bread, a child's lunch sack, or a chunk of meat snatched from a neighbor's countertop.

For all Sunshine's mischievousness in the city, during weekends and summers at our rural cabin, she invested herself in her true calling: chasing birds. She chased birds over sand and through water and woods, occasionally stopping to roll in a dead animal or receive a quick congratulatory pat from a family member. While in the city she spent her days trying to escape from us, in the country she always came when we called.

Sunshine was an Irish setter, born and bred to run and chase birds, and that's what she did. She wasn't too unlike the dogs who end up in animal shelters every day: full of energy with nowhere to direct it. Had we known better, we would have involved her in every activity under the sun followed by 5-mile runs. But we didn't, we just loved her and fretted over her incessant barking, digging, roaming, and food foraging. We just couldn't understand why she wasn't more like my mother's pekeapoo—Sen-Sen was perfectly content to spend the day sleeping.

Fortunately, animal education has come a long way since the 1970s, and many of us are realizing that it's not enough just to love our dogs; we need to provide them with physical and mental stimulation as well. Even those of us with enough foresight to adopt a so-called companion dog know that daily walks and playtime are required.

The bottom line is that if you expect to adopt or buy a working breed, then you must expect to provide the dog with something to do. Daily exercise is a start, but for many dogs you need to do more. Although I've always provided my cattle dog mix, Desi, with exercise, I know her life is far more fulfilling when she's also got a job to do. She's been at various times running buddy, uncertified therapy dog, and go-everywhere companion. She appointed herself the home guardian years ago and spends a good portion of every night stalking the perimeters of our home and yard—checking on each corner and giving out small warning barks when anyone strays too close. Invariably, if I get up during the night, I'll find her on our back porch, ears alert, and nose sniffing the air.

Desi truly found her calling at nine years old when we finally discovered agility. The weekly class gives her a jauntiness that she hasn't had in years; she seems to come alive as soon as we enter the field. Now, at 11 years old, she's thrilled to learn new obstacles and completes courses almost effortlessly. Yes, she's slower than the other dogs, and the hurdles are set low, but her tail wags the entire time, and that's what matters.

If I could do it all over, I would have involved Desi in agility when she was a super-energetic one-year-old whose favorite pastime was destroying my new clothes. I think if I'd involved my somewhat aggressive multimix, Tramp in SAR, she may have replaced some her fighting drive with hunting drive.

Finding a Job for Your Dog

Our knowledge of our dogs is always growing and expanding; unfortunately what we learn with one doesn't always come into play until the next. We aren't complete failures, however, until we give up altogether, and, as with Desi, there's always time to grow.

Whether your dog is an eight-week-old puppy or a 10-year-old grande dame, there's always time to give your dog a job, big or small. You'll be surprised how satisfying it is for both of you.

Pets can undertake many of the jobs I've described in this book; they require a level of time and commitment, however, that shouldn't be embarked upon lightly. Search and rescue can be a matter of life and death, while others, such as therapy work, really require that a team commit to following through with the relationships they make. For this reason, it's best not to look at any of the jobs I've discussed as hobbies per se. They require a level of activity that's far beyond most hobbies, and there are other dog activities that can be fulfilling without the level of responsibility. Among the hobbies, there are some that are more appropriate for individual dogs or dog breeds, but in theory, any dog can participate in any activity.

Before starting a canine sport, be sure your dog is healthy and capable of participating. Once she's vet-cleared, try a couple activities to see what your dog takes to. If your dog doesn't seem to be having fun, don't do that activity—try something else. There's absolutely no reason ever to force your dog to participate in an activity she doesn't enjoy. Not all trainers or activity coordinators are equally skilled or experienced. Look for a trainer with a few championships behind his or her dogs. This will tell you that the trainer knows what he or she is doing. Even if you're just doing an activity for fun, you want to be sure the trainer is aware of equipment safety and dog limitations. Weight pulling, for example, can cause serious injuries if a dog is asked to pull more than her capability, and agility can lead to falls if the dog is not properly acclimated to obstacles.

For dogs who were bred to pull, whether they be sled dogs or drafting dogs, there are a number of activities suited to their needs. Sledding, weight pulling, and skijoring are all popular sports that combine the drive to pull and run with tenacity and determination.

Sledding is no longer just for transportation, and if you live in an area with a snow pack, it's a great way to let your husky, or other high-drive breed, get her free-running fix. There are many hobbyist levels of sledding, and novices can participate in small one- or two-dog team races. The equipment, however, is expensive, and, as many mushers will tell you, the sport is addictive.

Dogs who love to pull can also get their release through weight-pulling or ski-joring. Weight-pulling is gaining popularity. You just need something heavy, a log or a tire, a harness, and a dog who loves to pull. Find a good trainer, however, to help you determine safety precautions and weight limits. Alaskan malamutes are common participants. Skijoring is a sport that combines cross-country skiing and pulling: the dog is hooked up to a harness and pulls the skier. Skijoring is an excellent job for a dog whose person isn't interested in buying a sled but is looking for a good canine activity—plus it's fun for the skier.

Like sledding, herding is a dog job that has also become a dog hobby. Many people with herding breeds are attracted to the sport and travel long distances to participate. Herding dogs really seem to come into their own on the field, and it's an indescribable feeling to watch your own dog's innate characteristics come into play. Watching the behavior that's been bred into certain dogs for hundreds of years is worth doing a herding proficiency test, although some herding experts caution against bringing out a dog's chase instinct if you do not plan to focus it on herding. Herding can be done on both a hobby and a competitive level. Many people only take classes once or twice a month for fun. Others become highly involved in trials. At a herding trial, the handler directs the dog to bring livestock from point A to point B. The higher the level of competition, the more obstacles the dog must navigate the livestock through.

Agility may be the best activity for a working dog to fulfill her skills in speed and precision and strengthen her bond with a human handler. Agility is a canine sport that truly took off in the 1990s. In fact, many participants would argue against calling it a hobby at all. Some of these folks spend their waking hours training for competition and every free weekend driving long distances to compete. Agility combines elements of many different types of work and allows the dog to use both her mental and physical powers. Dogs must go over, through, and around obstacles such as an A-frame, teeter, and tunnel in a certain order; the handler runs alongside the dog throughout the course. The goal is to complete the course in as little time with as few mistakes as possible. Speed, control, and agility are all skills that help dogs become stars of the sport, but even tiny Yorkshire terriers and huge Saint Bernards can participate.

Finding a Job for Your Dog

Flyball is another sport that combines speed and agility. It's a sort of relay race in which each dog must jump four hurdles; hit a ball box, which shoots a ball into the air; catch the ball; and then turn around and jump the four hurdles back to the start/finish line. There are four dogs on each relay team. Retrievers, with their natural fetching ability and athleticism, excel at this sport, but any dog can play and enjoy this game. In fact, flyball teams welcome fast small dogs because the hurdles are set based on the height of the smallest dog. The only requirement with flyball is that dogs must get along with other dogs. When they pass the dogs on the other teams, they are often facing one another at full speed, which can lead to scuffles.

In *schutzhund*, dogs combine tracking, obedience, and protection work. Essentially, this sport evolved from canine police work. In the tracking portion, the dogs search for and locate a scent article; in the obedience section, the dogs follow specific commands given by their handlers; in protection work, the dogs use a bite sleeve to subdue a suspect. *Schutzhund* is popular in Germany, especially among German shepherd fanciers, although rottweilers and Doberman pinschers participate as well. The sport is less common in the U.S., probably because of misconceptions about the protection work. As with all sleeve work, the dog is trained to bite and tug at a protective sleeve, with the sleeve being the reward. Finding a *schutzhund* club may be difficult, although not impossible.

For hunting dog aficionados, field trials and hunt tests are rapidly replacing real hunting. In field trials, hunting dogs compete against other hunting dogs, while in hunting tests, the dogs only work against their own best scores. Trials and tests are perfect for people with hunting breeds who don't have good hunting opportunities in their region or who aren't comfortable with hunting. It's also a great way to pit one dog's skills against another or test a dog's own skill. Usually no live fowl are used;

instead, dogs are tested on their ability to flush, retrieve, and scent discriminate through the use of dead birds (cold game) or rubber retriever bumpers. Occasionally, tethered live birds are used. Just as in hunting, the dogs must rely on both their natural instincts and the careful training provided by their handlers. Not only must a dog exhibit her skills in finding scent, but once on scent, she must show restraint and obedience by staying on point or flushing the bird. Finally, the dog is asked to retrieve the bird and bring it to her handler.

> **Whether your dog is an eight-week-old puppy or a 10-year-old grande dame, there's always time to give your dog a job, big or small.**

Going to ground is another hunting related activity. In eighteenth, nineteenth, and early twentieth century Britain, terriers were bred to pursue small quarry into their dens. The terrier structure is created for just this purpose: the stiff fur protects the skin from the sides of tunnels; the distinct terrier death-shake, which most terriers exhibit with their toys, was perfected for dispatching prey quickly; even the short, sturdy tail was bred into the dogs to allow their handlers an easy handhold for pulling a tenacious terrier out of a tunnel. Because most terrier owners aren't interested in actually hunting their dogs on foxes or badgers, so-called earth dog events were created to allow a dog to go to ground without killing any wildlife or risking injury in a tunnel cave-in or fight with prey.

Go-to-ground tunnels may be as simple as bales of hay stacked to create a tunnel or as complex as a liner being buried in the earth to simulate an animal's den. At the end of the tunnel, whether above or below ground, a captive-bred rat or other small animal is kept in a secure cage. Sometimes animal urine or other scent is used instead. The dogs are released and must chase the prey scent into the tunnel and bark to "mark" the quarry. Other earth dog events include lure coursing in which the terriers chase a mechanical furry animal. Go-to-ground events are only inclusive of terrier breeds.

Lure coursing is also a popular activity with the sighthounds. Although greyhound racing as an industry has come to represent almost everything that's bad in dog work, that doesn't mean your sighthound isn't bred to run. Many people with greyhounds, Afghan hounds, or salukis, among others, get involved in racing trials for fun. These are generally casual events where the dogs chase a mechanical rabbit. These dogs are at risk, however, of bone breaks from tripping in gopher holes and joint or muscle strains, and there have been cases of dogs getting caught in the rabbit mechanism. Advocates say the risk is worth watching their dogs' joy at running, but potential participants should do some research about the organization with which they wish to run their dog and have their dog cleared by a vet before participating.

Obedience is a simple activity in which any dog can participate. Although some obedience competitions are limited to dogs with AKC registration, there are also nonbreed oriented obedience trials. Learning the basics is a given, but teaching your dog long down-stays with distractions, scent discrimination, and how to do a figure eight while heeling can be fun and challenging activities, even if you don't compete. You'll also end up with a dog with a reliable recall and some impressive party tricks. The rub is that many working breeds get bored with the endless repetition that obedience entails. Give it a try, though, and if your dog isn't interested, try other methods to make the training fun or move on to another activity that she enjoys more.

Whatever you decide to do with your dog, the important thing is to have fun. If you have a working dog but don't want to join an organized activity, think of ways to keep your dog mentally and physically challenged. Give her a job to do at home such as fetching the morning paper or bringing you your keys. Take some of the ideas from SAR and teach your dog runaway games—run away with a favorite toy and teach her to bark for it. Then, graduate up to hiding with the toy and up the ante by hiding a friend.

To burn off working dog energy, take long walks or runs, but also think of ways to spice it up. Try bicycling with your dog or take a hike in the mountains. Go to a dog beach and get your dog swimming. A game of fetch in the water will make for a very tired pooch that night. It's important to remember that certain breeds have specific characteristics that may or may not fit into your lifestyle. A Border collie will herd, a terrier will dig, a husky will roam; participating in organized activities or providing a good varied schedule of activities will help channel some of these tendencies but not all of them.

If you want a house dog who doesn't want to play hard, get that kind of dog. There are many small companion dogs who are content with a walk around the block at night; or, consider one of the many senior dogs who are abandoned at shelters. These dogs are instant couch buddies and will reward you many times over for the effort you make. Allowing your dog to be the dog she is supposed to be is the key to both her and your happiness.

CHAPTER 17

TOWARD THE FUTURE

Since dogs and humans first crossed paths, we've manipulated them to serve us. We attempted to cull out the unmanageable dogs and bred the affectionate and loyal ones. Later, we turned to dogs for help in hunting and then in war—breeding fast, energetic, strong, and aggressive dogs. As our relationship progressed, we manipulated dogs into all types of forms. When we needed dogs to catch vermin, we bred terriers; when we needed dogs who ran birds out of their hiding places, we bred flushing dogs; when we needed dogs to fetch lines from boats, we bred Portuguese water dogs with webbed feet. We bred dogs to serve almost every purpose under the sun. And then about one hundred years ago, we gradually stopped using dogs for the purposes for which they'd been bred. We continued to breed for the looks of the dogs, but not for the work they were supposed to do, and we resented their need to chase or retrieve or pull or bark.

Breeds whose ancestors had full-time jobs are now expected to hang out in the backyard while we work. We ignore them or give them little exercise and are surprised when they dig or chew or bark. We expect our Irish setters to act like Chihuahuas. There are dogs who were bred as companion dogs, and they do their jobs smashingly, but unfortunately, many of the dogs we expect to be companion dogs were bred for other types of work. Given enough exercise and attention, it's quite possible for a working dog to make a great house dog, but without special considerations, the right dog in the wrong house can make for a disaster.

Working Dogs

Too often, we buy or adopt a cute little puppy on a whim, without putting any thought into the adult dog he will become. As working dogs enter adolescence, their breed instincts and high energy bring their genetic traits to new levels, and suddenly the family members who were positive they wanted that German shorthair, for example, find themselves overwhelmed. We are surprised when huskies roam, cattle dogs nip, and pit bulls fight. We are shocked when Jack Russell terriers dig holes in our prized gardens and greyhounds chase and kill rabbits. So we take dogs to shelters and tell the workers there that the dog is incorrigible, unmanageable, a real terror. Then we go on our way, and more likely than not, find another perfectly cute puppy, maybe a husky, maybe a Border collie, with whom we begin the process again. Maybe after one or two failures we learn our lesson and buy a shih tzu or stick to cats.

Unfortunately, the dogs pay for our trial and error. Many dogs who end up in shelters are euthanized, more than four million per year, and that's a good half of what it was in the early 1990s. Due to huge efforts on the part of animal advocates, fewer dogs are having accidental litters, and more people understand they have a responsibility to get their pets neutered. Spay and neuter education, however, does not address the issue of dog temperaments,

> **Too often, we buy or adopt a cute little puppy on a whim, without putting any thought into the adult dog he will become.**

something that animal welfare advocates realize may be just as important when addressing the reasons dogs end up in shelters. The fact is that it's not unwanted puppy litters that are ending up in urban shelters nowadays; instead, it's adolescent dogs, generally of breeds or breed mixes with strong working backgrounds. Shelters see a lot of rottweiler- and pit bull–types, but they also see a good number of Border collies and Australian shepherds, all dogs who live to work.

In the last part of the twentieth century, working dog advocates and animal welfare advocates began working together to try to keep these dogs out of shelters. If a working dog does end up in a shelter, advocates try to find them appropriate homes. As a result, many shelters and rescue groups now place appropriate dogs into working environments. Assistance dog organizations, particularly service and hearing dogs programs, routinely adopt animals from shelters.

Most of the organizations doing hearing dog work use shelter dogs, often high-strung terriers. Many service dog organizations also make use of homeless dogs,

Toward the Future

especially the organizations that do double duty by utilizing inmates or at-risk youths as trainers or puppy raisers. Those involved in these programs like to say they are a win-win-win situation. The trainer, recipient, and dogs all win, but I'd go further and say it's a four-time win scenario: the community also benefits from these programs,

with humane dog education and a successful rehabilitation program leading to healthier, happier, and safer animals and people. In the Prison Pet Partnership Program, in Washington State, female inmates are motivated by the work their once-unwanted canine partners can do.

Although organizations breeding for service, guide, and hearing programs will argue that well-researched genetic lines are vital, the statistics don't always bear this out. Whether they are rescue dogs or specially bred, only 25–30 percent of the dogs in most programs are actually placed with recipients.

The USDA recruits rescued beagles for their widespread Beagle Brigade, a program that uses the dogs to sniff out contraband agricultural products in an effort to keep dangerous pests out of the country. The USDA's Wildlife Services uses rescued Jack Russell terriers to detect and prevent brown snakes from leaving Guam and infesting new U.S. locales.

Many SAR dogs, both disaster and wilderness, got their working life start through the nod of an animal control officer or rescue worker. One disaster SAR group, NDSDF, gets almost all its dogs through rescues and shelters; not only because it can rescue an animal but also because it gets the best dog at the right time. "It gives us a dog at the right age without us putting a penny into it, and it saves a dog from having the incorrect life, whether it's digging up somebody's backyard because he's bored silly, or living in a kennel because no one knows what to do with him. Many of these dogs have the qualities that we need," says NDSDF founder, Wilma Melville. Other individual SAR handlers have adopted abandoned dogs, finding that the same personality that didn't work in the home environment was ideal for the high-energy, high-drive work required for SAR.

Why do rescued dogs make such good working dogs? Because they do what

they're supposed to do and they do it so well. Some dogs are pets by nature; their jobs are to be the best pets they can be, and they serve brilliantly by sitting in peoples' laps for hours on end or putting up with endless games of catch with the kids. But other dogs have different types of work in their background and hanging out in front of the hearth all day just isn't appealing.

There are times when dogs are abandoned because they are bought by irresponsible, ignorant people, and there are times when dogs are abandoned because they are bought by naïve people who feel out of control when their cute little puppies turn into high-energy teenagers. What so many prospective owners don't know or don't believe is that some dogs aren't satisfied to be just a pet dog; they also want a job.

Of the jobs discussed in this book, there are very few in which rescued dogs are not used. Spud, Carol Hummel's third cattle dog, had been destined for the death chamber for allegedly killing a cat, but his herding ways were welcome in the herd-friendly Hummel home. Mugsy, a U.S. Customs dog was handpicked from the Orange County Humane Society, and Beagle Brigade dog Brutus was hours from euthanasia when he was plucked from a Southern California animal shelter. Disaster SAR dog Manny, a Border collie, was rejected from a home because his typical Border collie energy was too much for his family. At age three, he ended up with NDSDF handler Ron Weckenbacher, who, although he admits Manny is a handful, is awed watching the Border collie work through chaos and fear, always coming back for more. Manny, of course, isn't the only rescued dog who worked at

Toward the Future

the World Trade Center. There were several other SAR dogs who were rescues, including Seth Peacock's Pupdog and Janet Linker's Ricky, a rescued rat terrier who was deployed with Washington Task Force One.

Julie Weibler's rescued dog, Zephyr, comes into his own when doing SAR work. Adopted when he was about six months old, he appeared to have been abused. His positive reinforcement comes from his SAR work and that's when he's happiest and most confident. This dog, mistreated in his early life and a potential statistic, has instead gone on to work on more searches than Weibler can count, recovering bodies and finding living victims as well.

All of these dogs are living examples of what could happen when the dogs we've bred don't fit into the lives we want them to lead. You can't fit a square peg into a round hole but once they're given the opportunity to be the dogs we made them, they shine.

Only a small minority of the dogs living in U.S. homes are actively working dogs, but these dogs can teach us a great deal about our pets and our relationship to them. Understanding working dogs—where they came from and how they serve us today—teaches us to value their capabilities and respect their sometimes inscrutable passions.

> **Why do rescued dogs make such good working dogs? Because they do what they're supposed to do and they do it so well.**

If a person knows that a Border collie was born to run for 8 to 10 hours a day, it may keep him or her from abandoning the hyperactive one-year-old dog to a shelter or from buying the fluffy puppy in the first place. Understanding our dogs' remarkable abilities also helps us to appreciate their value in our lives.

Although dogs have been used for work since they were domesticated, industrialization and urbanization were not kind to working dogs. Lives shifted away from agriculture and into cities, where there were fewer avenues for dogs' traditional work. During the last one hundred years, Americans have seen dogs largely as companions. Many urbanites have never even heard of working dogs, besides the ones who occasionally turn up on film or television.

Since the end of World War II, however, working dogs began to slowly resurface in the public view. Used by the military in almost every campaign in the Pacific and many in Europe, GIs returned having seen their capabilities. The folks at home saw the war dogs in news clips and returning soldiers heralded their bravery. Guide dogs also began to gain acceptance post–World War II, as young soldiers who had been blinded in battle embraced the use of guide dogs in order to continue independent and fulfilling lives.

Since then, dogs have slowly regained their footing as workers in modern-day America. As many farmers tried to hold onto or reclaim small farms, dogs reappeared as welcome and inexpensive helpers. Herding dogs relearned how to assist ranchers and farmers while flock protection dogs began to gain favor in part because of their endorsement by the USDA, which has advocated their use since the 1970s.

The success of guide dogs has led to dogs assisting the deaf and the mobility impaired as well as gaining popularity as therapy dogs. Quantitative research as to the positive medical benefit of dogs on humans has further increased their acceptance in the world of human health care. Researchers continue to explore the possibilities of cancer- or seizure-detecting dogs—exploring ways to train for these seemingly innate abilities.

Although the Swiss have used SAR dogs for centuries, it is only in the past 20 years that avalanche and wilderness dogs have gained popular use in the U.S. As we continue to experience natural and human-made disasters, disaster SAR dogs have become an accepted part of the landscape.

At airports, dogs inspect our bags for explosives, contraband agricultural products, and narcotics. They make our lives safer and, like many things today, less private. At schools, dogs have been used to search students for drugs, leading to lawsuits and questions as to when and where it is appropriate to use detection dogs.

The future of working dogs is in our hands. Right now we have the opportunity

Toward the Future

to embrace working dogs and place appropriate value on what they do for us—allowing them to do the work they were born to, but not manipulating them in harmful or degrading ways. It's also up to us to decide what work is appropriate for dogs: when does their work cross the bounds of propriety and when is it the best option for everyone involved.

September 11, 2001, brought life-ending, life-altering changes for everyone in the U.S. It taught us new ways of looking at the everyday things that surround us: airplanes and skyscrapers took on a new, sinister light; firefighters and New Yorkers took on the cloak of sainthood; and SAR dogs became a newly recognizable phrase to almost everyone in America.

On that day, a Port Authority dog died on duty, a guide dog led her blind handler down 78 stories, and disaster SAR dogs from all over the country were deployed to Washington, D.C., and New York. In the weeks and months that followed, therapy dogs provided posttraumatic support for the victims suffering the aftermath of the attack.

There's probably been no other time in American history when dogs so fully captured the attention of the American public. For whatever reason, the SAR dogs served as a sort of national catharsis. Watching dogs work in a place where every American wanted to be working helped us all feel part of the effort, and donating booties or money helped us feel connected.

Dog lovers contributed almost $1 million to one rescue organization in the months following the disaster, and, as opposed to the drop in donations experienced by many charities post–September 11, dog charities stayed somewhat stable. September 11 brought a new understanding for working and companion dogs. Anyone who's ever seen a working dog in action, of course, was not surprised by what the dogs did. If you've had a loved one

> **Although dogs have been used for work since they were domesticated, industrialization and urbanization were not kind to working dogs.**

found by a SAR dog, been guided by a guide dog, or seen the beauty of a herding dog delivering his flock, nothing a dog can do will astonish you.

As our urban and suburban communities have developed, we've adjusted dogs' skills for our current needs, just as we did thousands of years ago when we needed dogs for hunting and protection. In our homes, dogs serve as companions and guards, warning us of intruders. Herders and bird dogs work to clear birds off airfields and golf courses. And in less formal capacities, dogs are increasingly reappearing as part of our everyday lives outside the home. Offices have mascots and pet supply stores have resident tasters and toy testers. Dogs are even being used to sniff out termites.

Police dogs are now a normal, expected part of almost every police department in the country, helping to find more criminals, save more police officers and suspects lives, and bridging the gap between police and citizens. Police-dog handlers will tell you that a dog can be recalled, but a bullet can't; police dogs protect citizens and law enforcement officers equally. The San Diego Police Department has one of the largest canine units in the country because it has discovered that using dogs to subdue violent mentally ill offenders means fewer shootings.

> *If you've had a loved one found by a SAR dog, been guided by a guide dog, or seen the beauty of a herding dog delivering his flock, nothing a dog can do will astonish you.*

Working dogs, and as a result, companion dogs, are also gaining more respect from Americans and the worldwide community. In militarized countries, dogs help with demining, a dangerous job advocated by the HSUS because it helps cultures that traditionally abhor dogs to gain a new respect and humane standard for them. Military dogs, who have been routinely euthanized at the end of their usefulness for almost 50 years are finally receiving some of the recognition and treatment they deserve, although there's still a long way to go.

As we adjust our expectations of dogs, combining our impressions of our own pet dogs stretched out on the sofa with the image of a highly alert police dog on patrol, we learn to better adjust our lives to our canine companions. If we cannot adjust our lives to accommodate their needs, we at least learn to choose dogs who are better suited to our lifestyles. Once we understand and accept the drive and skills that we bred into dogs, we will be better able to serve them while they serve us.

No matter how well trained a dog is, he is not infallible; he is not a machine. As we come to depend on dogs more and more to keep us safe from explosives, narcotics, and agricultural pests, and as we depend on dogs to find our missing friends and family in almost any situation, it's important that we don't expect too much. If a dog is not 100 percent accurate, that doesn't mean he's not doing his job or that his uses are not valuable. It only means that as a living being, he isn't perfect. Still, he represents our best, most mobile chance to find victims, living or dead, and to find potentially lethal materials before they lead to a wide-scale disaster. Working dogs' skills depend on experienced and knowledgeable trainers and handlers.

Dave Kontny, head of the TSA Canine Program, is concerned by the number of new security dog agencies that have appeared in the wake of September 11. Some want to help; others are opportunists who hope to seize on a lucrative business opportunity. Whatever their motivations, if their training is not up to standards, then not only can their entrance into the field lead to a loss of respect for legitimate explosive detection dogs but it can lead to a loss of lives as well.

Conversely, it is often hard for humans to trust sensitive jobs to canine workers, but trust is the operative tool in all canine work. As Americans, we often put more faith in machines than in anything else, and unless we have seen firsthand the abilities of dogs, it is easy to second-guess a dog's alerts. Unfortunately, when we put our human hand into it, we bring our assumptions and our personal opinions into play. As Danny Turner of U.S. Customs points out, people don't suspect four-year-old children of having drugs in their backpacks, and that's why drug couriers use them. A dog doesn't discriminate—while a Customs officer is busy searching the guy with beady eyes and a four-day beard, the dog finds the drugs on an innocent-looking person. Dogs are also the ultimate witnesses because they have no prejudices; to a dog, a drug smells the same no matter who's carrying it.

Human skepticism can be a great hindrance to a SAR dog's work. If the task force system does not trust a dog's alert, there's no purpose to the alert. Unfortunately, because almost all canine handlers are civilians, other task force members sometimes dismiss them. That skepticism can be prevalent among the federal and local emergency systems, as well. The fact is, handlers say, dogs alert when there's something to alert on; it's that simple. They don't care that a victim should be here, or a body should be there, they only know where it is when they find it. If the emergency response system is not educated about SAR dogs' abilities, they will not give the alerts the significance they require.

Although we've come a long way in our appreciation of dogs' ability to help us prevent disasters and assist in their aftermath, we still require an appreciation of this work in a tangible, workable way. In the next disaster, and unfortunately, there always will be another, it's imperative that everyone, from the president on down, knows that a dog's work is only as good as a human's trust. If well-intentioned, ill-informed officials override dogs' alerts, the only result is fewer lives saved and fewer recovered bodies. As one handler says, "It's easy to train dogs; it's not easy to train people."

Despite the enthusiasm of Americans about disaster dogs post–September 11, few people actually become handlers. In October of 2001, Northwest Disaster Search Dogs had 30 volunteers eager to start training. By May that number had dwindled to three. Once potential handlers understand the depth of the commitment in any kind of SAR, few remain. Handlers commit at least five hundred hours a year in training, not to mention a $3,000–$5,000 yearly financial commitment. Unless an employer is sympathetic, handlers are not reimbursed for lost work time during a deployment or when they need to travel to out-of-state training sessions or tests.

> **Once we understand and accept the drive and skills that we bred into dogs, we will be better able to serve them while they serve us.**

Search and rescue handlers do it because they love it, but if the system doesn't work for them, they won't continue to do it. It's a sad statement that whenever handlers are deployed to a disaster site, many are lost from the program. Deployment issues, command-in-control problems, mismanagement of disaster sites, and inadequate posttraumatic counseling can all lead to disinterest in continuing SAR. For wilderness SAR, the problems are even greater because teams are so often deployed. When a team is called out 20 times in a month, arguments erupt within groups over financial support: Who should pay a gas bill? What if there is overnight lodging? Another thing that affects the longevity of SAR teams is the support that the handlers receive for the work they are doing. The dogs are happy to do it, and they always are rewarded for their efforts no matter what. Unfortunately, the handlers are not.

When a SAR team is called out, the situation is often chaotic and emotional for everyone: the family, other searchers, and the SAR team. If we expect to have a system in place with canine teams that spring into action to find our loved ones, dead or alive, we need to learn to express our gratitude to these volunteers, even when we are devastated. If not, they may not be available the next time. Too often, say handlers, they devote days to a search but are never thanked. Although they may understand the emotions that contribute to this, it doesn't motivate them to return.

Toward the Future

Issues over whether SAR teams should be professional or civilian, whether non-FEMA certified teams should be allowed onto disaster sites and how deployments should happen are all constant discussions that need to be addressed to ensure an adequate canine SAR system.

Now that we have seen what dogs can do, how they can shorten our work days, lengthen our lives, and increase our chances for survival, whether by preventing an explosion or a wholesale agricultural crisis, we can expect to see them in more and more capacities. Perhaps a dog will do your next termite inspection; maybe your dermatologist will employ a resident melanoma sniffer. Look around you. Dogs are at work almost everywhere you go—so quick and effective that you barely notice them.

Hopefully, our understanding of the ways dogs benefit us will work to both our and their advantage. If we can respect dogs as partners, we may be less likely to dump them in a shelter at a moment's whim. If we understand that we bred them to be the animals they are, we may not relegate them to the backyard in response to their quest for a job.

Doggy spas may soothe our guilt, but they probably don't do much for our dogs. Letting dogs be dogs often means letting dogs do the work they were bred for. Their ability to work, however, is only as good as our willingness to trust them, train them, care for them, and bond with them. Dogs and humans have shared their lives for more than ten thousand years; we chose them as much as they chose us. By domesticating dogs, we took on a responsibility that we can fulfill through caring for them and keeping them safe and happy. Our responsibility, however, also extends to allowing them to be the animals they are.

RESOURCES

ANIMAL ACTORS

**American Humane Association Film
and Television Unit**

15366 Dickens Street

Sherman Oaks, CA 91403

(818) 501-0123

Web site: www.ahafilm.org

Critters of the Cinema

P. O. Box 378

Lake Hughes, CA 93532

(661) 724-1929

Web site: www.crittersofthecinema.com

E-mail: info@crittersofthecinema.com

ANIMAL WELFARE

American Humane Association

63 Inverness Drive East

Englewood, CO 80112

(866) 242-1877

Web site: www.americanhumane.org

**American Society for the Prevention of
Cruelty to Animals**

424 East Ninety-second Street

New York, NY 10128-6804

(212) 876-7700

Web site: www.aspca.org

E-mail: information@aspca.org

Humane Society of the United States

2100 L Street NW

Washington, D.C. 20037

(202) 452-1100

Web site: www.hsus.org

People for the Ethical Treatment of Animals

501 Front Street

Norfolk, VA 23510

(757) 622-7382

Web site: www.peta.org

**Royal Society for the Prevention of
Cruelty to Animals**

Wilberforce Way

Southwater

Horsham, West Sussex RH13 9RS UK

International number: +44 870 3335 999

Web site: www.rspca.org.uk

ASSISTANCE DOGS

Assistance Dogs International, Inc.

P.O. Box 5174

Santa Rosa, CA 95402

Web site: www.adionline.org

E-mail: info@adionline.org

Canine Companions for Independence

P.O. Box 446

Working Dogs

Santa Rosa, CA 95402-0446

(800) 572-2275

Web site: www.caninecompanions.org

E-mail: info@caninecompanions.org

Dogs for the Deaf

10175 Wheeler Road

Central Point, OR 97502

(541) 826-9220

Web site: www.dogsforthedeaf.org

E-mail: info@dogsforthedeaf.org

Guide Dogs for the Blind

P.O. Box 151200

San Rafael, CA 94915-1200

(800) 295-4050

Web site: www.guidedogs.com

E-mail: information@guidedogs.com

Guide Dogs of America

13445 Glenoaks Boulevard

Sylmar, CA 91342

(818) 362-5834

Web site: www.guidedogsofamerica.org

E-mail: mail@guidedogsofamerica.org

**International Association of
Assistance Dog Partners**

38691 Filly Drive

Sterling Heights, MI 48310

(586) 826-3938

Web site: www.iaadp.org

E-mail: info@iaadp.org

**National Education for
Assistance Dog Services**

P.O. Box 213

West Boylston, MA 01583

(978) 422-9064

Web site: www.neads.org

E-mail: info@neads.org

**San Francisco Society for the
Prevention of Cruelty of Animals**

Hearing Dog Program

2500 Sixteenth Street

San Francisco, CA 94103-4213

(415) 554-3020

U.S. Council of Dog Guide Schools

625 West Town Street

Columbus, OH 43215

(614) 221-6367

**Washington State Correctional Center
for Women Prison Pet Partnership
Program**

P.O. Box 17

Gig Harbor, WA 98335

(253) 858-4240

E-mail: ppppsd@yahoo.com

Resources

BREED REGISTRIES

American Kennel Club

260 Madison Avenue

New York, NY 10016

(212) 696-8200

Web site: www.akc.org

E-mail: info@akc.org

United Kennel Club

100 East Kilgore Road

Kalamazoo, MI 49002-5584

(269) 343-9020

Web site: www.ukcdogs.com

DETECTION DOGS

Animal & Plant Health Inspection Service

4700 River Road

Riverdale, MD 20737-1232

(301) 734-8892

Web site: www.aphis.usda.gov

E-mail: APHIS.Web@aphis.usda.gov

Beagle Brigade

4700 River Road

Riverdale, MD 20737-1232

(866) SAFEGUARD

Canine Enforcement Training Center

(888) USA-DOG1

Web site: www.cbp.com

E-mail: canine@customs.treas.gov

Marshall Legacy Institute

K-9 Demining Corps

2425 Wilson Boulevard

Suite 313

Arlington, VA 22201

(703) 243-9200

Web site: www.marshall-legacy.org

E-mail: info@marshall-legacy.org

Transportation Security Administration Canine Explosives Unit U.S. Department of Transportation

Office of Civil Rights

Mail Stop: TSA-6

400 Seventh Street SW

Washington, D.C. 20590

Web site: www.tsa.dot.gov

E-mail: k-9@tsa.dot.gov

U.S. Customs Canine Enforcement Program

National Canine Program Headquarters

(202) 927-3827

U.S. Fish and Wildlife Service

Web site: www.fws.gov

E-mail: contact@fws.gov

Working Dogs

HUNTING DOGS

The Bird Dog Foundation, Inc.

Bird Dog Museum

P. O. Box 774

Grand Junction, TE 38039

(901) 764-2058

Web site: www.fielddog.com

E-mail: sportdogctr@aol.com

MILITARY DOGS

Department of Defense Military Working Dog Center

Lackland Air Force Base Public Affairs

37TRW/PA

1701 Kenly Avenue

Suite 4

Lackland AFB, TX 78236-5157

(210) 671-2907

Quartermaster Museum—War Dogs OQMG USA Quartermaster Center

1201 Twenty-second Street

Fort Lee, VA 23801-1601

(804) 734-4203

Web site: www.qmfound.com /War_Dogs.htm

U. S. Army Quartermaster Corps Remount Branch

3901 A Avenue

Fort Lee, VA 23801

(804) 734-3767

Web site: www.quartermaster.army.mil

E-mail: qmweb@lee.army.mil

Vietnam Dog Handlers Association

Web site: www.vdhaonline.org

War Dog Memorial Fund

760 East Parkridge Avenue

Corona, CA 92879

(877) WAR-DOGS

SEARCH AND RESCUE DOGS

Colorado Search and Rescue

222 South Sixth Street

Room 409

Grand Junction, CO 81501

(970) 248-7310

Federal Emergency Management Administration

FEMA 500 C Street SW

Washington, D.C. 20472

(202) 566-1600

Web site: www.fema.gov

King County Search Dogs

7300 Perimeter Road S.

Room 143

Seattle, WA 98108

Web site: www.wa-sar.net/kcsd

National Disaster Search Dog Foundation

323 East Matilija Avenue

Suite 110-245

Ojai, CA 93023

Resources

(888) 646-1242

Web site: www.ndsdf.org

National Urban Search and Rescue Response System

500 C Street SW

Washington, D.C. 20472

(202) 566-1600

Web site: www.fema.gov/usr

Northwest Disaster Search Dogs

P.O. Box 2083

Redmond, WA 98073

Web site: www.ndsd.net

E-mail: ndsd@ndsd.net

THERAPY DOGS

American Red Cross

431 Eighteenth Street NW

Washington, D.C. 2000

(202) 303-4498

Web site: www.redcross.org

E-mail: internet@usa.redcross.org

The Delta Society

580 Naches Avenue SW

Suite 101

Renton, WA 98055-2297

(425) 226-7357

Web site: www.deltasociety.org

E-mail: info@deltasociety.org

Hand-in-Paw, Inc.

Village East Shopping Center

5342 Oporto Madrid Boulevard S.

Birmingham, AL 35210

(205) 591-7006

Web site: www.handinpaw.org

E-mail: handinpawinc@aol.com

Intermountain Therapy Animals

P.O. Box 17201

Salt Lake City, UT 84117

(877) 485-1121

Web site: www.therapyanimals.org

Paws with a Cause

4646 South Division

Wayland, MI 49348

(800) 253-PAWS

Web site: www.pawswithacause.org

E-mail: paws@ionline.com

Therapy Dogs International

88 Bartley Road

Flanders, NJ 07836

(973) 252-9800

Web site: www.tdi-dog.org

E-mail: tdi@gti.net

BIBLIOGRAPHY

Bogle, L. S. "Therapy Dogs Seem to Boost Health of Sick and Lonely," [online]. *National Geographic News* [cited 8 August 2002]. Available from World Wide Web: <http://news.nationalgeographic.com/news.html>.

Budiansky, S., "The Truth About Dogs," *Atlantic*, July 1997.

Caras, R.. *A Celebration of Dogs*. New York: Crown Publishing Group, Inc., 1984.

Coppinger, R., and L. Coppinger. *Dogs*. New York: Scribner, 2001.

Coren, S., *The Pawprints of History: Dogs and the Course of Human Events*. New York: The Free Press, 2002.

Derr, M., "If You're a Bear, These Dogs Will Give You Pause," *Smithsonian*, May 1999.

Dold, C., "For Rescue Dogs 'Nothing's Better than a Live Find,' " *Smithsonian*, August 1997.

Foote, T., "A Good Dog Knows What to Do," *Smithsonian*, October 1999.

Handwerk, B. "Detector Dogs Sniff out Smugglers for U.S. Customs," [online]. *National Geographic News* [cited 12 July 2002]. Available from World Wide Web: <http://news.nationalgeographic.com.html>.

Hotz, R. L. "Those New Tricks Came from Old Dogs." *Los Angeles Times*, 22 November 2002, sec. 1A.

Lange, K. E., "From Wolf to Woof," *National Geographic*, January 2002.

Phillips, A., "Dogs: A Love Story," *National Geographic*, January 2002.

Querna, B. "U.S. Beagle Brigade is First Defense Against Alien Species," [online]. *National Geographic Today* [cited 7 June 2001]. Available from World Wide Web: <http://news.nationalgeographic.com.html>.